Contents

Your qualification   v

Guide to qualification content   vi

About our exams and your study commitments   vii

How to use this book   viii

Book features   ix

Supplier Relationships   x

Chapter 1

1   *The dynamics of relationships in supply chains*   1

1.1   Differentiate between different types of commercial relationships in supply chains   2
- Internal and external relationships   2
- The relationship spectrum   5
- The relationship life cycle   10

1.2   Appraise portfolio analysis techniques to assess relationships in supply chains   16
- Matrices to identify supply, supplier and purchaser positioning   16
- Developing value-adding relationships with strategic suppliers   24
- Developing action plans   28

1.3   Identify the competitive forces that impact on relationships in supply chains   30
- Sources of competitive advantage   30
- Competitive forces: sources of competitive rivalry, bargaining power of buyers and suppliers, threat of new entrants and potential substitutes   38
- STEEPLE factors that affect supply chains (social, technological, economic, environmental, political, legislative and ethical)   43

1.4   Compare the sources of added value that can be achieved through supply chain relationships   47
- The link between relationships as a process and the achievement of added value outcomes   48
- Sources of added value: pricing and cost management, improving quality, timescales, quantities and place considerations in procurements from external suppliers   49
- The link between organisations in supply networks   59

Chapter 2

2   *Understanding processes and procedures for successful working with stakeholders*   63

2.1   Analyse the purpose of organisational procedures and processes in sourcing goods and/or services   65
- Achieving value for money   65
- Supplier identification, assessment and selection   71
- Award stage – selection and awarding criteria   75

2.2   Compare team management techniques to ensure positive stakeholder relationships   80
- Positive relationships through positive contributions   80
- Overcoming resistance   83
- Identifying conflict and coping processes   86

Contents •

- Cross-organisational teams   88
- Stages of team development – forming, storming, norming, performing   90
- Summary   93

2.3 Compare the practical considerations of stakeholder management   **93**
- Accurate cost modelling   93
- Reduced impact of price fluctuations   95
- Early supplier involvement in product and/or service development   97
- Knowledge transfer and access to innovation   99
- Common metrics to drive change for both organisations   101
- Improving risk management and continuity of supply   104

2.4 Identify the process for terminating stakeholder relationships   **106**
- Reasons for termination   107
- The process of termination   108
- Relationship impacts – amicable *v.* hostile   111
- Legal considerations – finances, confidentiality, IPR, security, employee rights   112
- Succession issues – continuity of supply   116

Chapter 3

3 Understanding the concept of partnering   **121**

3.1 Analyse the concept of partnering and where it is a suitable approach   **122**
- The three types of partnering   122
- Partnering *v.* 'traditional' contracting agreements   124
- The drivers for partnership sourcing   127
- Advantages for purchaser and supplier   129
- High spend   132
- High risk   134
- Technically complicated supplies   135
- New services   136
- Fast-changing technology   137
- Restricted markets   138

3.2 Appraise the process of partnership implementation   **139**
- Identify items potentially suitable for partnership sourcing   139
- 'Sell' the philosophy to senior management and other functions of the organisation   141
- Define the standards that potential partners will be expected to meet   146
- Establish joint commitment to the partnership   149
- Reviews and audits   153

3.3 Identify the reasons why partnerships fail   **155**
- Poor communication   156
- Lack of senior management support and trust   159
- Lack of commitment by one or both partners   161
- Poor planning   162
- Lack of value-added benefit   164
- Changes in the market   166
- Corporate cultural differences   168
- Logistics and distance barriers   170

Glossary   177

Index   182

Supplier Relationships

[L4M6]

Core

Study Guide

Level 4
Diploma in Procurement
and Supply

Printed and distributed by:
The Chartered Institute of Procurement & Supply, Easton House, Easton on the Hill, Stamford, Lincolnshire PE9 3NZ

info@cips.org
www.cips.org

Every attempt has been made to ensure the accuracy of this study guide; however, no liability can be accepted for any loss incurred in any way whatsoever by any person relying solely on the information contained within it. The study guide has been produced solely for the purpose of professional qualification study and should not be taken as definitive of the legal position. CIPS cannot be held responsible for the content of any website mentioned in this study guide. Specific advice should always be obtained before undertaking any investment.

ISBN: 978-1-86124-293-8

A CIP (Catalogue in Publication) catalogue record for this publication is available from the British Library.

All facts are correct at time of publication.

Author: Leanne Richards (MCIPS)

CIPS would like to thank Professor Douglas Lambert for his invaluable contribution on the subject of partnerships, and for permission to reproduce 'The Partnership Model', and 'The Collaboration Framework'.

First published in 2019 by CIPS

Editorial and project management by Haremi Ltd.
Typesetting by York Publishing Solutions Pvt. Ltd., INDIA
Index by York Publishing Solutions Pvt. Ltd., INDIA

Every effort has been made to trace all copyright holders, but if any have been inadvertently overlooked, the Publishers will be pleased to make the necessary arrangements at the first opportunity.

Your qualification

CIPS qualifications are regulated internationally to ensure we offer a recognised, professional standard in procurement and supply. CIPS Level 4* Diploma in Procurement and Supply is a vocationally related professional qualification. Formal recognition is included within the regulatory frameworks of an increasing number of countries such as the UK (England, Wales and Northern Ireland), UAE (including Dubai) and Africa (including Zambia). Further information on this recognition and the details of corresponding qualifications levels for other international qualifications frameworks are detailed on our website. CIPS members can have the confidence in our regulated qualifications, which reliably indicate the standard of knowledge, skills and understanding that you, as a learner, are required to demonstrate.

A step up from the Level 3 Advanced Certificate in Procurement and Supply Operations, the Level 4 Diploma in Procurement and Supply is a stepping stone to study on the CIPS Level 5 Advanced Diploma in Procurement and Supply. The content has been written using the CIPS Procurement and Supply Cycle as its focus, which presents a cyclical process of key steps faced by those procuring goods or services. The Diploma offers the most common entry route to the profession and should be used by learners to develop a professional 'tool box' which learners can apply in the practical environment and further develop at Levels 5 and 6.

In this way successful learners will possess transferable workplace skills, developing their operational and tactical abilities as they strive for managerial roles and responsibilities. It is aimed at those in the profession who have procurement and supply activity at the heart of their role. Learners will be expected to provide advice and guidance to key stakeholders on the performance of organisational procedures and processes associated with procurement and supply and will aspire to manage developments in and improvements to the related functions. Transferable skills are those such as communication, teamwork, and planning and completing tasks to high standards, all enable the learner to add value to the organisation.

Entry level	Entry level	Highest Entry level		
Level 2 Certificate in Procurement and Supply Operations	Level 3 Advanced Certificate in Procurement and Supply Operations	Level 4 Diploma in Procurement and Supply Operations	Level 5 Advanced Diploma in Procurement and Supply	Level 6 Professional Diploma in Procurement and Supply

Next steps

This qualification provides progression to the CIPS Level 5 Advanced Diploma in Procurement and Supply.

Level 5

* Refers to levels within the UK RQF. Other regulatory bodies may have different corresponding levels

 Based on the Tactical competency level of CIPS Global Standard

Guide to qualification content

What will I study?

Eight CORE modules make up 60 required credits

60
Credits
required for
completion

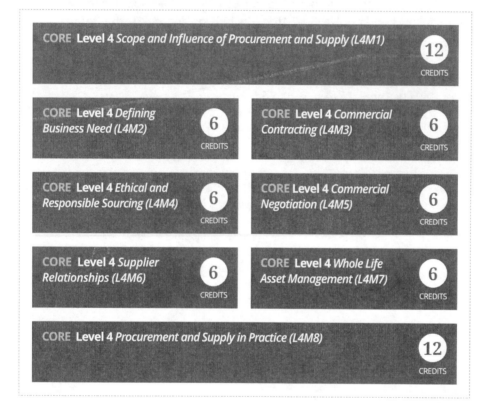

CORE **Level 4** *Scope and Influence of Procurement and Supply (L4M1)* — **12** CREDITS

CORE **Level 4** *Defining Business Need (L4M2)* — **6** CREDITS

CORE **Level 4** *Commercial Contracting (L4M3)* — **6** CREDITS

CORE **Level 4** *Ethical and Responsible Sourcing (L4M4)* — **6** CREDITS

CORE **Level 4** *Commercial Negotiation (L4M5)* — **6** CREDITS

CORE **Level 4** *Supplier Relationships (L4M6)* — **6** CREDITS

CORE **Level 4** *Whole Life Asset Management (L4M7)* — **6** CREDITS

CORE **Level 4** *Procurement and Supply in Practice (L4M8)* — **12** CREDITS

Who is it for?

This qualification is the essential toolkit for anyone planning a career in procurement and supply. Developed and written using the Procurement and Supply cycle** as its focus, it is at the same level as the first year of an undergraduate degree course. It is suitable for those in operational roles or those managing or supervising the procurement and supply function who want to develop their career and work towards MCIPS Chartered Procurement and Supply Professional.

What will I learn?

You will learn about making procurement and supply happen within an organisation, and you will be equipped with an essential range of knowledge and tools that you can apply immediately in your workplace. Learn how to apply practical, theoretical and technical knowledge, gain a clear understanding of procurement and supply and develop the ability to address complex, non-routine problems.

On completion, you will be able to analyse, interpret and evaluate relevant information and ideas and have an informed awareness of differing perspectives and approaches within the profession. You will also be able to review the effectiveness and appropriateness of methods, actions and results.

Entry requirements

This is the only entry point onto our Diploma qualifications. A minimum of at least two A-levels (or international equivalent) or a CIPS Level 3 Advanced Certificate qualification is required. Alternatively, you will need a minimum of two years' relevant experience in a business environment.

Credit values

To gain a qualification you are required to complete a total number of credits. This is a way of quantifying the required number of study hours. 1 credit is equivalent to 10 hours of study. Each module is given a credit value of 6 or 12 credits.

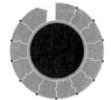

* The Procurement cycle is the cyclical process of key steps when procuring goods or services.
www.cips.org/en-gb/knowledge/procurement-cycle/

Total credits required for completion **60**

About our exams and your study commitments

Objective Response exam format (OR)

These questions allow you to select a response from a list of possible answers. You will find these types of exams across all our qualifications levels and they are marked by computer and then moderated by CIPS examiners.

Constructed Response exam format (CR)

These questions require you to create or 'construct' a response to the question such as an essay or case study. You will find this type of exam in our diploma level qualifications and they will be marked by subject expert examiners.

Your total qualification time (TQT)

600
TQT HRS

The TQT indicates the overall number of guided learning hours, additional self-study and assessment time that is required.

Guided learning hours (GLH)

250
GLH HRS

It is expected that you will undertake 250 GLH. The definition of guided learning hours is: 'A measure of the amount of input time required to achieve the qualification. This includes lectures, tutorials and practicals, as well as supervised study in, for example, learning centres and workshops'.

Self-study requirement (SSR)

335
SSR HRS

Additionally, we recommend that you also commit to at least 335 SSR hours. This includes wider reading of the subject areas and revision to give yourself the best preparation for successfully achieving the qualification.

Total exam time

15
HRS

All the modules in CIPS qualifications are assessed by an examination.

How to use this book

Welcome to this study guide for Supplier Relationships. It contains all the information needed to prepare you for the assessment in this module.

This study guide follows the order of the module specification and each chapter relates to one of the learning outcomes below. You can also see the assessment criteria for each learning outcome.

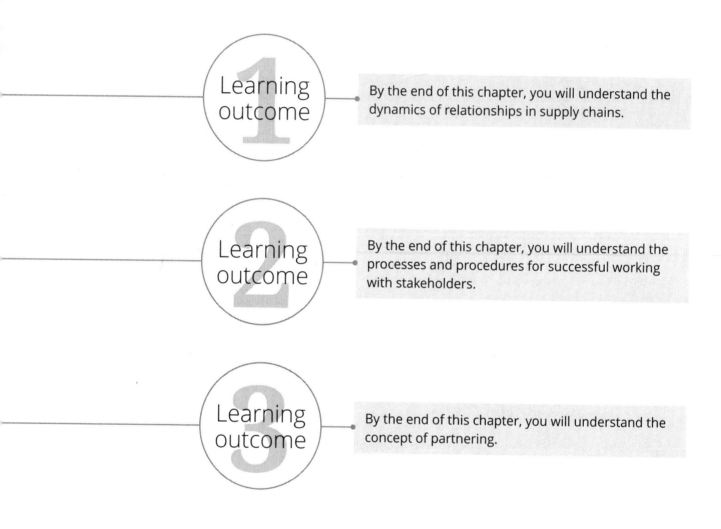

Learning outcome 1

By the end of this chapter, you will understand the dynamics of relationships in supply chains.

Learning outcome 2

By the end of this chapter, you will understand the processes and procedures for successful working with stakeholders.

Learning outcome 3

By the end of this chapter, you will understand the concept of partnering.

Book features

Throughout this book there are a number of features to aid your learning and simplify your revision. Take a look at the different features you will find in the book below.

Glossary
These are the key terms and their definitions

> *Remember*
> This information is important, so you should make a note of it.

> *Check*
> These revision questions give you a chance to check you understand the content in this chapter.

> *Apply*
> These tasks give you a chance to test out your knowledge and understanding.

> *Recap*
> This information will summarise sections from previous chapters.

> Case study
> These case studies will relate the content you have learned to real-world examples.

> *Recommended reading*
> These books can give you more understanding on the subject.

Link to CIPS knowledge where members will be able to access additional resources to extend your knowledge, plus links to online eLearning content including videos, audio and interactive quizzes to recap and test your knowledge and understanding.

End of chapter assessments

At the end of each chapter in the book there is a set of exam-style questions to prepare you for your assessment.

End of Chapter Assessment

IDENTIFY

1. The National Health Service (NHS) in the UK is an example of an organisation from which sector?

   a. Public   c. Third

   b. Private   d. Primary

C

CORE MODULE

**CIPS GLOBAL
STANDARD**
1.2 • 1.4 • 2.1
6.3 • 9.3

OR

**OBJECTIVE
RESPONSE EXAM**

1.5
HRS

**EXAM DURATION
HOURS**

60
HRS

**MODULE
LEARNING
TIME**

6
CREDITS

Supplier Relationships
[L4M6]

Module purpose

On completion of this module, learners will be able to analyse the dynamics of supplier relationships, examine the processes and procedures for working with stakeholders and appreciate the concept of partnering.

Module aim(s)

In any organisation, a significant element of the procurement and supply function is based around decisions to source activity from external suppliers. Once agreements have been established the relationship established with the supplier is paramount to overall success. At its highest level outsourcing can take the form of a partnership or joint venture. This module is designed for those who have responsibility for maintaining and managing relationships with stakeholders and suppliers and for those who may be faced with establishing and developing formal partnerships.

Credit value

CHAPTER 1
The dynamics of relationships in supply chains

Learning outcome

By the end of this chapter, you will understand the dynamics of relationships in supply chains.

Chapter overview

1.1 Differentiate between different types of commercial relationships in supply chains

You will understand:
- Internal and external relationships
- The relationship spectrum
- The relationship life cycle

1.2 Appraise portfolio analysis techniques to assess relationships in supply chains

You will understand:
- Matrices to identify supply, supplier and purchaser positioning
- Developing value-adding relationships with strategic suppliers
- Developing action plans

1.3 Identify the competitive forces that impact on relationships in supply chains

You will understand:
- Sources of competitive advantage
- Competitive forces: sources of competitive rivalry, bargaining power of buyers and suppliers, threat of new entrants and potential substitutes
- STEEPLE factors that affect supply chains (social, technological, economic, environmental, political, legislative and ethical)

1.4 Compare the sources of added value that can be achieved through supply chain relationships

You will understand:
- The link between relationships as a process and the achievement of added value outcomes
- Sources of added value: pricing and cost management, improving quality, timescales, quantities, and place considerations in procurements from external suppliers
- The link between organisations in supply networks

Supplier relationship management (SRM)
Process for identifying all interactions with key suppliers and then managing them in a way that increases the value from the relationship for both parties

Introduction

This chapter begins by looking at relationships within supply chains. For procurement departments this will involve day-to-day management of supplier relationships. Supplier relationship management (SRM) is one of the key skills required to successfully control an organisation's spend. When relationship development and subsequent management is done well it should result in added value, improved supply chain performance and risk mitigation.

Supplier relationship management originated in the Japanese automotive industry in companies such as Nissan, Toyota and Honda. SRM is key in industries where a large proportion of a finished product or service is provided by external suppliers.

It is not necessary or beneficial to develop close relationships with an organisation's entire supplier base. SRM is about selecting the most beneficial type of relationship for each of the organisation's requirements. Over time, buyer–supplier relationships evolve through a number of phases, and so supplier development also needs to be considered as part of SRM.

1.1 Differentiate between different types of commercial relationships in supply chains

The procurement and supply department will have many different types of commercial relationships, making it beneficial to be able to classify these relationships and review their current status. A buyer needs to consider what the optimum type of relationship might be for each part of the supply chain and put strategies in place to achieve this.

Internal and external relationships

Internal supplier
A supplier that is part of the same company as its customer. It provides the products or services that co-workers within the organisation need in order to do their job

External supplier
A supplier that is independent of the organisation and provides products or services to it

Make-or-buy decision
The action of choosing whether to manufacture a product or provide a service in-house or purchase it from an external supplier

When we think about a supplier we typically think of an organisation that is external to our own. However, within supply chains an organisation may choose to use an internal supplier rather than an external supplier. Both types of supplier may provide products, services or both.

Internal suppliers

The use of an internal supplier is often referred to as 'in-house', that is, the internal supplier is an in-house supplier. The choice to use an internal supplier is based on a corporate decision linked to the make-or-buy decision. Procurement has a key role to play in supporting the business to make this decision. To help your understanding of internal suppliers we will look at a brief example.

Imagine that an advertising company is developing a marketing campaign. As part of the campaign the advertising company must develop a new website. Instead of finding an external web design supplier to undertake this work the advertising company uses its internal IT team to develop the website.

The make-or-buy decision is a key part of the sourcing process. Will an organisation manufacture a product or provide a service itself, or will it outsource this to a supplier or external organisation? Products or services produced by an internal supplier are usually those that are considered core to the business and therefore are not suitable to be produced by an external supplier.

Producing the products or services in-house allows the organisation to keep a greater degree of control over the process than if this was outsourced to an external supplier. This can be key for products or services that are time-critical or subject to frequent design changes.

These core products and services are likely to be the aspects of a business that provide it with a competitive advantage. **Competitive advantage** is discussed in more detail in section 1.3. The decision whether to make or buy must be linked to the overall strategy and future plans of the organisation.

> *Remember*
> An internal supplier normally produces products and services that are core to the organisation.

1.1 L01

Whether a product or service should be made or bought must be fully analysed in order to make the best decision for the business. When making the decision it will be necessary to try and anticipate future developments in both the market and the business. The procurement department, along with key internal stakeholders, will need to compare the costs of producing the product or service in-house with the cost of procurement from an external supplier.

Non-price factors such as quality should also be included in the review. The decision involves achieving the best balance between cost and flexibility. One of the non-price factors which requires detailed review is the risk using an external supplier could create. This is covered in greater detail in 'External suppliers' later in this section.

There are several advantages for a business using an internal supplier.

- Greater control and continuity of supply, as there is less dependence on parties that are external to the business.

- The relationship between customer and supplier is likely to be stable and long term, as they are part of the same organisation. As a result, they should also share the same culture and values, which supports relationship building.

- Improved quality control due to having a higher degree of control over the manufacturing process.

- Potential lower costs as no external supplier margin is added to the cost of the product or service and there will be no, or limited, transaction costs.

- Intellectual property (IP) is protected from passing to competitors. This is often key in the technology and food industries.

There can also be disadvantages to using an internal supplier.

- Unless the price is benchmarked against external supplier offerings then there is no guarantee that the internal supplier is providing value for money.

- When the product or service is created in-house, the internal supplier will have both fixed and variable costs. However, when using an external supplier, as the buyer is only paying for the product or service when it is required, there are effectively only variable costs.

- As no money is changing hands the internal supplier may be less motivated to meet the required performance standards.

Stakeholder
In terms of procurement, stakeholders are people who have an active interest in or a concern about what is being procured. They will be affected by the outcome of the procurement, for example, via changes to their job role or working practices. The level of stakeholder interest/concern will vary, as will their power to act on it

- In order to ensure the products and services provided by the internal supplier are up to the standards that could be sourced from external suppliers, the procurement organisation must continually invest in the internal supplier. An example of this would include investing in new machinery. There is an opportunity cost to this investment as perhaps the greater value could be obtained investing in other aspects of the business.

In many cases, following a full review of the current situation, it may not be possible for an organisation to produce a product or service itself or to continue the production of this internally. This could be due to various different factors.

- High costs of production if the required volumes are low.

- Legislative barriers, for example, permits or licences are required for some services such as asbestos removal.

- Skill shortages in areas that are key to producing the product or service.

An internal supplier should be evaluated, reviewed and managed in the same way as an external supplier. This should correct or prevent any poor performance that could have a negative impact on the final product or service. Effort should also be spent on maintaining positive working relationships with an internal supplier.

Poor service from an external supplier could lead to a company reversing its make-or-buy decision and insourcing the production of a product or service so that it is back in-house. However, the decision should not be taken lightly; insourcing can be very costly for an organisation.

External suppliers

Selecting, having a contract with and managing an external supplier are the three main reasons for the existence of the procurement and supply department. When an external supplier is selected, particularly for complex contracts, the decision is made based on several factors. These factors include, but may not be limited to, purchase price, delivery lead time, quality of product or service, and the previous experience of the supplier.

When reviewing whether or not to use an external supplier, an organisation needs to fully evaluate the risks of doing so. Supply chain risks are many and varied. Risks can include supplier insolvency, delivery delays, natural disasters, human rights issues and political instability. Risks are often enhanced if a decision is made to source products or services from an external supplier in a foreign country. This is particularly the case where the supplier is located in a country that has lower standards of labour law than those of the buying organisation.

The work that the procurement department undertakes to review a supplier during the selection process aims to protect the organisation from these risks. For example, in order to protect against the use of child labour a contract may include the right for the procurement organisation to undertake spot audits of a supplier's factory. When developing relationships with a supplier, procurement will have to consider the need to protect the reputation of their company.

There are a number of advantages to using an external supplier.

Economy of scale
The trend of cost per unit being reduced as output increases due to factors such as increased bargaining power and the cost of tooling being shared between larger numbers of units

- An external supplier is often an expert in its field. This could potentially lead to innovation that an internal supplier would have been unable to achieve.

- As a result of the first point, an external supplier may be more cost effective, and they may also be able to benefit from economies of scale if they are producing the same product or service for multiple customers.

- Using an external supplier frees up internal resources that could be used on core activities and creates greater value for the business.

- The external supplier may be more flexible to meet changing levels of demand.

- An external supplier is useful for items where a small volume is required and the costs of internal production are prohibitive.

However, there are also disadvantages to using an external supplier.

- Depending on the nature of the product or service there will be a degree of dependency on the supplier, which increases risks.

- Potential damage to the buyer's reputation if the external supplier engages in unethical behaviour such as the use of child labour.

- Cost and risk of transportation.

- Risk of relationship issues – an organisation may view an external supplier as critical, but the supplier may not have the same opinion of the relationship, or the wrong supplier may be selected. This is discussed in more detail in section 1.2.

> *Remember*
> When making a decision to use an external supplier the buyer must evaluate all of the risks carefully.

When an external supplier is ready to produce products or services, a key role of the procurement and supply department will be to manage the relationship for the duration of the contract. The type of relationship that is entered into will depend on a number of factors around supplier positioning (see section 1.2).

The relationship spectrum

The first step in actively managing supplier relationships is to classify the relationships that are currently in place. This enables the procurement team to ascertain where efforts need to be focused in order to develop supplier relationships that will both be beneficial and drive value for the business.

Classification can be done by using the supplier relationship spectrum (see figure 1.1). The spectrum ranges from adversarial relationships through to collaborative co-destiny relationships. In reality an organisation will have multiple types of supplier relationships, as it is not possible or desirable to create strategic relationships with every supplier.

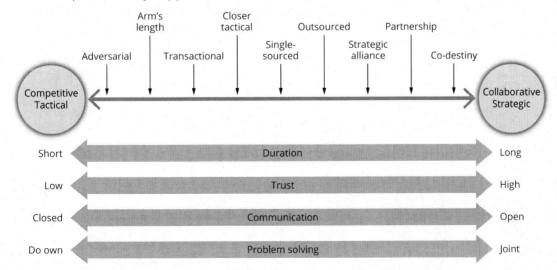

Figure 1.1 Supplier relationship spectrum (Source: www.procurement.govt.nz/ procurement/guide-to-procurement/plan-your-procurement/positioning-yourself-in-the-market/)

Pareto principle
Also called the 80/20 rule, this states that 80% of the outputs come from 20% of the inputs

Using the Pareto principle an organisation can prioritise its efforts. Approximately 80% of an organisation's spend will be with around 20% of its supplier base, which should be an organisation's strategic key suppliers. They will be the suppliers with the contracts that have the greatest values and the highest levels of risk. Therefore, spending time on developing relationships with these suppliers is likely to result in greater benefits for the business, rather than developing a relationship with a supplier that provides low-value goods or services.

An organisation will generally have a large number of suppliers that provide non-core products or services as part of a low-value, low-risk contract. This could be a supplier that provides stationery or office cleaning services. This type of supplier is needed but the service it provides is often transactional in nature. Also, a failure to supply this type of product or service would have a minimal effect on the buying organisation. There is also likely to be a large number of suppliers of this type in the market, and therefore it would be easy for a buyer to switch to an alternative supplier. There would be little benefit in developing relationships with them so they remain at arm's length.

As a buyer, it is key to understand which type of relationship will best suit a supply situation. However, each supplier will have its own view of the relationship, and it will not always be the same as that of the buying organisation. This is discussed further in section 1.2.

> *Remember*
> The following mnemonic can help you remember all the different types of relationships that are part of the relationship spectrum.
>
> **A**mazing **A**nnie **T**ried **C**ooking **S**ome **O**nions **S**adly **P**eeling **C**ried

As the relationship types move along the spectrum from competitive to collaborative, generally the relationship features shown in table 1.1 increase.

Relationship feature	Reason for increase
Duration of the relationship/contract	If a supplier is of key importance to a buyer, the buyer will want to lock them into a longer-term agreement/relationship in order to secure the supply and price.
Trust between the parties	As two businesses become more involved in each other's activities, trust will develop between the staff working on the contract.
Communication in terms of both frequency and detail	If a requirement has significant importance to a business it will need to communicate to the supplier regularly to ascertain key information such as delivery lead times, any potential issues, etc. In a more strategic relationship, information exchange will be two-way.
Levels of innovation	If a contract is long-term a supplier is more likely to want to work with a buyer to make improvements that will drive value for both parties, such as moving to an electronic ordering system and therefore eliminating waste.

Table 1.1 Relationship features

As you move from left to right along the spectrum, the importance of maintaining the relationship between the buying organisation and the supplier increases. This will have an effect on the **negotiation tactics** employed by both parties.

Cornelius and Faire (1989)[1] stated that there are three basic ways that conflict can be worked out. This can be applied to supplier negotiation situations.

The following three methods have been described using the analogy of a pie.

- **Win-lose** – one party gets what they want at the expense of the other party. For example, the buyer gets a bigger piece of the pie and the supplier gets a smaller piece. This will leave the supplier dissatisfied with the outcome and the buyer satisfied.

- **Lose-lose** – neither party gets what they really want. Both the buyer and the supplier get a smaller piece of the pie than they wanted.

- **Win-win** – parties are able to get to a position that is beneficial for both. This has also been referred to as "expanding the pie" (Jap, 1999).[2] Productive discussions may enable both parties to get additional value from the negotiation by expanding the possible options available.

In some situations the outcome of the negotiation is more valuable to the buyer or supplier than creating a close working relationship. The best example of this is achieving a cost saving on a non-core product or service that could be purchased from one of several suppliers. If the relationship fails with one supplier, it is fairly simple to source from one of the other suppliers in the market. When negotiating in such a situation, a buyer is more likely to negotiate harder in order to get the best deal, resulting in a win for the buyer and a loss for the supplier – a win-lose situation. This situation will lead to the development of adversarial buyer–supplier relationships.

Alternatively, maintaining the relationship may be equally important to both parties. As such, both will be more tactful in their negotiation strategy, keeping in mind that they will be working together in the future. In these situations, a buyer and a supplier may be able to come to a mutually beneficial deal – a win-win situation.

> *Remember*
> When negotiating, a buyer will use different tactics depending on the relationship it wants to establish with the supplier.

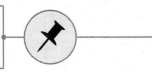

The nine relationship types included in the relationship spectrum model are described in more detail below. The characteristics of the different relationships, their benefits and drawbacks are also outlined.

Adversarial relationships

- The outcome of the deal, for example, in terms of price, is more important than maintaining the relationship over a long-term period. Both parties are trying to extract the maximum value out of the deal for themselves. The gain of the buyer, for example, will be at the expense of the supplier's profit margin.

- Typically, these suppliers will be providing non-core products and services, or the buyer may procure a one-off item.

- These relationships are characterised by poor communication, a lack of trust, and short-term or one-off contracts.

Leverage
To use the market to one's best advantage. For example, leveraging spend involves the buyer reviewing the total spend for a product or service, e.g., across multiple business areas or sites. The spend will then be combined into one contract, which will increase the potential contract value with the supplier, increasing the buyer's power to negotiate a better deal

Arm's-length relationships

- This type of supplier would be used infrequently, and contracts tend to be short term. As such, the time and effort taken to develop a more collaborative relationship is not justifiable.

- Both parties act independently of each other; avoiding dependency can enable a supplier to leverage the market to achieve the best possible price.

- An example of this type of supplier is low-level construction trades on a building site.

Transactional relationships

- This type of relationship is similar to an arm's-length relationship. However, the frequency or volume of the purchase is higher but the service or products are still low value and low risk.

- This type of relationship is characterised by markets that have a number of competing suppliers. This allows buyers to undertake regular competitive tender processes in order to secure the best price.

Closer tactical relationships

- The time and resources required to develop a collaborative relationship are not justifiable, but the buyer needs to ensure that it is dealing with a competent supplier.

- In some tiered supply chains this type of supplier may co-ordinate the activities of other suppliers.

Single-source relationships

- A single-source relationship is one where an organisation purchases a product or a service exclusively from one supplier. The aim is to obtain commercial benefits such as volume discounts or greater levels of quality.

- Single-source decisions are usually made at a strategic, top management level. Procurement and supply managers need to determine whether and how much value single-source relationships would add (Leenders et al., 2002).[3]

- Offering a supplier exclusivity requires a high level of trust. This type of relationship creates risk for the buying organisation due to the level of dependence they will have on the supplier.

- This type of relationship should not be confused with a sole source supplier. With a sole source situation there is only one supplier that is able to fill the requirement. Van Weele (2010)[4] notes that in the presence of dependency, good relationships between a buyer and a supplier are key in order for companies to achieve their goals.

Outsourced relationships

- Outsourcing describes a situation where a service previously carried out in-house by internal staff is transferred to a supplier.

- The main aim behind outsourcing is reducing costs, particularly staffing overheads. Often a supplier is able to provide a service or manufacture a product at a cheaper cost than the buying organisation could itself.

- In many cases contracts are outsourced to a supplier operating in lower-cost economies where labour costs are much lower.

- Typically, a business will only outsource non-core activities. Outsourcing the non-core activities enables the buying organisation to focus on its core competencies.

- TUPE legislation is important here (UK only).

Strategic alliance relationships

- This type of relationship describes a situation where two or more suppliers join together to deliver a joint offering, such as a new product. Each company will maintain its own autonomy.

- The aim is that working together will be mutually beneficial and will bring benefits quicker than if an organisation worked alone. The relationships may also involve sharing resources.

Partnership relationships

- Partnership working with a supplier is beneficial when procuring a high-risk, high-value product or service, or in a market where there are few viable suppliers.

- Working in this way will enable the supplier to have a much greater understanding of the buyer's needs. This is likely to benefit buyers in innovative developments, improvements in quality and reductions in waste.

- Both parties will keep the other informed of future plans and the relationship is long-term. There is commitment from the top management on both sides.

- The relationship is equal in terms of the balance of power. Both parties understand the need to work together. Maintaining the relationship is more important than individual gain.

TUPE legislation
TUPE stands for Transfer of Undertakings (Protection of Employment). TUPE regulations protect the rights of the employees where work they were employed to undertake is transferred to a new business

Case study

Toyota partnerships
Toyota is a world leader when it comes to SRM. Over the years it has developed long-term partnerships with key suppliers. Managing relationships with its key suppliers is a constant and ongoing process. Procurement leads the relationship-building process, which is managed via the following.

- **Key performance indicators (KPIs)**
- Company-to-company reviews
- Management of internal requests/concerns – with procurement as the main contact
- Regular and transparent communications

Toyota uses SRM to drive value from the relationships and generally shares any savings on a 50/50 basis with suppliers.

Key performance indicators (KPIs)
These are measurable values that will enable a buyer to track how well a supplier is performing. KPIs are tracked over time and will enable the buyer to decide when remedial action may be needed to improve performance

Co-destiny relationships

- The buyer organisation and the supplier organisation will be very closely linked. They make decisions about their future together and choose to share a common destiny.

- This results in a high level of interdependence between the two parties.

- Joint ventures are an example of a co-destiny type of relationship.

Remember
There are nine types of relationship that make up the relationship spectrum. As you move from left to right on the spectrum the level of closeness and collaboration increases.

Apply
Think about the supplier relationships in your current organisation. For five supplier relationships that you have knowledge of, try to locate where you think they would be on the relationship spectrum.

Summary

The type of relationship that develops between a buyer and a supplier will be closely linked to the levels of power that the buyer and the supplier have within the marketplace. There will be situations where a buyer can actively develop the type of supplier relationship that will be beneficial to their business. In other cases the supplier will have the balance of power and will impose the relationship type that they want to have on the buyer. This is discussed further in section 1.3.

Check
List all nine types of relationships that make up the relationship spectrum.

The relationship life cycle

Just like the relationships that each of us have in our personal lives, supplier relationships will also pass through a relationship cycle. Supplier relationships will evolve and change over time. A new supplier will be on-boarded and other supplier relationships will be terminated. Some relationships will pass through the cycle quicker than others. Therefore, during this time the supplier relationship management process will also evolve (Wagner, 2011).[5] The model below depicts a typical supplier relationship life cycle.

Figure 1.2 Relationship life cycle (Source: JAGGAER)

Qualification

The relationship life cycle will begin with the buyer searching the marketplace for a suitable supplier to meet their business requirement. Once the buyer has selected a suitable list of potential suppliers they will begin the on-boarding process by undertaking supplier qualification and selection activities. This is covered in more detail in section 2.1. There are two main processes that buyers use to on board and select suppliers.

- **Request for information (RFI)**. An RFI might be used if a buyer is unsure about the number of suppliers in the marketplace or whether there are a large number in the market. Additionally the buyer may be unaware of the potential capabilities that suppliers can offer. The RFI process will be used to shortlist or pre-qualify suppliers for the next stage of the process.

- **Request for proposal (RFP)**. In some cases a buyer will go straight to the RFP stage without undertaking an RFI if there are a known, small number of suppliers in the marketplace and the scope is well defined. An RFP will be used by a buyer when there is competition in the marketplace. It will enable the buyer to select the best supplier to deliver the products or undertake the service. Selection and evaluation are discussed in more detail in section 2.1.

Carter's 10 Cs is a key model that buyers can use to support them in building effective selection and qualification processes. Table 1.2 identifies each of the 10 Cs and then details what type of information would be collected relating to that point. The first seven listed were part of the original model. The model was expanded at a later date to include the final three.

Number	Area of evaluation	Benefits of information
1	Competency	The buyer will want to check that the supplier has delivered similar products or services and is competent to perform the task(s). The buyer may also ask the supplier to provide references to evidence its competency.
2	Capacity	The supplier will need to have sufficient capacity to provide the required volume of products or service levels. Buyers will also check whether the supplier is able to flex up or down if the requirement is variable.
3	Commitment to quality	A supplier will need to demonstrate how it manages quality, such as through an internal system or a third-party accredited system such as ISO 9001.
4	Control of processes	There are various aspects of control of processes, like the internal processes and procedures, that the supplier has. In some industries, control will be governed by legislation, e.g., catering and food production.

Liquidity ratio analysis
Referred to as 'financial ratios' – using information from a supplier's published financial statements

Whole life costing
A process that involves the buyer reviewing the costs of a product or service throughout its whole life. This will include the initial cost of the product, set-up, day-to-day running, maintenance, repair and disposal costs. This is generally applied to the purchase of equipment and machinery to assess which item will offer the best value for money over its expected life

Number	Area of evaluation	Benefits of information
5	Cash	A buyer needs to ensure that the supplier is financially stable, with sufficient cash flow, and therefore not likely to go out of business. This can be checked using credit reports such as those provided by Dun & Bradstreet. The buyer may also carry out liquidity ratio analysis.
6	Cost	This refers to the price submitted by the supplier. In some cases it may be necessary to look at whole life costings.
7	Consistency	The buyer will be looking for a supplier that is able to perform consistently, perhaps who is able to produce the product or service at the required quality consistently.
8	Culture	Carter felt that the supplier should have the same values and ways of operating as the customer. This would serve to support relationship development. The issue of having a supplier with a compatible culture becomes more important the further the relationship moves to the right along the spectrum.
9	Clean	This is very important in industries such as construction and heavy manufacturing, where breaches of environmental legislation are more likely and could result in costly fines.
10	Communication	How will a supplier communicate with the buying organisation? This needs to be in the format that the buying organisation requires. This point also includes the use of IT software and hardware.

Table 1.2 Carter's 10 Cs

A supplier may not always welcome this process, which can be both costly and time consuming, and there is no guarantee that its proposal will be successful. However, this process is also time consuming for the buying organisation. With the move towards e-procurement platforms, many qualification and selection processes are now undertaken electronically. This has removed the administrative burden for both parties.

Risk management
A process involving risk identification, assessment and management

Segmentation and risk management

Following the qualification process, segmentation and risk management is the second phase of the cycle. The products that a supplier provides will be segmented and classified to ensure that the correct relationship type is developed with each supplier. Segmentation is covered in detail in section 1.2. Ongoing risk management will also need to be carried out, especially for strategic contracts.

1.1 L01

Supply chains themselves have their own risks, such as the following.

- A key supply chain partner going out of business
- A supplier using child labour, causing reputational risks
- An event such as flooding, or a supplier staff strike, affecting deliveries of component parts

Risk management is an ongoing process that links to supplier relationship management. In more strategic relationships a buyer and supplier will need to work together to manage risks in order to ensure the survival of the relationship. In strategic relationships the level of interdependence between the parties is usually higher. Risk management is covered in greater detail in section 1.2.

> *Remember*
> The relationship life cycle involves the following stages.
>
> - On-boarding
> - Qualification
> - Segmentation and risk management
> - Performance management
> - Development and innovation
> - Phase-out (if required)

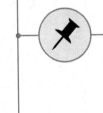

Performance management

In the same way that an employer will hold appraisals with its employees at the end of the year, a procurement department will complete reviews with each supplier. Supplier performance measurement is the assessment of a supplier's current performance. This may be assessed against the required standards, the supplier's previous performance and how it compares to other suppliers delivering a similar service. This is often undertaken as part of the contract management process and will involve the use of key performance indicators (KPIs), which may include the following.

- **Safety**
  - Lost time injury frequency
  - Total injury frequency
  - Near miss incidents/accidents
- **Quality**
  - Stock accuracy
  - Pick accuracy
  - Stock loss/damage
  - Obsolescence
  - Shrinkage
- **Delivery**
  - Percentage of products delivered in full on time
  - Percentage of products with a defect
  - Goods receipt discrepancies
  - Compliance to paperwork
  - Conformance certificates

- **Cost**
  - ○ Cost to budget
  - ○ Output
  - ○ Continuous improvement
  - ○ Waste/recycle revenue stream
- **Morale**
  - ○ Attendance/absence
  - ○ Employee/supplier survey/opinion results
- **Environment**
  - ○ Waste to landfill
  - ○ CO_2 emissions

To be successful, this process will also need to involve the internal business stakeholders affected by the purchase of the product or service. In a manufacturing company it could be the production manager. These stakeholders will have key information on how well the supplier is performing.

This process is likely to include regular contract management/review meetings. The regularity of these meetings will depend on the importance of the product or service. Strategic contracts may have reviews as often as once a month, whereas other contracts may only have annual reviews. These review meetings can be used as a tool to support the development of supplier relationships when developing closer relationships is the buyer's chosen strategy.

Development and innovation

Supplier development
The process of working with a supplier to improve its processes and/ or the products and services it delivers. The aim of supplier development is commercial benefits for the buying organisation; however, there will also be benefits for the supplier

Supplier development is also a key part of the relationship life cycle. Supplier development is a time-consuming and resource-intensive process. Therefore this activity will only be undertaken with an organisation's strategic suppliers (or those that are potentially strategic) such as those that the buyer has developed partnerships with.

Before a buyer begins a programme of supplier development activities it should review the activities against the vision and objectives of the buying organisation. Supplier development should be viewed as a two-way process. It will require a commitment of time, effort and resources from both parties. Both parties must have a mutual desire to achieve the objectives of the supplier development programme.

Here are various reasons why a buyer might undertake supplier development activities.

- Previous performance issues with a key supplier resulting in quality issues that need to be addressed.

- The buying organisation needs to improve its performance, for example, by reducing waste in order to become more competitive in the marketplace.

- The buyer wants the supplier to adopt some of its own technologies such as ordering systems, and the supplier will require support to do this.

- The buyer wants to develop new products and services.

A supplier development programme should result in measurable benefits. Without these measurable benefits neither party will be able to track progress against the objectives. It would also be difficult to ascertain when the end goal has been reached. As a supplier development programme is a journey that both the buyer and supplier embark on, the process will involve elements of change management.

Supplier development can result in a number of benefits for both the buyer and the supplier.

- It can reduce costs for a buyer and supplier.

- Working together can result in elimination of waste from the supply chain, again reducing costs.

- Long-term security of business can serve to increase the motivation of a supplier, which could lead to innovative benefits.

There is no standard approach for supplier development. A buyer will need to select a method that will best achieve its objectives and suit the relationship that it has with the supplier.

Case study

Nestlé

In 2005 Nestlé India established a dedicated supplier development department. The aims were sourcing more raw materials locally due to high import barriers, overcoming quality and food safety issues, and creating a wider, more flexible supply base. By 2009 the team had:

- secured more local sources of supply

- avoided ten single-supplier situations

- developed over 70 Indian suppliers to meet its specification

- achieved large savings

- provided technical assistance to suppliers to improve quality and safety as well as access to better technology.

This programme has since been replicated by Nestlé in other countries.

(Source: www.Nestle.com)

As is the case with all types of relationships, the relationship between a buying organisation and a supplier will eventually come to an end, with the supplier being phased out. The end of the relationship could be due to several reasons.

- The contract comes to a natural end and there is no longer a requirement to purchase that product or service.

- The contract is re-tendered and another supplier is able to provide a more competitive offer.

- The contract with the supplier is terminated due to a **material breach** such as poor performance.

- The supplier becomes insolvent – this can also be classed as a material breach of contract and would enable the buyer to formally end the relationship.

The reason for the end of the relationship will affect the nature of the phase-out period. If the contract came to a natural end then the phase-out will be planned. However, if a supplier has become insolvent the buyer will quickly have to find a

Material breach
A material breach of contract is a failure of performance. This can be on the part of either the buyer or the supplier. This failure is considered so great that it gives the other party the right [?] to terminate the contract and/ or sue for damages depending on the situation

replacement and build relationships with a new supplier. In contrast, if a competitive tender process has been run and an existing supplier has lost a contract, the phase-out could be hostile. To avoid this, a buyer should carefully detail any required handover processes in their contracts with a supplier. This should also cover management of the TUPE process.

> *Remember*
> There are six phases to the relationship life cycle.
>
> - On-boarding
> - Qualification
> - Segmentation and risk management
> - Performance management
> - Development and innovation
> - Phase-out (if required)

> *Check*
> - What are the benefits and drawbacks of using an internal supplier?
> - What are the benefits of supplier development for the buyer?

1.2 Appraise portfolio analysis techniques to assess relationships in supply chains

There are a number of portfolio analysis techniques that can be used by a buyer to support the development of sourcing and supplier relationship strategies. These include the following.

- Supply positioning (the Kraljic model)
- Supplier preferencing model
- Market management matrix

Each of these portfolio analysis techniques is discussed below.

All of these techniques have benefits and drawbacks that should be considered carefully when using the tools in practice. Action plans can then be developed, ensuring that buyer–supplier relationships are developed in a way that will help to achieve the desired strategies.

Matrices to identify supply, supplier and purchaser positioning

Section 1.1 discussed the fact that an organisation is likely to have a portfolio of relationships to match its portfolio of products and services. Due to resource and time constraints it is not beneficial or possible to have a close relationship with each supplier. As a result, a company will need to analyse and segment its portfolio of products and suppliers in order to assess its current position and identify where it needs to make improvements in order to obtain greater value for the buying organisation.

Undertaking a positioning exercise has a number of benefits for the buyer, the procurement department and for the wider business that the function serves.

- Allowing a buyer to focus on leveraging the available resources by identifying both sourcing and relationship opportunities that may be able to add value (see sections 1.3 and 1.4)

- Identifying opportunities to develop competitive advantage (see section 1.3)

- Providing a framework for decision-making and action planning for the buyer

- Improving risk management, by helping the business to identify which products and suppliers pose a vulnerability

However, the process of using these techniques is time-consuming and will require a procurement resource that could potentially be more effectively used on other procurement tasks. Therefore, when undertaking the portfolio analysis and segmentation, the buyer should set some clear objectives around what they are trying to achieve. Below are three examples of procurement objectives and how these could be supported by the use of portfolio analysis.

- Identifying opportunities to move non-contract spend on to a contract and as a result reduce costs. This could be achieved by undertaking a Pareto analysis (also known as ABC analysis) of the top non-contract suppliers.

- Identifying an organisation's key products and suppliers. This could be achieved by using a Kraljic model to identify which items are strategic.

- Developing value-adding relationships with strategic suppliers. This could be done by reviewing where the strategic suppliers are on the supplier preferencing model to assess whether more collaborative relationships are possible.

Identifying opportunities to move non-contract spend onto a contract

Pareto analysis

Pareto analysis was defined briefly in section 1.1. Vilfredo Pareto was an economist and sociologist during the late 19th and early 20th century. Pareto analysis, also referred to as the 80/20 rule, applies not only to economics and its related disciplines but also to much of the natural environment.

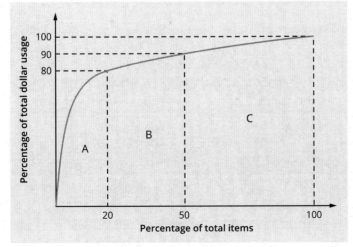

Figure 1.3 ABC analysis (Source: adapted from www.resourcesystemsconsulting.com)

ABC analysis can be used to look at the costs of a product or service. Cost is a key consideration of the procurement department; reducing costs is often a KPI for the procurement team. Using Pareto analysis can assist with achieving this objective. Cousins et al. (2008)[6] explained that, for example, 20% of the products used to manufacture a car will make up 80% of the costs. Outlined below is the application of ABC analysis (see figure 1.3).

- A items account for 80% of cost and 20% of volume.

- C items represent low-cost and high-volume items.

- B items are in the middle.

This analysis will show where the costs sit. Spend data is crucial in order to make the correct procurement decisions. Spend analysis brings several benefits including reduced costs, lower inventory levels and improved supplier management, and it allows the refocusing of resources on strategic issues.

> *Remember*
> Pareto analysis and ABC analysis are based on the 80/20 rule.

Based on the above analysis, the time, attention and resources of the procurement team should be focused on the A items. If 80% of the spend is with 20% of suppliers, the procurement team will need to focus on these relationships. This will give a better return on the invested time and resources.

Pareto analysis is useful for targeting a buyer's efforts in order to leverage better outcomes and add more value for the wider business. Once the analysis has been carried out and the strategies put in place, they will then reduce the spend on the procured products and services found in the 20%. Thus the purchases move down the ranking and out of the 20% range to be replaced by another product or service from the remaining 80%.

The downside of this type of analysis is that it does not consider the impact of the categories or the market complexity. Also it does not provide strategic recommendations, it has no real guidelines and therefore it is not a portfolio technique (van der Schans, 2014[7] and Gelderman, 2000[8]).

Pareto analysis will allow the procurement team to make a more accurate judgment when plotting products and services on the financial axis (horizontal) of the Kraljic model (see below).

Risk in the context of the Kraljic model

Risk
A situation that involves exposure to danger

Before moving on to discuss the Kraljic model we need to take a look at **risk** and risk management. Although this is a wide field of study in its own right, we will briefly touch on the concept of risk management here, as supply risk forms the second axis (vertical) of the Kraljic model. We have already defined risk management, but the concept of risk also needs to be defined and explained.

In order to ensure survival, businesses need to actively manage the risks that could affect them. Risk can be internal or external to an organisation. The monitoring of both types of risk is covered in section 1.3 on STEEPLE analysis.

In order to effectively manage risks, these should also be identified and classified by a business. A business can use a risk register to record and manage all of the possible risks that might have an impact on it. Procurement as a function will have its own risks. Many of these risks will affect the wider business. This is especially true in the manufacturing sector, as procurement is responsible for managing the inputs for the manufacturing process. Without these crucial inputs the manufacturing process may come to a stop, which could have serious implications for the buying organisation.

There are various different types of risk that could affect procurement. Some of these are related to the inputs from the supplier and some are related to buyer–supplier relationships. Zsidisin (2003)[9] states that risks tend to arise from individual supplier failure and market factors.

- Supplier failure can relate to problems with quality, delivery, relationship and price.
- Market characteristics relate to demand and the number of suppliers in the marketplace.

Once risks have been identified they should be classified according to the size of the impact that they could have on the business as well as the likelihood that the risks could occur. A risk score can be calculated using the simple formula:

$$\text{Total risk} = \text{Likelihood} \times \text{Impact}$$

For example, a flood could pose a very high risk to a business' supply chain (4 out of 5). However, flooding that is extensive is rare (1 out of 5), so the likelihood would be low.

Risks should be scored both on impact and likelihood in order to fully assess the situation. To continue with the example used above, the:

$$\text{total risk} = 1\ (\text{likelihood}) \times 5\ (\text{impact}) = 5\ (\text{out of a possible 25}).$$

The higher the degree of potential risk, the more a business will want to gain control of the sourcing process and ensure continuity and quality of supply. Once the business risks have been identified and classified the business will look at whether or not they can be mitigated. Having strong relationships with a supplier can support a business with mitigation should one of the risks occur. For example, if there is a supply shortage, generally a supplier will ensure that its key customers' orders are fulfilled first.

Identifying an organisation's key products and suppliers

The Kraljic model

The **Kraljic model** is a well-known positioning model. This key model will be an influential part of your procurement and supply studies and the work that you undertake for organisations. You may have already come across this model in your earlier studies.

The Kraljic model, developed in 1983 by Peter Kraljic, is a simple model. It was first introduced in an article called 'Purchasing must become supply management'.[10] It is used to distinguish between different types of procurement strategies depending on the value of the products or services being purchased, balanced against the risk of the purchase. The aim of the model was to enable a buyer to maximise its buying power whilst minimising risk to the organisation. Despite the age of the model it remains highly relevant today.

The model allows a buyer to classify its purchases and select appropriate procurement strategies for each type of product or service. This is therefore likely to lead to more effective decisions based on market and supplier knowledge. The model plays a key part in category management, as a buyer can use it to segment all of the products and services that form part of its category.

Category management
The spend in an organisation is broken down into groups (categories) of related products and services, e.g., construction, IT, facilities management. For example, an IT category would include contracts for software, and hardware such as laptops/printers/ servers, telecoms and IT consultancy

The model demonstrates the need for procurement to be viewed as a strategic rather than a transactional operational function. Over the last few decades, the view of procurement has changed in many organisations. In many businesses it is now viewed as a strategic function. As more and more companies focus on their core business and enter into contracts with an external supplier, procurement has become more important. This is also due to the fact that procurement can have a huge effect on the financial performance of a company (van Weele, 2000[11]) by reducing the cost of inputs. The cost of inputs can affect a company's profits significantly.

All organisations have strategic suppliers and these suppliers need to be managed in a different way to the transactional suppliers. The Kraljic model can be used to create a long-term strategy for the procurement department or, as mentioned, for an individual category or area of spend. An important part of this strategy involves selecting which suppliers to focus relationship management efforts on.

> *Remember*
> The Kraljic model can be used to develop procurement strategies.

The Kraljic model as shown in figure 1.4 consists of two axes. The first is financial risk (vertical axis), ranging from low to high. The second is supply risk (horizontal axis), also ranging from low to high. These classification results produce a two-by-two model with four categories/quadrants.

- **Vertical axis = financial risk.** This includes issues such as the impact on profit of an item measured against criteria such as volume, percentage of total purchase cost, quality and business costs, relative value and profitability. These risks are internal to a company.

- **Horizontal axis = supply risk.** This includes issues such as the number of suppliers in the marketplace, delivery risks and issues associated with technological developments. This also links with Porter's Five Forces model, which is covered in detail in section 1.3. The issues in the Porter's Five Forces model will affect the supply risk and the level of market complexity. These risks are external to a company.

Leverage suppliers	Strategic suppliers
Vast competition Low cost to switch suppliers Often utility services e.g., electricity	Critical supplier to an organisation Responsible for core products and services
Routine suppliers	**Bottleneck suppliers**
Low-value items Lots of work associated with these suppliers Lots of variety available e.g., stationery suppliers	Holds monopoly in marketplace Little or no other options Low-value items

(Vertical axis: Cost impact — Horizontal axis: Risk impact)

Figure 1.4 Based on The Kraljic matrix of different supplier types

The Kraljic model contains four quadrants: routine, bottleneck, leverage and strategic. The segment into which a product or service is plotted will indicate the type of sourcing approach that should be applied and the level of resources that will be required in order to develop or maintain the relationship.

Table 1.3 outlines each of the segments in the Kraljic model. It gives an example of the type of products or services that might fall within each quadrant, what the issues are regarding that quadrant, and the types of procurement strategy that could be used, as well as the type of relationship strategy.

1.2 L01

> *Remember*
> The Kraljic model has four quadrants – routine, bottleneck, leverage and strategic.

Quadrant	Routine – low risk and low value
Examples	Stationery supplies
	Consumables
	Materials such as maintenance, repair and operation (MRO)
	Low-level temporary labour
Issues	Can be time-consuming compared to the value due to the volume of orders and requisitions
	On a day-to-day basis can distract a buyer from more strategic/value-adding activities
Strategy	Use tactics to leverage savings and reduce costs, e.g., **reverse e-auctions**/use of procurement cards
	Optimise ordering process and stock holding (Gelderman and van Weele, 2002[12])
	Use online catalogues to improve efficiency
	Standardise products as much as possible to increase volumes
	Construct framework agreement/**call-off contracts** to reduce burden of tendering
Relationship strategy	Adversarial
	Arm's length/transactional

Quadrant	**Bottleneck** – high risk and low value but relatively rare in terms of the supply market
Examples	**OEM** parts
	Computer chips
Issues	Prone to supply risk such as limited availability
	Potential storage issues
	Likely to be a small number of suppliers in marketplace
	Can seriously affect the delivery of the product or service
Strategy	Secure long-term supply contracts with clauses regarding late delivery charges for delivery failure
	Look for alternatives in the marketplace (Lysons and Farrington, 2006[13]) – this is likely to be difficult in the case of OEM parts
	Focus on managing the procurement process
Relationship strategy	Single-source, long-term contracts

Reverse e-auction
An electronic procurement process that involves suppliers competing against each other by reducing their prices. The supplier that submits the lowest price will win the auction

Call-off contract
An overarching agreement in respect of price, terms and conditions that allows a buyer or user department to 'order/ call off' products or services as required over a period of time. These types of contract are useful where volume over a period of time is unknown

Consortia procurement
When a group of separate organisations come together to procure products or services. This allows them to leverage their buying power. This is common in the public sector

Quadrant	**Leverage** – market risk is low and the cost or value is high
Examples	Product-specific materials
Issues	Unit cost management is important due to volume
	Can have a large impact on profit due to the high value
Strategy	Obtaining the best deal via competitive tendering due to nature of market
	Target pricing and product substitution where possible (Gelderman and van Weele, 2002[14])
	Enhancing buyer power by engaging in consortia procurement
Relationship strategy	Closer tactical
	Outsourced

Quadrant	**Strategic** – high risk and high impact on profitability
Examples	Major outsourcing providers such as IT
Issues	Dependent on small number of suppliers
	Could severely affect profits
	Likely to be important for gaining/maintaining competitive advantage
Strategy	Long-term relationships as changing the source of supply likely to be costly or difficult
	Balancing power and co-operating with supplier
Relationship strategy	Strategic alliance
	Performance-based partnerships (Lysons and Farrington, 2006[15]) with single or sole sources
	Co-destiny

Table 1.3 Kraljic model quadrants

Check
What are the four quadrants of the Kraljic model? Can you draw the model?

Kraljic example
A component of a machine could have a relatively low cost to purchase, but it could be a high-risk item. For example, if a delivery is late it could potentially stop production. Stopped production would result in delays in meeting customer timescales, which could be costly for a business. It would also lead to downtime, which is costly. A product with a low cost and high risk would be categorised as a bottleneck product. In this case, ensuring continuity of supply is critical.

Case study

Products and services can move to different quadrants of the model overtime, particularly as a result of developing appropriate supplier relationships and strategies. Once segmentation has been applied, a buyer may realise that its non-critical, transactional supplier is actually in the leverage quadrant and should have a closer, more tactical relationship. Action plans can then be put in place to move to the desired situation (see later in this section).

Lysons and Farrington (2006)[16] suggest undertaking the following practical steps in order to carry out the segmentation analysis.

- Make a list of all purchases in descending order of value, i.e. highest-value products and services first.

- Evaluate the supply risk and market complexity for each item or service on the list.

- Evaluate each item on the model based on the above analysis. Which segment of the model fits a product or service best?

- Regularly review the position of each product/service in the model to assess risks and identify any new opportunities.

Segmenting the products and services that an organisation buys will also support supplier relationship management. With regard to the products and services that are classified as 'strategic', these suppliers would be the key ones to target for relationship building and development. Cousins et al. (2008)[17] noted that it is important to remember that the Kraljic model segments services/products and not companies. It is possible that a supplier may provide a range of services that cross into two, three or even all of the quadrants of the model. The buyer will need to use its professional judgment to decide the positioning of these products and services.

> *Remember*
> In order to segment the supply base the buyer should make a list of all products and services in ascending order of value and then evaluate the risk of supply for each item. Following this, each product or service should be positioned on the model and the model should be reviewed regularly.

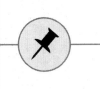

Use of the Kraljic model to segment the products and services that an organisation procures has a number of benefits.

- The model is simple to understand and apply.

- It can be applied across all industries and company types.

- It can result in a buyer/procurement department having a better understanding of the importance of each of the products or services to the business. This is especially true in terms of the cost of the item and the risk in the supply chain. A buyer may uncover risks that it was previously unaware of.

- It can assist in deciding what is the optimum relationship strategy for each purchase/supplier, e.g., the model will illustrate the likely bargaining position that the buyer will have.

- It can provide an additional insight into strategic issues (Gelderman and van Weele, 2003[18]).

However, there are some limitations of the Kraljic model.

- Supply markets are complex. As a result it is not always easy to classify products or services into one of the four quadrants.

- There is an element of subjectivity regarding where products and services are located within the model.

- Overtime there are likely to be changes in the marketplace; therefore, the analysis is only a snapshot in time.

- The analysis applies to the products or services being purchased and not the supplier. This will be discussed shortly when we learn about supplier preferencing, below.

- Not all supply risks arise within the buyer–supplier relationship; there are also risks that are external to this. (See section 1.3 for more on external risks.) In addition to this, not all risks can be mitigated by developing relationships.

- It has a limited academic foundation (Luzzini et al., 2012[19]).

Apply

Think of five products or services that your organisation procures and plot them on the Kraljic model. Consider whether your current strategy for procuring these items fits their position in the quadrant.

Developing value-adding relationships with strategic suppliers

Supplier preferencing model

In order to develop successful strategies for managing supplier relationships, a buyer also needs to take into account a supplier's perspective of the relationship. Before entering into a commercial relationship, a supplier will also be reviewing the benefits and potential drawbacks of the relationship. One key consideration for each supplier will be whether the business relationship will be profitable. Sometimes a buyer is not an attractive customer for the supplier; for example, the buyer's business may be unprofitable or the buyer may be known in the market for not paying its suppliers on time. It is important for a buying organisation to be viewed as an attractive customer because this will support them in gaining a competitive advantage (Bew, 2007[20]). It is also important for a buyer to be aware of a supplier's perception of them in formulating its negotiation strategies.

Some suppliers may be keen to develop relationships with a buyer, whereas others may not. Some buyers may wish to develop a partnership with suppliers, but some suppliers may have no interest in forming a closer relationship. Therefore, supplier preferencing is also an important segmentation tool. Developed by Steele and Court (1996), the supplier preferencing matrix allows a buyer to understand how suppliers view the buying organisation and its requirements. The matrix is based on two axes (see figure 1.5).

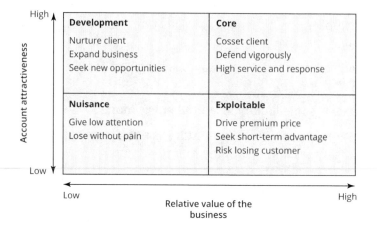

Figure 1.5 Supplier preferencing matrix (Source: adapted from: '12 Steps to key account management portfolio analysis', Part 2, Fig. 2, by Professor Malcolm McDonald MA(Oxon) MSc PhD DLitt DSc, Emeritus Professor, Cranfield University School of Management)

1. The vertical axis is the attractiveness of the account. A supplier will be keen to associate themselves with a high-profile buyer such as the Olympic Games projects. A buyer needs to ensure that its business is viewed in a positive light by the suppliers in the marketplace. There are various other elements linked to this set out below.

1.2 LO1

- Profitability – the more profitable a buyer's business is, the more attractive the business is as a customer.

- Further opportunity for growth and development with the buyer.

- Stability of future contracts – predictable requirements with good forward planning will be attractive to suppliers.

- The general reputation of the buyer in the market.

- Ethical trading practices. For example, a supplier is often keen to do business with public sector organisations as they offer better payment terms – 30 days instead of 60. A supplier may avoid a customer if they are known to have long payment terms.

- Willingness to collaborate on projects, including sharing risks and costs with a supplier.

2. The horizontal axis is the relative value of the business. In general, the greater the value of the business, the more important a buyer will be to a supplier. They will be a **preferred customer**. Small volumes of business may be too costly for a supplier to administer and will therefore be less attractive.

Preferred customer
A buying organisation that a supplier treats better than other customers, for example, in terms of product quality and availability, delivery or/and prices

> *Remember*
> The supplier preferencing model looks at how the supplier views the relationship with a buyer.

The following quote demonstrates the benefits for a buyer if they are viewed by their supplier as a core customer.

> *[75%] of suppliers say they regularly put most preferred customers at the top of allocation lists for materials or services in short supply, 82% say that their customers consistently get first access to new product or service ideas and technologies and a resounding 87% of suppliers offer unique cost reduction opportunities to their most preferred customers.*

(Source: Bew, 2007[21])

Table 1.4 looks at each quadrant of the supplier preferencing model in turn, considering the actions that a supplier may take and the buyer's responses to these actions if the supplier is providing a strategic product or service.

Quadrant	Actions a supplier may take	Potential buyer's responses if a key product/service (strategic)
Nuisance – little profit for supplier Customer difficult or expensive to service	Decide to stop dealing with the buyer and withdraw from the relationship Service levels and/or quality may be poor Raise prices and push into exploitable quadrant	Try and move into the development quadrant. Could do this by looking at areas of business that the supplier might find attractive, such as being involved in a prestigious project

Quadrant	Actions a supplier may take	Potential buyer's responses if a key product/service (strategic)
Exploitable – supplier in position of strength	Regular price increases and lack of negotiation on terms and conditions Supplier is seeking short-term advantage Will not go out of its way to service the buyer	Try to move into the core quadrant by looking at areas of business that the supplier might find attractive, such as being involved in a prestigious project
Development – customer has potential for growth	Provision of good customer service. Supplier is proactive, regularly going the extra mile in an attempt to win more business from the buyer Competitive pricing provided	Move into core area by rewarding supplier's efforts with additional business (if possible) Undertaking supplier development activities
Core – customer very important	Provision of great customer service in order to defend and retain the business Supplier drives innovation Receptive to a close relationship	Review regularly to ensure position as a core customer is ongoing

Table 1.4 Supplier preferencing quadrants

Overtime, a buyer can become less attractive to a supplier for a number of reasons. Steinle and Schiele (2008)[22] noted that the principle of customer attractiveness is most important if there is a scarcity of suppliers in the marketplace. In these cases, a supplier can be more particular about which buyers and organisations they sell to, as supplier power is high. Marketplace structures and supplier power are discussed in more detail in section 1.3.

> *Remember*
> The supplier and the buyer may not always have the same view of the relationship. This could lead to potential risks for the buyer, especially if the supplier views it as a nuisance or exploitable.

Relationship marketing
This looks at long-term term customer engagement including customer loyalty

Research undertaken on buyer–supplier relationships has generally focused on this topic from the perspective of the buyer (Hallikas et al., 2005[23]). However, it was noted by Grönroos and Helle (2012)[24] that even if businesses had conflicting and differing ambitions and goals, according to **relationship marketing**, the possibility to achieve mutual gain does exist.

There are a number of advantages to applying the supplier preferencing model.

- It provides the supplier view. Therefore, once both Kraljic and supplier preferencing have been undertaken the buyer will have a fuller picture of the best strategy to help it move to the desired relationship.

- It may provide the buyer with information it was unaware of; for example, it may not have realised that its suppliers view it as exploitable. Once the buyer is aware of this it can take action to improve how it is viewed by the marketplace.

However, there are also a number of limitations of this model.

- As with the Kraljic model, the supplier preferencing model is a snapshot in time.

- Although some information about services provided can be quantified, such as KPI reports, this supplier preferencing model is subject to the judgment of the buyer.

Check
What are the four quadrants of the supplier preferencing model? Can you draw the model?

1.2 LO1

Market management matrix

Both models can be combined by using the market management matrix. This will give a more holistic view of supply positioning and supplier preferencing. The model was developed by Steele and Court (1996)[25] (see figure 1.6) and shows the 16 possible outcomes.

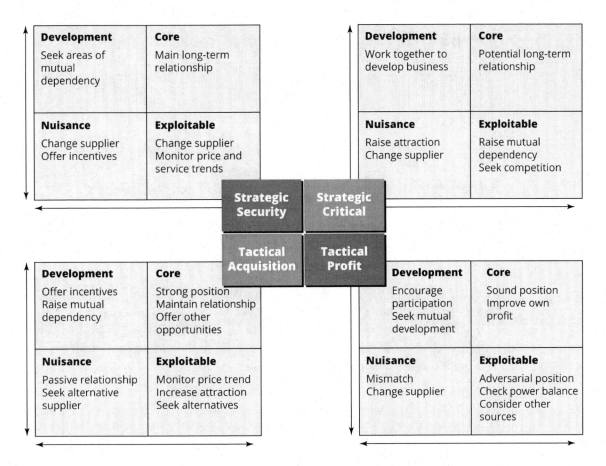

Figure 1.6 Market management matrix model (Source: PMMS Consulting Group, model developed in Steele, P.T. and Court, B,H. Profitable Purchasing Strategies: A Manager's Guide for Improving Organizational Competitiveness through the Skills of Purchasing, London: McGraw-Hill Press.)

This model helps a buyer to understand where its requirements are and how it is viewed by the market. Ideally these two items should match up, but this is not always the case. If the buyer understands the current situation, plans can be made and actions taken to progress the buyer/supplier relationship and therefore get a better procurement outcome.

Ideally, each supplier that provides the buyer with its strategic critical requirements will also view the buyer as a core customer. However, this may not always be the case. The views of the buyer and the supplier may conflict. The most vulnerable position for a buyer to be in is where a supplier of strategic critical products and services views it as a nuisance or exploitable.

If the buyer–supplier relationships are not aligned, a buyer will need to take action to reduce its risk exposure. The buyer will need to influence the supplier to align its perceptions of the relationship with the buyer's objectives for the relationship (van der Schans, 2014[26]). The model helps a buyer to examine and manage the marketplace. It could indicate the actions that a buyer could take (see figure 1.6).

> *Remember*
> The management matrix model combines the Kraljic model and the supplier preferencing model.

The management matrix model attempts to provide some practical advice on which strategy a buyer should adopt after it has judged the position from its own point of view (Kraljic model) as well as from the supplier's perspective (supplier preferencing) (van Weele, 2010[27]). There are various benefits of using this model.

- It offers a further chance to minimise risks and maximise opportunities by showing, for example, which suppliers may be open to partnership development, avoiding wasted resources.

- It can indicate when action should be taken, for instance when a change of supplier might be required if the buyer is viewed as a nuisance or exploitable.

- It can indicate where a change of relationship rather than a change of supplier might be required.

Limitations of this model include the fact that, as with the other models, it is a snapshot in time and buyer–supplier relationships can change.

Developing action plans

The portfolio management tools outlined above are very useful for developing procurement strategies. Once the process of segmenting the products and services that a company buys and the supplier base has been undertaken, a procurement team will be able to start developing action plans. The action plans can turn the models that have been developed into a tool for strategic change.

The segmentation process will provide information that the organisation can use to make informed choices about the type of relationships that it should have with each supplier. However, in order to ensure that these strategies are relevant, the details from the models should be supplemented with additional information. Such information could include the company's overall strategy, market data and details about an individual supplier. This additional information will help to avoid threats and missed opportunities (van der Schans, 2014[28]). A buyer may discover that a new supplier has entered the marketplace, and this might allow the buyer to move away from a supplier that is treating it as a nuisance or exploitable.

As mentioned above, the action plan should take into account the supplier's view of the buyer. It should also consider the power that both the buyer and the supplier have in the marketplace. This needs to be considered to ensure that time and resources are not spent on attempting to develop a relationship with a supplier that has no interest in doing so.

In some cases, the relationship that a buyer has with a supplier may already be on the right-hand side of the relationship spectrum model. The business will need to ensure that this is maintained in order to cultivate the ongoing value. In other cases, a supplier relationship on the spectrum may currently be offering no value and could in the long-term be detrimental to an organisation's procurement strategies. An example of this is when a supplier providing strategic products or services views the buyer as exploitable. Supplier action plans can then be developed and used to move these suppliers to a more desirable position on the spectrum.

For example, as noted above, a strategic supplier may view the buyer as exploitable or a nuisance. An example of a supplier action plan in this case would include moving the supplier up into the development or core quadrant. The plan could include the following actions.

- Increasing the volume/value of business with the supplier if this is possible and desirable. There are risks associated with single sources of supply. Increasing the volume/value of business with a supplier could be done by aggregating volume from smaller contracts. The more of the buyer's business a supplier has, generally the more important the relationship will be to the supplier.

- The buyer could also involve the supplier in innovation and development programmes to create new products and services or generate greater value from existing products and services. A supplier is likely to view such an invite as a route to greater volumes and values of business in the future.

- The buyer could work with the supplier to understand why they are viewed as a nuisance. For example, a supplier may be frustrated with the buyer's ordering process and system. The buyer can then work on such issues to improve the working relationship.

The implementation of action plans will need to form part of a structured process. Where a business is in its supplier relationship management journey will depend on the type of plan used. If little SRM activity has been undertaken, a more **transformational** approach and plan may need to be implemented. This will include elements of change management. In order to develop the action plan, procurement will need to include key internal stakeholders such as the operations, sales and marketing teams to create a **cross-functional** working group.

The first task will involve reviewing current SRM activities and defining each of the existing relationships. The segmentation tools discussed in this section will allow a business to define the current status of the relationships. Following this, the team will need to develop a road map showing where they would like each of the relationships to move. This will include developing strategies and objectives that will enable progress to be measured and tracked.

> *Remember*
> The insights provided by the positioning models should be used to develop supplier relationship management action plans.

The action plans will also include plans for communication and collaboration. For example, in order to move from being a development customer to a core customer, a buyer may need to change the way it communicates with the supplier. There are various different mechanisms that could be used for this, including regular review meetings with suppliers. These could naturally form part of the current contract management process. Technology could also be used to support this process, including the use of extranets and web portals. Such plans are also likely to include supplier development activity (see section 1.1).

Once an action plan has been created it should be monitored and evaluated against the desired outcome at regular intervals in order to assess the progress made. This could be done as part of a **Plan Do Check Act (PDCA)** cycle. Buyers need to review whether there is a return on investment of the time spent developing supplier relationships.

1.3 Identify the competitive forces that impact on relationships in supply chains

Competitive forces are constantly at play within a marketplace. They evolve and change overtime as industry structures change. These market changes will affect supply chains, particularly in terms of supplier and buyer power. The distribution of power between a buyer and supplier has a direct impact on relationship management.

Sources of competitive advantage

Competitive advantage
Putting an organisation in a strong position against its competition

Companies strive to gain competitive advantage over others in the marketplace to ensure the survival of their company. If a company cannot compete it will cease to exist. Therefore, companies need to ensure that they obtain a profitable and sustainable position in the market.

This is particularly important in markets where there are a large number of companies fighting for market share, for example travel agencies and insurance companies. However, competitive advantage should not be confused with market leadership. Having the biggest share of the market does not always result in the largest profits. The selection of a competitive strategy is therefore of great importance.

Competitive strategies

Porter (1985)[29] stated that there were two elements to selecting a competitive strategy.

- The attractiveness of industries for long-term profits
- Factors that determine relative competitive position within an industry

Competitive strategy involves both a company's response to the marketplace and its attempt to shape that marketplace for its own gain. The ability to secure competitive advantage will allow a company to generate greater profits than its rivals.

There are many potential sources of competitive advantage. Several of these sources are the result of relationships that have developed between a buyer and supplier. Competitive advantage should be sustainable and not eroded by competitors or changes in the marketplace overtime.

Porter stated that there were three generic strategies for achieving above-average performance within a market.

1. Cost leadership

- A company sets out to become the lowest-cost producer in the marketplace.
- The company could do this by pursuing economies of scale by standardising its product or by obtaining proprietary technology; the company must exploit all sources of cost advantage.
- These types of companies typically sell a standard or budget product.
- If there is more than one cost leader in a market, rivalry will be fierce.
- There are several examples of companies following this strategy across all industries, e.g., Aldi (low-cost food), Ryanair (low-cost flights) and Primark (low-cost clothes).

2. Differentiation

1.3 L01

- A company will seek to be unique in a way that is valued by buyers.

- Differentiation could be based on the product itself, its distribution to the marketplace or its marketing strategy.

- Due to the uniqueness of products/services the company is able to charge a premium price.

- The price premium that a company charges must exceed the costs of creating the unique offering.

- In contrast to cost leadership there can be more than one successful differentiation strategy in a marketplace.

- Examples of companies following this strategy are Waitrose (premium food), Emirates (premium flights) and Burberry (premium clothing).

- These types of companies should still follow cost reduction strategies so long as they do not sacrifice differentiation.

3. Focus (separated into cost focus and differentiation focus)

- A company selects a segment within the marketplace and focuses its strategy on that.

- In **cost focus** a company seeks a cost advantage in its target segment.

- In **differentiation focus** a company seeks differentiation in its target segment.

- It is possible to have multiple focus strategies operating successfully in a market if they are all targeting different segments.

- A company adopting this strategy should be careful not to compromise its plan for short-term growth.

- Examples of focus strategy include The Body Shop (focus on animal welfare and vegan food), and the Free From supermarket product ranges (focus on foods that are free from dairy or gluten).

- In some industries, however, there may be few opportunities for focus.

These strategies are shown below in figure 1.7, which illustrates that both cost leadership and differentiation focus on the whole market. Cost focus and differentiation focus are targeting niche markets.

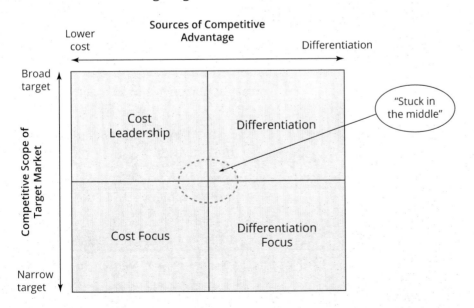

Figure 1.7 Porter's generic strategies model (Source: Porter, M.E. (1980). Competitive Strategy: Techniques for Analysing Industries & Competitors. The Free Press, NY)

Case study

Cost leadership and differentiation strategies – travel market

An example of cost leadership is a travel company selling holidays at a lower price, for example budget holidays. By selling at lower prices the travel company will be able to achieve additional volumes of sales and therefore profits. This could be achieved by brokering high discounts with hotels and airlines.

An example of differentiation is selling luxury holidays to unusual destinations such as Madagascar or the Galapagos Islands. The travel company is able to sell its products or services at a premium price by differentiating them from the offerings of the rest of the market.

Remember

Porter stated that there were three generic strategies for competitive advantage.

- Cost leadership
- Differentiation
- Focus

The type of strategy employed by a company will be directly affected by its culture and the type of leadership and management used. Planning is also a key part of gaining a competitive advantage. Once a generic strategy has been chosen at a corporate level it should then be fed into each of the functional areas, which will develop a plan for achieving these objectives. Table 1.5 shows objectives that are relevant to procurement.

Generic strategy adopted	Procurement department's objectives
Cost leadership	• Achieve high percentage of savings/reduce costs • Improve economies of scale • Review market for new suppliers to improve competition • Look at opportunities to source from low-cost countries • Look at opportunities to standardise/use substitute products • Reduction of waste – this could include supplier development activities
Differentiation	• Source a supplier that is able to support the 'unique' element of the products/services • Involve the supplier early in the process to add as much value as possible for the buyer • Achieve high percentage of savings/reduce costs

Generic strategy adopted	Procurement department's objectives
Focus	• Source a supplier that is able to support the needs of the niche buyers (applicable to both cost and differentiation focus) **Cost focus:** • Select a supplier that enables the buying organisation to be able to offer the product or service at a cost the market can afford – this may include low-cost country sourcing • If cost focus is chosen, earlier supplier involvement (ESI) may be used to reduce waste of rework (if a design has to be altered to fit a niche market) **Differentiation focus:** • Again, the use of ESI to add as much value as possible, especially if the product is innovative

Table 1.5 Procurement objectives

Porter classes a company that engages in each of the three generic strategies but fails to achieve competitive advantage with any of them as 'stuck in the middle'. This position is highlighted by the blue ellipse in figure 1.7. This is a dangerous place to be. This company will typically be less profitable than its competitors in the industry who are successfully undertaking one of the three strategies.

However, it is possible for a company to create two different business units with different generic strategies – one pursuing cost leadership and the other differentiation. A good example of this is Qantas Group, which owns both Jetstar and Qantas. Jetstar is its budget airline offering a range of no-frills flights following a cost leadership strategy, whereas Qantas is a premium airline offering a luxury travel option to its passengers.

What enables a company to obtain competitive advantage today may not be the same in the future, as markets and the world constantly evolve and change. Each of the three strategies involves an element of risk, and they are each vulnerable to attacks by competitors. Poor strategic choices can also weaken a company's competitive advantage.

In addition to the three generic strategies outlined by Porter there are other elements of a business that can develop a company's competitive advantage.

- **Human resource management, staff and skills.** An organisation's workforce is one of its biggest assets. This is especially the case in technological and creative industries such as advertising and computer game development. Tacit knowledge of employees is something that cannot be easily replicated by another company. In order to protect their best employees, companies often put a non-solicitation clause in their contracts to prevent companies that they work with from attempting to poach their best staff.

- **Organisation culture and structure.** In order to drive the organisation forwards employees will need to work towards a shared mission and set of objectives. Both the culture and the structure of an organisation provide focus for employees to ensure that the company's objectives are met. The leadership of an organisation will have a strong impact on its culture and structure. If there is poor leadership in an organisation there will be a lack of focus on creating competitive advantage.

Tacit knowledge
The vast amount of unwritten knowledge that is held in the minds of people. This knowledge has not been taught, but is based on previous experiences, observations, thoughts and feelings

- **Processes and practices.** There is another way that companies can secure a competitive advantage. Processes and practices that are difficult for competitors to replicate prevent the development of substitute products and services. This is discussed in greater detail below. These processes and practices could enable a supplier to be the first to market with a new product. Therefore they are able to benefit from being able to charge a premium price until other competitors enter the marketplace.

Competitive advantage

In 1855, inventor Henry Bessemer took out a patent on a process for the mass production of steel. It became one of the most valuable patents in history. The process reduced the cost of producing steel from £40 per ton to £6 per ton, therefore resulting in a competitive advantage.

(Source: www.inventioncity.com/henry-bessemer)

Case study

- **Products and intellectual property.** Intellectual property is key in technological and design industries. A good example is Apple and the products it produces. Apple produces multiple different technological products which share the same operating system and applications. Since the launch of the Apple iPhone, other similar products have entered the marketplace. However, there was a competitive advantage to being the first.

- **Capital.** Access to financial capital, whether this is obtained from retained profits, business loans or the sale of shares, can offer a competitive advantage. It can be used to help a business to invest in technologies and processes that will enable it to either get to market first or produce at a lower cost. However, newly developed industries are less capital intensive than industries developed in the past such as steel making.

- **Natural resources.** Access to natural resources such as mineral ores or sources of power generation can also act as a competitive advantage. For example, a food producer may be able to gain competitive advantage from being located in an area that has fertile soils and sufficient rainfall. This producer will be able to grow a greater volume of healthier crops than farmers located in other geographical areas.

- **Technology.** The development of technology has accelerated since the second half of the 20th century, and having access to the most advanced technology is a competitive advantage. This area includes information technology (IT), which has resulted in the creation of a number of new markets. As noted by Michael Porter (1985),[30] technological innovations can have important strategic implications for companies and industries as a whole.

In order to achieve competitive advantage a company can develop externally focused or internally focused strategies. One such externally focused strategy that links directly to supplier relationship management is the development of a strategic alliance. A successfully implemented and managed strategic alliance could bring significant competitive advantage to a company.

Apply

Think about a company you or someone you know works for and their closest suppliers. Which of the three generic strategies do you think they are following? What evidence is there to show this?

The value chain

Another key model that describes competitive advantage is Michael Porter's (1985)[31] value chain. The value chain is a set of activities and processes that an organisation must undertake in order to create value for its customers.

> " *The ultimate value a firm creates is measured by the amount customers are willing to pay for its products or service over and above the cost to the firm of carrying out its value-creating activities.* "

(Source: Michael Porter, 1985[32])

An organisation needs to create this 'value' to enable it to sell its products for more than the sum of their costs and achieve the required margin. Value should be added at each step of the value chain. The more value an organisation is able to create, the more profit it will generate for its shareholders and owners. The enhanced value is then passed on to customers, thus consolidating a company's competitive advantage. The model is shown in figure 1.8.

> " *Each activity within a value chain provides inputs which, after processing constitute added value to the output received by the ultimate customer.* "

(Source: Lysons and Farrington, 2006[33])

Co-operation and the process of creating value for both buyers and suppliers is the main objective for undertaking supplier relationship management.

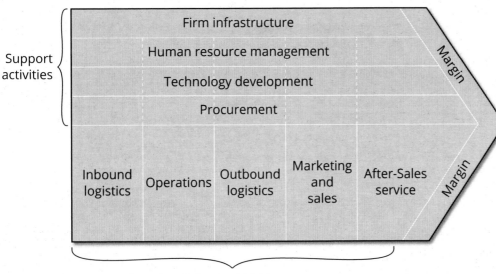

Figure 1.8 Porter's value chain (Source: Porter, M.E. (1985). Competitive Advantage: creating and sustaining superior performance. The Free Press, NY)

Sources of competitive advantage lie all along the value chain. The activities are split between primary activities, which contribute directly to the creation of the product or service, and support activities. The support activities are those back-office functions that support the business in its efforts to become more efficient. These activities are interdependent and will affect each other. The value chain enables a company to understand which activities add value and which are wasteful and could therefore be eliminated.

> *Remember*
> The value chain is made up of primary activities and support activities. The procurement department is a support activity.

When analysing a company's value chain the following steps should be taken.

- Split all activities within the company's value chain into primary and secondary activities.

- Review each area, looking for processes that are wasteful, for example, double handling of invoices by the procurement function.

- Consider the linkages among the activities that are important for competitive advantage, e.g., could procurement be used to reduce the cost of outbound logistics?

Table 1.6 shows the value chain of one of the biggest global companies: Starbucks coffee shops.

Type of activity	Area of the value chain	Starbucks example
Primary activities	Inbound logistics	Coffee beans are transported to storage sites and beans are roasted, packaged and sent to distribution centres
	Operations	Operates globally; stores are either directly owned or franchised
	Outbound logistics	Little or no presence of intermediaries in product selling
	Marketing and sales	Invests more in product quality and customer service than aggressive marketing strategies
		Commonly offers samples in stores as a way of marketing new products
	Service	Aims to build customer loyalty via good service levels
		Has invested heavily in equalities training in all US stores
Support activities	Infrastructure	Includes support functions such as finance and legal as well as the overall management of the company
	Human resource management	The workforce is considered a key part of Starbucks' success
		Staff are motivated via generous benefits and incentives and the good work culture, feeding into achieving happy staff and positive customer service experiences
	Technology	Used for processes and also to connect with its customers, who will often use Starbucks as office/meeting space due to free access to wireless computer networks, and ordering is available via an app
	Procurement	Company-appointed coffee buyers procure coffee beans directly from farmers
		Procurement is not outsourced to a third party, demonstrating that it is a core function

Table 1.6 Starbucks value chain (Source: adapted from www.investopedia.com)

As shown above, procurement is listed as one of the secondary activities in the value chain. There are a number of ways in which procurement can help to add value and generate a bigger margin for organisations.

- Selecting a supplier and negotiating the best deal for the raw materials/inputs and logistics, thereby reducing the cost of these inputs

- Developing relationships with a key supplier to ensure continuity of supply of inputs

- Managing quality of inputs by monitoring supplier performance

- Managing inventory and stock control

- Supporting the other support functions by sourcing products and services that the organisation requires in order to undertake these functions

The five rights of procurement

The procurement department is able to specifically add value by ensuring that it achieves the five rights of procurement. The five rights of procurement are principles describing the ideal outcome from buyer–supplier relationships. Table 1.7 lists and defines the rights, and provides an example to show why each is an important principle.

Right	Definition	Example of importance
Place	Achieving delivery of the products/services to the right place, packaged and transported in a way that ensures their safe arrival	Delivery of the inputs to the wrong place could cause delays in production and affect the reputation of the company.
Quality	Ensuring that the products and services purchased are of the correct quality and **fit for purpose** – in some industries there are strict quality standards	There is a need to strike a balance between price and quality. If defective products reach the customer this could affect the reputation of the company.
Quantity	Purchasing the correct quantities	This is a balance between having enough stock for production and having too little. Not enough stock could cause a stop in manufacturing, resulting in costly downtime and delays for customers. Too much stock could result in additional storage costs and reduced cash flow.
Time	Ensuring the delivery of the products or services on the correct date and at the correct time	Late delivery of inputs could result in production delays; delivery too early could result in stock-holding issues and reduced cash flow.

Fit for purpose
The product or service is capable of doing what it was designed to do

Right	Definition	Example of importance
Price	Achieving the right price for the products and services Prices should be fair, competitive and affordable	If the price paid for the inputs is too high this will reduce the margin that the organisation is able to achieve; too low and quality could be compromised. This is especially key in markets where prices are subject to large changes.

Table 1.7 The five rights of procurement

In some cases, there needs to be a trade-off between the 'rights', examples of which are given here.

- In order to obtain products at the right price a procurement team may need to buy at volumes that are beyond the optimal stock levels. This may not be the right quantity for the buying organisation's day-to-day requirements. It may therefore cause additional stock-holding costs and reduced cash flow.

- In order to ensure that products are of the correct quality, a procurement team may need to purchase from one of the more expensive suppliers in the marketplace and might not be able to secure the right price.

All of the five rights are key objectives for the procurement department. These rights will often form part of the key performance indicators that procurement must meet in order to support the overarching business strategy. However, there are many other factors that a procurement department must consider when sourcing products such as risk, sustainability, etc. For this reason there is some suggestion in procurement and supply literature that the five rights of procurement are an outdated concept.

> *Remember*
> The five rights of procurement refers to procuring goods and services in the right quantity, at the right quality, to be delivered at the right time, to the right place, at the right price.

Competitive forces: sources of competitive rivalry, bargaining power of buyers and suppliers, threat of new entrants and potential substitutes

There are a number of competitive forces operating in the marketplace. Each of these forces can affect the development of buyer–supplier relationships, and are described below.

Porter's Five Forces model

All of the competitive forces mentioned above (e.g., competitive rivalry, potential substitutes, etc.,) are captured in Porter's Five Forces model. Porter's model is an example of micro-environmental analysis.

Figure 1.9 shows the five competitive forces that determine the attractiveness of an industry. The rules of competition are embedded in these five competitive forces and they determine the ability of a company to make a profit in a marketplace, as the five forces influence prices, costs and required levels of investment.

1.3 L01

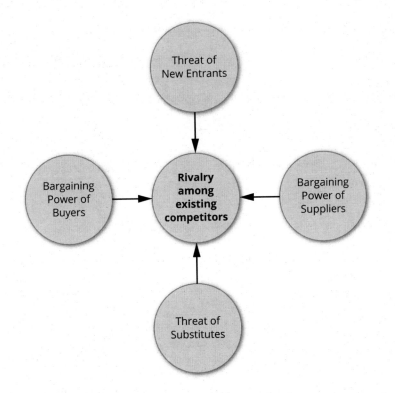

Figure 1.9 Porter's Five Forces model (Source: Porter, M.E. (1980). Competitive Strategy: Techniques for Analysing Industries & Competitors. The Free Press, NY)

The strength of these five forces can vary from industry to industry and can evolve overtime. Some industries, such as pharmaceuticals, will be more profitable than others and therefore the structure of an industry can affect the levels of profitability. Every industry is unique and will have its own distinct structure. The actions of industry leaders can have a disproportionate impact on structure because of their size and influence over suppliers, buyers and other competitors in the market.

Rivalry among existing competitors

This is located at the centre of the model (figure 1.9). The extent of this competition depends on the type of market in existence. There are several types of market.

1. **Monopoly**

- In situations where there is a **pure monopoly** there is one large supplier in the marketplace; in reality this situation is rare.

- Buyers that are procuring in this market have to **sole source** the required products and services from this supplier.

- Examples of monopolistic markets include utilities (water).

- In the UK the Competition Commission monitors proposed **mergers** and **acquisitions** within the economy closely to try to prevent such situations.

- In this type of market, the bargaining power of the supplier is strong and the buyer's bargaining power is weak.

2. Oligopoly

- In these cases the market is dominated by a few large suppliers as the costs of entering the marketplace are so great.

- An example is the oil industry.

- The actions of one company can significantly affect the others in the market.

- Again, supplier power is strong; however, the presence of alternative sources of supply improves the position of the buyer.

- Governments have responded to oligopolies with laws against price fixing and collusion.

3. Imperfect competition

- In this situation there are a number of suppliers in the marketplace, but they are not selling similar services and products (products are heterogeneous). Therefore competition is not strong.

- Each seller could be following a differentiation strategy.

- Monopoly and oligopoly are types of imperfect competition.

4. Monopolistic competition

- Companies in the market offer similar products or services, but they are not perfect substitutes.

- Companies have the same low level of market power and all are **price makers**.

- Generally demand is highly price elastic.

5. Perfect competition

- The market is characterised by a large number of suppliers selling identical products and services (products are homogeneous). There is also a large number of buyers.

- Perfect competition is a hypothetical market where competition is at its greatest possible level.

- There is perfect knowledge of the market; all buyers and customers have perfect and instant information on prices, usage and cost.

- There are no **barriers to entry** or exit of the marketplace.

- All companies are **price takers**, they cannot influence the price charged for the products.

- There is a cost for companies of competing, for example advertising and marketing campaigns.

Table 1.8 summarises these market types.

Price elasticity
A measure of the change in demand for a product or service in relation to changes in its price. If a product is price elastic, the more the price is reduced the more demand will rise. Generally for a product to be price elastic there will need to be a number of substitute products. Price elasticity of demand (PED) is a measure of how responsive the demand for a product is in relation to its price

Type of market	Supplier power	Buyer power	Example
Monopoly	Very high	Very low	Utilities such as water
Oligopoly	High	Low	Oil and gas companies
Imperfect competition	Weakening	Strengthening	See examples for monopoly and oligopoly

Type of market	Supplier power	Buyer power	Example
Monopolistic competition	Strengthening	Weakening	Possible where supplier can differentiate, such as restaurants and hotels
Perfect competition	Low	Very high	Agricultural produce

1.3 L01

Table 1.8 Market typology overview

Rivalry between companies in a market can be affected by a number of factors.

- Industry growth or decline
- Product differences/brand identity
- Switching costs – if the costs of switching between products are low for buyers, then rivalry will be more intense
- Diversity of competitors
- Exit barriers

> *Remember*
> Porter's Five Forces model is made up of the rivalry in the marketplace, the threat of substitutes, barriers to entry and the relative power of buyers and suppliers.

Threat of new entrants

As the market types move from monopoly in the most extreme case towards greater competition, the threat of new entrants moving into the marketplace increases. Once new companies enter the market, competition will increase. In some markets, especially those that are highly capital intensive such as oil and gas extraction, the barriers to entry for new companies are too great to make it achievable. Barriers to entry include but are not limited to the following points listed here.

- Economies of scale
- Access to capital and high start-up costs, for example costs for equipment
- Licences and permits – costs of these and how difficult they are to obtain
- Strong brand identities already dominant in the marketplace
- High switching costs for buyers to switch to alternative products or services
- Access to distribution networks
- Government policy; for example, some governments will attempt to protect their national industries by imposing various tariffs on imported products

Threat of substitute products or services

This links to barriers to entry. When there are fewer barriers to entry in a marketplace, it is more likely that new businesses will enter and develop substitute products or services. Buyers can often put up their own barriers by the way they define their requirements. Therefore, the way the procurement organisation's requirements are defined will either encourage or discourage substitute products/services. Encouraging substitutes will create more competition, which will result in better-quality products and services and lower pricing.

Often companies will have to defend themselves against a substitution threat. An example of this is the mobile telephone industry. Apple was the first company to launch a smartphone – the iPhone. It was closely followed by a number of companies which used substitute Android technology including Samsung and Sony, and by Microsoft with phones that used Windows technology. There are various factors that affect substitution.

- Relative price performance of substitutes – if substitutes are cheaper, buyers are more likely to switch products

- Switching costs for buyers

- Buyer propensity to substitute and how they evaluate the economic benefits

Power of suppliers

Supplier power is at its highest in monopolistic markets where the supplier is dominant. This is often the case in the supply of **OEM (original equipment manufacturer)** equipment. When it comes to upgrading the equipment or procuring parts, the buyer has little or no choice but to deal with the OEM. Supplier power is strong when the following factors occur.

- A supplier can differentiate its offering

- Switching costs for buyers are high

- There is a lack of substitute products or services

- There are a number of suppliers in the marketplace (concentration)

When supplier power is strong, suppliers may have little or no reason to invest in building a relationship with the buying organisation.

Power of buyers

Buyer power and leverage are at their highest when there is competition in the marketplace and the buyer is dominant. If there are several suppliers in the marketplace and the buyer decides to run a competitive tender exercise, the suppliers will need to compete in order to win the business. Buyer power influences the prices that suppliers can charge.

In some cases specifications can be written in a way that increases the leverage and power of the buyer. For example, removing branded products from the specification and including the options for equivalent non-branded substitutes can have this effect. Such processes should result in the buyer obtaining a competitive price for the products or services being tendered. However, buyers need to carefully review prices to ensure that they are not abnormally low and the supplier is not going to cover its costs. If the price is too low it could be unsustainable for the supplier, which could lead to the buyer facing an unexpected price rise or, in extreme cases, the supplier going into administration.

Buyer power is affected by a number of different factors.

- The number of buyers in the marketplace versus the number of suppliers – at one extreme this is a monopsony

- The volume of purchases made by buyers

Monopsony
A market with only one buyer

- Costs for buyers
- Availability of information for decision-making
- Ability to **backward integrate**
- Substitution of products and services

1.3 **L01**

Backward integration
A situation where the buying organisation purchases one of its suppliers of raw materials. The raw materials supplier is further back in the supply chain. For example, a paper factory buying a forest plantation

The model shown in figure 1.10 was developed by Cox in 2000 and it demonstrates the effect of buyer and supplier power.

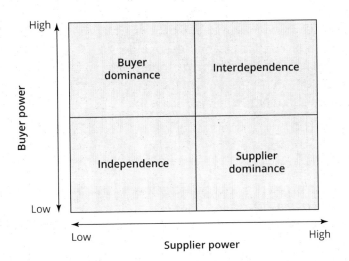

Figure 1.10 *Model of buyer and supplier power (Source: based on Cox et al., 2000)*

The level of power held by a buyer or supplier is an important consideration when developing supplier relationship management strategies. Where either the buyer or the supplier has high power relative to the other, they will be dominant in the relationship. However, where both the supplier and the buyer have low levels of power, there will be a dependence on each other, which brings an element of risk for both parties. Conversely, where both have a high level of power they will be interdependent on each other, and this can also bring a level of risk.

> *Check*
> In what circumstances is buyer power likely to be high?

STEEPLE factors that affect supply chains (social, technological, economic, environmental, political, legislative and ethical)

You may know the term PESTLE analysis. However as 'ethical' has been added, the acronym has changed to STEEPLE. This model analyses potential external influences and risks (macro-environmental) that could affect a company or a marketplace. The influences are separated into seven themes.

STEEPLE analysis should be used to guide and support strategic decision-making, ensuring an organisation is ready for any potential changes in its external environment. It could be used to support the strategic planning undertaken by the procurement department, for example in its category management plans or when planning for any changes in its supply chain and environment. The seven elements of STEEPLE analysis are described below.

> *Remember*
> STEEPLE analysis looks at risks that are external to a company.

Social

The social element of the analysis relates to demographic (population) trends. For example, in the UK and the majority of Western Europe there is an ageing population. It is important for businesses to understand these trends as they will affect workforce planning and buying patterns. This could be seen with the ageing population in the UK which has marked the rise of the 'grey pound', referring to money spent in the economy by elderly consumers.

Consumer tastes and buying habits also change overtime. What is fashionable or popular today may not be the same in a year's time. Businesses need to monitor this when reviewing their strategic plans for their product lines.

Trends, including lifestyle choices such as getting married and buying property later in life, will also affect consumer patterns.

Cultural norms will affect a company's external environment. However, these will differ significantly from one country to another.

Technological

There has been a high rate of innovation in technology in recent decades, especially in the areas of artificial intelligence, automation and robotics, which has reduced the number of people employed in some industries.

Companies now have access to large amounts of data, and how that data is stored, processed and managed needs to be carefully considered.

The huge rise of social media such as Facebook, Instagram, LinkedIn and Twitter since the early part of the 21st century has affected consumerism and the way companies communicate with their customer base.

The emergence of **disruptive technologies**, which have changed the structure of a market or the way that a product is consumed by customers, have had a major impact on companies' external environment. Examples of a disruptive technology would include the taxi ordering app Uber. As a result of Uber, taxi companies have had to change the way they take bookings and operate in order to remain competitive.

Disruptive technologies
New or enhanced technologies that replace or affect existing technology, making it obsolete. An example is cloud computing services, which are a disruptive technology for in-house servers

Economic

This area covers matters concerning finance such as exchange rates, interest rates, increases to the national minimum wage, the introduction of the living wage, changes to pensions and maternity/paternity entitlements.

Increases in any of the above-mentioned areas can cause increases in a business' cost base and therefore an impact on its profit margin.

The economic health of the country in which a company is trading also needs to be considered. Countries pass through the **business cycle** (figure 1.11). There are boom periods when the economy is buoyant and consumer spending is high, followed by decline and recession periods which are characterised by higher levels of unemployment and reduced consumer spending.

Business cycle
The rise and fall over time of output in an economy as measured by gross domestic product (GDP)

Now that the world is more interconnected, what happens in one country can have a direct effect on the financial fortunes of another country. This is the result of **globalisation**.

1.3 L01

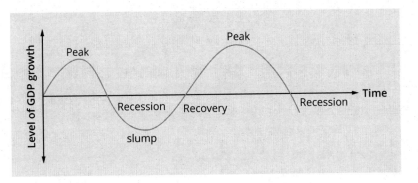

Figure 1.11 The business cycle

Globalisation
The process by which the world is becoming more interconnected, which means that events in one location are shaped by things that happen many miles away

Environmental

Businesses, particularly those involved in heavy industry and traditional manufacturing, have a direct effect on the natural environment, for example via carbon emissions and disposal of waste.

The majority of governments around the world are now seeking to reduce their carbon emissions, improve their waste management and reduce the amount of material sent to landfill. In the first few months of 2018 there was a large drive towards reducing the consumption of plastics, which are polluting the oceans and threatening marine life.

There is a link between environmental factors and legislative factors, as a number of laws have been passed all round the world in an effort to protect the natural environment.

Natural disasters such as earthquakes, volcanic eruptions and hurricanes are also environmental threats to a business. Following the 2011 earthquake in Japan and the resulting tsunami, a number of global supply chains were seriously affected.

More and more companies are looking to source 'green' (environmental) products to meet consumer demands, and this aspect links to the sociocultural element of the STEEPLE model.

There has been a large move towards sustainable energy including wind, solar, tidal and biomass power.

Corporate social responsibility (CSR) encompasses policies for environmental benefits and ethical sourcing (see below).

Political

The political theme relates to the current government, its stability and its policies, particularly those that affect trade and industry. This will include global trade agreements and restrictions such as tariffs and import duties.

Legislative

Changes in legislation will affect the way that a business operates. This can result in cost increases in order to ensure that the organisation is compliant.

Corporate social responsibility (CSR)
A business approach that contributes to sustainable development by delivering social, environmental and economic benefits for all stakeholders. The CSR policy may cover fundraising for charity, ethical behaviour, social and environmental policies, etc.

In order to avoid any financial penalties due to non-compliance, organisations must keep up to date with changes in legislation that could affect their business.

Companies that are operating internationally will be required to meet the legislative requirements of the countries in which they operate.

Ethical

Ethical sourcing
Ensuring that products are obtained in a responsible and sustainable way that demonstrates respect for the people who produce them and for the environment

Ethical sourcing is a concept that has developed in recent decades, as consumers have become more concerned with the processes involved in manufacturing the products and services that they buy.

It involves ensuring that the business acts in an ethical manner and considers the effects that it has on its employees and customers, the local community and the environment in which it operates. Ethical issues also cover other aspects such as use of child labour, modern-day slavery, protecting local environments, etc.

> *Remember*
> STEEPLE analysis covers the following areas: social, technological, economic, environmental, political, legal and ethical.

STEEPLE analysis in practice

There are some overlaps between some of the elements of STEEPLE analysis. Positive changes in the external environment can be considered as opportunities for a business. Negative environmental changes will pose risks for a business. Although the external environment will always contain risks and threats to a business, supply chain relationships can help to mitigate the impacts.

Table 1.9 is an example of STEEPLE analysis undertaken by a car manufacturer based in the UK. Its main consumer base is the UK, and it sources components from Europe, China and the UK.

STEEPLE letter	STEEPLE area	STEEPLE analysis
S	Social	The UK economy is growing and therefore consumer spending on expensive products such as cars is high. Growth is predicted to continue. As a trend, there is a growing number of cars per household as parents buy their teenage children cars and elderly people continue to drive for longer.
T	Technological	Improvements in automation may lead to the business being able to reduce its workforce in some areas.

STEEPLE letter	STEEPLE area	STEEPLE analysis
E	Economic	The company has decided to source from China and some parts of Western Europe to take advantage of the lower costs of production. There is a concern currently about the recession in China.
E	Environmental	The company has been working towards reducing the waste it produces.
P	Political	There is much uncertainty around what type of trade deals the UK will broker with Europe.
L	Legislative	New pieces of legislation will affect the company, including the new General Data Protection Regulation (GDPR). This will affect how the company manages its marketing database.
E	Ethical	There have been a number of cases of human rights violations by Chinese suppliers. Therefore, processes will have to be put into place to ensure that these are not repeated.

Table 1.9 STEEPLE analysis undertaken by a car manufacturer

> *Check*
> What are the seven elements of STEEPLE analysis? Give one example from each of the seven areas.

Dynamic and uncertain environments as well as growing demands may increase the willingness of a business to engage in more collaborative relationships. Buyers should also keep a close eye on market risks that could affect the supply chain as well as their own business.

1.4 Compare the sources of added value that can be achieved through supply chain relationships

Procurement is a key part of the value chain, as demonstrated in the diagram of Porter's model in section 1.3. There are various ways in which procurement can add value for the business by making sourcing decisions that will result in better outcomes.

The link between relationships as a process and the achievement of added value outcomes

Added value
Non-cash releasing benefits generated via procurement processes and supplier relationship management

Return on relationship investment (RORI)
The financial benefits for a buyer of establishing, developing and maintaining buyer–supplier relationships

Building successful business relationships will involve a conscious process by both the buyer and the supplier. Added value outcomes refers to the range of benefits derived by a buyer, supplier, stakeholder or user. **Added value** is the business case for justifying spending time and resources on building relationships with suppliers. The time spent on developing these relationships has to deliver value for the business.

There is a strong link between developing successful supplier relationships and achieving added value outcomes. Developing relationships is an ongoing process. This process starts with segmentation, and then reviewing where the relationship needs to be in order to add value for the buying organisation. Plans will then need to be put in place to get the relationship to the desired state. Following this, relationships will need to be maintained in order to ensure that they continue to deliver benefits.

A buyer should be able to leverage the relationship with a supplier to achieve valuable outcomes for the business. The buyer needs to ensure that it gets a positive **return on relationship investment (RORI)** for the time and effort involved in this process. This value could take many different forms (see below).

As part of this process a buyer needs to consider the long-term outcomes with each supplier. Adding value for the buyer's business by pushing a supplier to deliver added value could be detrimental to long-term relationships. This links back to the discussion about the 'pie' in section 1.1. In order to achieve added value for both parties the pie should be expanded rather than merely divided up.

Increasingly procurement teams need to be able to demonstrate the value that they can bring to the wider business. This will enable procurement to build its profile in the business. There has been strong growth of procurement as a profession and as a key, strategic function of the business rather than just a back-office, administrative process.

As discussed in section 2.1, segmentation enables the selection of the most beneficial relationship for each type of supplier. This information can then be used to develop a strategy and action plan to bring the relationship to the most beneficial point. The type of supplier you are working with will depend on the type of added value that is achievable. If a buyer is working with one of its partner suppliers the buyer is likely to be able to extract more value from the relationship than when dealing with an arm's-length supplier. However, the process of measuring the value achieved is difficult, as some of the benefits may be intangible.

The process of developing positive relationships will support achieving added value outcomes. Procurement can support the delivery of a number of added value benefits.

- Cashable savings and/or cost avoidance, which can have a direct impact on internal budgets. This could be achieved by working with the supplier to reduce waste. This will increase profitability for the buyer and the supplier.

- Competitive advantage over others who are not reaping the benefits created by collaborative relationships.

- Thorough risk management – a greater knowledge of supply chain partners and their risks will improve this process. As discussed below, the value network is interconnected; what affects a supply partner also has effects on its downstream partners.

- Improved business efficiency, for example by improving the processes involved in the touchpoints between the buyer and its suppliers. This could include developing e-catalogues with suppliers for high-volume items to reduce the administrative burden for both parties.

- Improved corporate social responsibility (CSR).

The value chain was discussed in section 1.3, and what now follows is a discussion of value networks. A value network is a set of connections between organisations interacting with each other which benefits the entire group. Value networks have been described as 'economic ecosystems', with members (buyers and suppliers) relying on each other to support and increase value. In this way, a buyer **and** supplier are more likely to serve the needs and interests of consumers and therefore gain competitive advantage in the marketplace (Fearne et al.[34]). Development of value networks may also be a reaction to the competitive environment.

As well as products and services moving through the value network, information is also shared. The rise of information technology has made this process easier and more cost effective. As a result, value networks can be virtual. This concept is discussed in more detail below.

> *Remember*
> The relationships between a buyer and a supplier can add value for both parties. Examples of this added value include reduced costs and improved quality.

Sources of added value: pricing and cost management, improving quality, timescales, quantities and place considerations in procurements from external suppliers

Various different types of added value can be generated from the relationships that a buyer has with its external supplier. Some of these have been discussed above. These types of added value are the target outcomes of successful supplier relationship management. (See Porter's value chain in section 1.3 and the Remember box below.)

> *Remember*
> The value chain key points are as follows.
>
> - An organisation will add value to its inputs in order to create value for the customer.
> - This will generate margin (profit) for the company.
> - The activities in the value chain are interdependent; what affects one will affect the other.
> - Waste across the value chain should be eliminated.

The sources of added value are linked to the five rights of procurement which were discussed in section 1.3. The procurement department will manage the process for obtaining all of the raw materials, inputs and services that an organisation requires in order to produce the finished products. The five rights of procurement are as follows.

- The right quantity
- The right quality
- The right time
- The right place
- The right price

> *Remember*
> The following is an easy way to remember the five rights of procurement.
>
> Remember your Ps and Qs.
>
> - Place
> - Price
> - Quantity
> - Quality
> - Time (Don't forget!)

In order to deliver the five rights, a procurement department will need to ensure that it understands the needs of the business. The areas of the sourcing process where procurement can add value are discussed below.

Pricing and cost management

Achieving reduced costs for inputs and generating savings is traditionally what the procurement department has been associated with. There are various ways in which procurement can influence the pricing that is achieved for a product or service.

- Reducing the unit cost paid for the product or service
- Getting additional products or services for the same price; generally these are referred to as value adds
- Increasing the payment terms, for example moving from 30 days to 60 days; this can improve the cash position of the buying organisation
- Mitigating a price increase that a supplier requests

There are two main ways that a supplier can price a product or a service. The most common method that a procurement department will encounter is either one of the two points listed here.

- **Cost-based pricing.** Total cost plus mark-up calculated for profit
- **Marked-based/demand pricing.** Pricing that stimulates demand for a product

The procurement team needs to ensure that it is aware of any market factors that may cause increases in price. This could include, for example, increases in the minimum wage.

Specification development

One of the first elements in managing the cost of inputs is to work with the user department and other key internal stakeholders on the specification of the requirements. The following are the elements to consider.

- Ensuring that the user department has not over-specified the requirement
- Making sure that the specification is clear and unambiguous, that prices are not being overinflated due to uncertainty
- Ensuring that all spend with a supplier is captured under the contract and in line with agreed rates
- Reviewing whether any products could be substituted for non-branded alternatives
- Involving the supplier early on in the process (see section 2.3)

Competitive tender

Following the specification stage, if there is sufficient competition in the marketplace the procurement department will competitively tender the requirements in order to get the best price. As discussed above, the greater the number of suppliers in the market, the more leverage the buyer will have to negotiate the best deal possible for the business. In some cases tenders are evaluated on a price only basis. In other cases tenders will be evaluated on a mix of both price and quality criteria. Quality criteria would include evaluation based on product/service quality, whether the right quantity can be provided, and whether the supplier can deliver to the right place at the right time. This process is discussed further in section 2.1.

Once the tenders have been received the procurement department will evaluate the responses. The evaluation team should ideally be made up of a mixture of the procurement/commercial team and the internal stakeholders that will be using the procured products or services.

Figure 1.12 shows the **price–cost iceberg**. The price is what the supplier will include as part of the tender process. This price will be made up of various costs, which may or may not be visible to the buyer (the invisibles are shown as being below the waterline in figure 1.12). These costs may be included with other costs, so it can be difficult to accurately compare one supplier to another. In order to achieve greater visibility of total costs a buyer may request that a supplier undertakes **open book costing**.

Open book costing
Where the supplier allows the buyer access to its finances so the buyer knows what the costs are

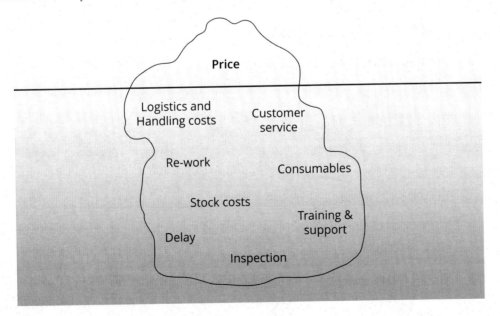

Figure 1.12 Price–cost iceberg (Source: adapted from Baily, P., Farmer, D., Crocker, B., Jessop, D. and Jones, D. (2015), Procurement Principles and Management, Harlow: Pearson)

Historically a supplier did not divulge what its final price was made up of. Open book costing is a key method that can be used to see what makes up a supplier's price. It is logical for the buyer to want to be able to review how the supplier's costs are made up, looking at labour rates, materials costs, overheads and percentage of profit margin, etc., as well as whether any contingency has been included. Including a contingency sum is a common practice in the construction sector, especially where there are fixed price contracts. A buyer needs to be able to understand what the overhead element of the pricing is made up of to ensure that they are not being double charged for certain elements.

Open book costing is a process that would only be undertaken with strategic and partnership-type suppliers. These suppliers are more likely to be receptive to being involved in this process. A supplier that occupies the adversarial/arm's-length sector of the spectrum would not engage in such activities with a buyer.

In some cases, in order to ensure that all costs of a project are accounted for, a buyer may look at the whole life costing (WLC). Whole life costing is a concept that was introduced earlier in this chapter. It generally applies more to the purchase of products than services. There are a number of elements that make up whole life costing and they are listed below. A number of costs captured as part of whole life costing are those that are shown as being invisible on the price–cost iceberg (figure 1.12).

- Pre-acquisition costs, for example surveys
- Cost of procurement process
- Transport/delivery/insurance during carriage
- Actual cost of an item
- Operating and maintenance costs over the life of the item
- Disposal costs/residual value at end of the life cycle of the item

There are limits to whole life costing. Costs included for processes that will happen in the future such as disposal costs are only estimates. These costs may increase by the time a business needs to dispose of an asset. In addition to this, not all of the costs that will occur during the life of a product can be forecast. Undertaking the WLC exercise itself can be costly and time consuming.

> *Check*
> What is open book costing? What type of relationships are needed with the suppliers in order for them to endorse open book costing?

E-sourcing

Once the tender is complete, a buyer may decide to enter into an e-auction with several shortlisted bidders. This only applies to suitable quadrants of the Kraljic model, generally to products and services that sit within the routine or leverage categories. There are various types of e-auction, the most popular being a reverse auction. The auction can be used by a buyer to drive further cost savings following a tender process. There are other elements of automation that can result in savings including e-catalogues and procurement cards.

Negotiations

Negotiations with a supplier often follow the tender process, and this is a key area where procurement can add value. As discussed in section 1.1, the type of negotiations entered into will depend on the type of relationship the buyer envisages going forward. If a buyer and supplier have undertaken open book costing this will put the buyer in a strong negotiating position. In order to achieve the best price, it is important that a buyer prepares fully for supplier negotiations. In negotiations the buyer must ensure that it does not erode the supplier's profit margin. If that happens, the contract may not be sustainable in the future.

Some suppliers may include value add items in a tender process. These can be difficult to evaluate and assign a value to. It is important to remember that these added value outcomes must be achieved in a manner that is compliant with the companies' procurement and contract policies. In the case of public sector organisations, for example those operating within the European Union, they must meet with the Contract and Procurement Regulations (2015) and be achieved in a fair and transparent manner.

Contract management

Procurement can add value by actively managing the contracts once they have been awarded. Very often once a contract is signed, it is filed away. If procurement actively manages the contract to ensure that the supplier delivers the commitments it agreed to in the signed contract, it will achieve greater value for the company. These supplier commitments could include a fixed price for a fixed period of time and adherence to the relevant key performance indicators.

> *Remember*
> In terms of cost management, procurement can add value via careful specification development, competitive tender, e-sourcing and negotiations, and contract management.

Improving quality

Quality is another area where the buyer can add significant value for the organisation. The type and quality of the specification used are important aspects of this. There are two key elements when considering the quality of products and services.

- Whether they are fit for purpose
- Whether the products or services meet the specification

There are generally two different types of specification: a conformance specification and a performance specification. The latter is also referred to as an output-based specification. However, in reality, specifications may have elements that relate to both conformance and performance.

Type of specification	Description	Advantages	Disadvantages
Conformance specification	Detailed description of what the product or part must consist of The supplier must conform to the specification Mainly used for products – inputs based	Easy for the supplier to understand and enables the buyer to detail technical information	Limits the supplier's freedom to innovate
Performance specification	Describes what it expects a part, material or service to achieve Mainly used for services – outputs based	Easier to draft, which may be relevant if the buyer has little knowledge of the product Encourages innovation from the supplier, which may add value and could also widen the supplier base	The burden is placed on the supplier to ensure that the outcomes are achieved

Table 1.10 Types of specification

> *Apply*
> Review some recent specifications used by your organisation. Try to identify whether they are conformance or performance specifications or a mixture of the two.

There are several ways value can be added when quality is improved on. Poor quality comes at a cost.

- Cost of the organisation undertaking rework to products that may include faulty components
- Cost of downtime
- Poor-quality products/services reaching the end customer, affecting the reputation of the buying organisation

Regarding the element of quality, procurement and the supplier relationship activities can add value in a number of ways. The first is to ensure the selection of a supplier that can provide a good-quality product or service. This also involves making sure a good-quality specification is issued to a supplier, as discussed above. It can also involve the appraisal of the supplier's quality policy and whether or not it has any externally accredited quality standards such as ISO 9001, and how it manages quality in its own supply chains.

In order to ensure quality standards are met, they need to be managed. Although this may be undertaken by a different department, procurement still needs to be involved in this process because it is the link between the buying organisation and the supplier. There are four processes involved in ensuring the right quality: quality planning, control, assurance and improvement. Once a contract has been put in place procurement will be involved in the monitoring of KPIs, which usually include KPIs linked to quality and provision of service levels.

> *Remember*
> There are two main types of specification – conformance and performance.

It is important to distinguish between quality control and quality assurance. Quality control, which is usually developed first, is the process of controlling variation. It is used to verify the quality of the output. Quality control is often undertaken by spot checking a sample of the parts, products or services produced. Quality assurance, which is usually developed later, is the process of managing quality. This involves various systems and processes. The spot checking of service delivery could be undertaken by using a 'mystery shopper' to ensure that the supplier is delivering the service as specified. In addition to the above points, procurement can also add value in its involvement in the quality audits of suppliers.

Case study

UK horse meat scandal and quality control
In 2013 the horse meat scandal broke in the UK. Several of the large supermarkets were found to have beef products on sale that were contaminated with horse meat. Products were quickly removed from the shelves. This was a quality issue, with the out-of-specification horse meat having made its way into the final product.

Food testing was later tightened following this issue. This is an example of quality control. This quality control issue had huge repercussions for the companies involved. For example, £300 million was wiped off the value of Tesco, as customers lost trust in the quality of the product.

(Source: www.theguardian.com/business/marketforceslive/2013/jan/16/ horse-meat-tesco-market-value-shares

Value engineering, also referred to as value analysis, is another process that can add value for businesses. This involves a review of the current product or service including the specification, its component parts and the processes used for manufacturing in order to create the optimum product or service at the lowest total cost. This process is linked to early supplier involvement (see supplier development in section 1.1, and section 2.3). Procurement can assist this process by supporting relationship management activities with regard to supplier improvement initiatives.

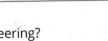

> *Check*
> What is value engineering?

Timescales

On-time delivery is a key part of ensuring that the business and manufacturing process are able to remain operational. Delivery on time is often a KPI that suppliers are measured against. The products and services need to arrive at the right time in order to avoid the issues listed below.

- Production bottlenecks or stoppages, which could have a number of negative effects.

- Lost time costs – when a company is not producing it will still be paying overheads and the salaries of the staff involved in the manufacturing process. It may have to pay staff overtime to catch up after stoppages, which would be an additional cost.

- Late delivery by a supplier could result in the company delivering late to its customer. This could result in reputational damage and financial costs if the contract included late delivery clauses.

Lead times for delivery are very important, especially in manufacturing environments. A buyer needs to liaise with stakeholders to ensure that the correct lead times are included in tender documents and contracts. There are a number of ways that lead times could be shortened.

- Paying higher prices for shorter delivery times. The cost of this and the benefits for the business need to be carefully weighed up.

- Simplifying transaction processes such as the time taken to convert a purchase requisition (PR) to a purchase order (PO).

- Working with suppliers to reduce waste in the cycle of ordering, such as delays caused by double handling on the supplier side.

- Holding more stock. There is a cost to this, including the cost of storage and the opportunity cost of the money tied up in the stock. The business will also need to assess its cash flow before agreeing to increase the stock holding.

Expediting can be used to chase up orders and ensure that deliveries are received on time and at the correct quality. If there are delivery issues, problem solving techniques should be used to find out the root cause of any scheduling difficulties. The buyer should then work with the supplier to prevent these issues happening again in the future.

The location products and services are sourced from will have a big impact on lead times. For example, products sourced from foreign countries will have a far greater lead time than those sourced from the same country where the products are being manufactured. More risk is introduced into the process when the product has further to travel to get to the buyer. Buyers need to weigh this up carefully. Getting a product from a low-cost country might result in the right price, but if there are delays in delivery, it could lead to extra costs and risks to the business.

Apply

Imagine you are a buyer. Think of some examples as to how late deliveries may affect your business and if the risk of buying products from foreign countries is worth the saved money?

Quantities

Procurement can add value by ensuring that the supplier provides the right quantities of a product or service. Ensuring that the quantity is right is linked to

1.4 L01

demand management. Again, the correct information is needed from the user departments. Quantity is more relevant to a buyer so procuring products and raw materials than to those buying services.

As mentioned previously, quantity is one of the five rights of procurement. Ensuring the right quantity of goods is received by the buying organisation also includes stocking and store management policies and practices. Most organisations will be required to hold at least some stock. For products that occupy the bottleneck quadrant of the Kraljic model, more stock may be needed as part of contingency and risk management. There are a number of reasons to hold stock.

- Holding stock can ensure continuity of supply if unforeseen events occur, such as natural disasters, which can severely affect global supply chains.

- It can reduce long lead times and ensure production can continue in the short-term.

- Potential discounts may be available for buying in bulk. This will need to be evaluated against the costs of stock holding. This is linked to economies of scale (see section 1.1).

- Holding stock can protect against price fluctuations. This is more applicable to commodity items such as metals.

- Stock holding can support demand management. This will require the involvement of internal stakeholders such as operations, and marketing and sales. Demand management could be based on historic demand forecasts.

Although there can be benefits of holding stock, there are also a number of costs associated with it.

- The cost of storage space, such as warehouses – the more stock stored the bigger the space required.

- Cost of capital – businesses will need to have the cash flow to buy a large amount of stock in advance.

- Obsolescence, depending on the product – some items such as food have expiry dates. In markets where technology changes quickly, there is a risk that stock can be held for too long and be superseded by a new product. This also has a negative financial impact on the business.

- Opportunity costs – the money invested in the stock could potentially have been better invested in alternative projects.

Getting the correct amount of stock is a fine balancing act. Too much, and cash flow that may be needed by the business is tied up. Too little, and the business risks running out of key parts and materials, which could result in production downtime and delays for the customer. This can be costly depending on the nature of the contract.

Sometimes the management of stores falls within the remit of the procurement teams; other times it may be within other departments such as operations. When deciding on the level of stock to hold, the operations team will need to engage closely with procurement in order to calculate the most economical order quantity for each part or material. In order to ensure that the right quantities of products are available, procurement will need to review market availability. This is very important for commodity items, as these could suffer from scarcities.

One method of ensuring that the correct quantities of stock are available at all times while avoiding the cost of stock holding is to buy using just in time (JIT) methods of stock holding. This is a practice that was originally developed in the 1970s by Taiichi Ohno in Japan. It is often referred to as the Toyota production system and is used

Just in time (JIT)
A system that works alongside Lean manufacturing. In order to reduce waste in the supply chain, JIT makes sure that stock is not held unnecessarily in inventory

widely in the automotive industry. The aim of JIT is to hold zero inventory, not just in the buyer's business but across the supply chain (Hutchins, 1999[35]). This method provided a competitive advantage for the Japanese car market.

> *Remember*
> Stock holding can reduce risks but it can also increase costs.

Supplies and components are pulled through a system when and where they are needed, helping to reduce waste (Aghazadeh, 2003[36]). Close, long-term relationships will need to be developed with a supplier in order to make such a system work and to reduce the risk of stockout. The benefits of JIT include cost savings, improved cash flow and better utilisation of space. However, JIT is not appropriate for all businesses and does not allow for the risk of unexpected events that can affect supply chains, such as natural disasters.

JIT

Due to depreciation alone, in 1993 Dell lost about 10% of the value of each new computer by allowing them to sit, unsold, in a Dell warehouse. In 2001 the company lost less than 1%, and managed to reduce stock-holding costs by nearly 9% by implementing a JIT system.

(Source: Atkinson, 2005[37])

Case study

Procurement can also add value by developing contracts with a supplier that is able to offer **vendor managed inventories (VMI)**. This describes a situation where the supplier is responsible for the amount of stock that the buyer has. The vendor will review the buyer's stock levels, and based on forecasts it will replenish the stock to the required levels, making decisions on both the volume of products and the time of replenishment. When the stock is located at the buyer's site this is known as **consignment stock**. The growth of this concept was fuelled by developments in information technology. However, there are higher costs associated with this. The level of dependence created by this will require the creation and management of a strategic relationship between the buyer and supplier.

Place considerations in procurements from external suppliers

It is absolutely necessary to provide clear information to a supplier regarding where the product is to be delivered. This could be done in a number of ways including the quote or tender documents, the contract and the purchase order (PO). The right place also includes considerations around the right type of packaging and handling in order to avoid damage, as well as the most appropriate form of transport for the products and services in question.

There are various different types of distribution methods including road, rail, sea and air transport. Different levels of risk are associated with each of these methods which will affect the type of relationship that is developed with each supplier.

If a product is being sourced from overseas this will affect the type of relationship that is developed with the supplier. This is due to the fact that sourcing from a foreign country will extend the delivery lead times and add more risk. There are also likely to be additional challenges to developing relationships such as language barriers, different business culture and different time zones. The development of technology such as e-mail, video conferencing and Skype has made developing relationships with overseas suppliers a much easier process than previously. It has also substantially reduced the costs of maintaining these types of relationships.

> *Remember*
> There are various ways that procurement can add value for the buying organisation through the way it manages and builds relationships with external suppliers. This includes pricing and cost management, improving quality, timescales, quantities and place considerations.

The link between organisations in supply networks

Due to the links between organisations a company's value chain does not exist in isolation. As a result of this, value-adding activities continue beyond the borders of an organisation. This is the value network. Because of the interconnections there is a need to manage the links between each company involved in the network in order to ensure that the activities add value. These supply chain linkages are developed when relationships are built between buyers and suppliers.

Developing relationships with a supplier is a process that is key for **supply chain management (SCM)**. Supply chain management is another procurement concept that emerged in the Japanese car manufacturing industry. Yeo and Ning (2002) describe enhancing trust among supply chain members as an essential concept of supply chain management. They also described a collaborative attitude among all supply chain members as an effective driver of SCM. Key to this is developing successful relationships with supply chain partners.

The links between networks or supply chains also include concepts such as **Lean** production. This connects directly with two of the five rights – quality and timeliness. It is used to reduce the stock levels held by a company to the minimum and push parts through the system as fast as possible to cope with any variations in demand (Marsh, 2011[38]).

Agile is another process that requires strong links between the buyer and supplier. It was developed in response to external pressures from volatile markets and short product life cycles which require businesses to bring new products to the marketplace faster than ever before. As is the case with other concepts such as SCM and Lean, close buyer–supplier relationships are required for agile supply chains to be effective. Goldman (1993)[39] noted the importance of co-operation as one of the key principles of agile supply chains. Agile supply chains require a wide network of suppliers, so buyers will have to carefully review how strategic each product is to ensure that the correct type of relationship is developed.

Supply chain management (SCM)
The ongoing development and monitoring of a supplier and the links between supply chain members to ensure that the buyers' and end customers' needs are met

Agile
An agile organisation is one that has systems and processes that enable it to react quickly to changes in its environment

Remember
Value networks are interconnected. If a risk affects one company, it is likely that it will have an effect on the other members of the value network.

The topics of quality planning, control and assurance were touched on above. These concepts come together in **total quality management (TQM)**, a concept developed by Deming. This process is designed to improve quality at every level within an organisation (Reid and Sanders, 2010[40]). Carter et al. (1998)[41] noted that buyer–supplier relationships in organisations that operated successful TQM differed from those that did not in the following three areas.

- These companies had more formal mechanisms for interacting with a supplier.

- Integration was important, including formal reward and recognition programmes, level and quality of interaction between procurement and a supplier, the degree of supplier training, and the degree of formal evaluation of procurement personnel based on their involvement with a supplier.

- Companies that attempted to exert influence over a supplier were less successful than those that used co-operative approaches.

Early supplier involvement also falls into this area, but this is covered in more detail in chapter 2.

Chapter Summary

This chapter has introduced the concept of supplier relationship management. The different types of relationship that a buyer could have with a supplier have been discussed, and when each might be appropriate. Some key models have been covered, including the relationship spectrum, the Kraljic model, supplier referencing, Porter's Five Forces and Porter's value chain, and how these can be used to build relationships and action plans. You have also learned about the concepts of value and how relationships with a supplier can result in competitive advantages for a business.

End of Chapter Assessment

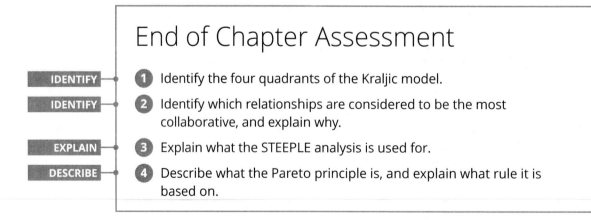

IDENTIFY — **1** Identify the four quadrants of the Kraljic model.

IDENTIFY — **2** Identify which relationships are considered to be the most collaborative, and explain why.

EXPLAIN — **3** Explain what the STEEPLE analysis is used for.

DESCRIBE — **4** Describe what the Pareto principle is, and explain what rule it is based on.

References

1 Cornelius, H. and Faire, S. (1989), *Everyone Can Win: How to Resolve Conflict*. Sidney: Simon & Schuster

2 Jap, S. D. (1999), "Pie-expansion efforts: collaboration processes in buyer – supplier relationships", *Journal of Marketing Research*, Volume 36, Issue 4, pp. 461–475

3 Leenders, M. R., Fearon, H. E., Flynn, A. and Johnson, P. F. (2001), *Purchasing and Supply Management*. New York: McGraw-Hill

4 Van Weele, A. J. (2010), *Purchasing & Supply Chain Management: Analysis, Strategy, Planning and Practice*. Andover: Cengage Learning EMEA

5 Wagner, S. M. (2011), "Supplier development and the relationship life-cycle", *International Journal of Production Economics*, Volume 129, Issue 2, pp. 277–283

6 Cousins, P., Lamming, R., Lawson, B. and Squire, B. (2008). *Strategic Supply Management: Principles, Theories and Practice*. Harlow: Pearson Education

7 Van der Schans, F. (2014), "Improving the buyer attractiveness for suppliers", Erasmus University

8 Gelderman, C. J. (2000), "Rethinking Kraljic: towards a purchasing portfolio model, based on mutual buyer–supplier dependence", *Danish Purchasing & Logistics Forum*, Volume 37, Issue 10, pp. 9–15

9 Zsidisin, G. A. (2003), "A grounded definition of supply risk", *Journal of Purchasing and Supply Management,* Volume 9, Issue 5–6, pp. 217–224

10 Kraljic, P. (1983), "Purchasing must become supply management", *Harvard Business Review,* Volume 61, Issue 5, pp. 109–117

11 Van Weele, A. J. (2000), *Purchasing and Supply Chain Management: Analysis, Planning and Practice*. London: Thomson Learning

12 Gelderman, C. J. and van Weele, A. J. (2002), "Strategic direction through purchasing portfolio management: a case study", *Journal of Supply Chain Management*, Volume 38, Issue 1, pp. 30–37

13 Lysons, K. and Farrington, B. (2006), *Purchasing and Supply Chain Management*. Harlow: Pearson Education

14 Gelderman, C. J. and van Weele, A. J. (2002), "Strategic direction through purchasing portfolio management: a case study", *Journal of Supply Chain Management*, Volume 38, Issue 1, pp. 30–37

15 Lysons, K. and Farrington, B. (2006), *Purchasing and Supply Chain Management*. Harlow: Pearson Education

16 Ibid.

17 Cousins, P., Lamming, R., Lawson, B. and Squire, B. (2008). *Strategic Supply Management: Principles, Theories and Practice*. Harlow: Pearson Education

18 Gelderman, C. J. and van Weele, A. J. (2003), "Handling measurement issues and strategic directions in Kraljic's purchasing portfolio model", *Journal of Purchasing and Supply Management*, Volume 9, Issue 5–6, pp. 207–216

19 Luzzini, D., Caniato, F., Ronchi, S. and Spina, G. (2012), "A transaction costs approach to purchasing portfolio management", *International Journal of Operations & Production Management*, Volume 32, Issue 9, pp. 1015–1042

20 Bew, R. (2007), "The New Customer of Choice Imperative: Ensuring Supply Availability, Productivity Gains, and Supplier Innovation", *92nd Annual International Supply Management Conference*

21 Ibid.

22 Steinle, C. and Schiele, H. (2008), "Limits to global sourcing?: Strategic consequences of dependency on international suppliers: Cluster theory, resource-based view and case studies", *Journal of Purchasing and Supply Management*, Volume 14, Issue 1, pp. 3–14

23 Hallikas, J., Puumalainen, K., Vesterinen, T. and Virolainen, V. M. (2005), "Risk-based classification of supplier relationships", *Journal of Purchasing and Supply Management*, Volume 11, Issue 2–3, pp. 72–82

24 Grönroos, C. and Helle, P. (2012), "Return on relationships: conceptual understanding and measurement of mutual gains from relational business engagements", *Journal of Business & Industrial Marketing*, Volume 27, Issue 5, pp. 344–359

25 Steele, P. T. and Court, B. H. (1996), *Profitable Purchasing Strategies: A Manager's Guide for Improving Organisational Competitiveness Through the Skills of Purchasing*. London: McGraw-Hill

26 Van der Schans, F. (2014), *Improving the buyer attractiveness for suppliers*, Erasmus University

27 Van Weele, A. J. (2010), *Purchasing & Supply Chain Management: Analysis, Strategy, Planning and Practice*. Andover: Cengage Learning EMEA

28 Van der Schans, F. (2014), *Improving the buyer attractiveness for suppliers*, Erasmus University

29 Porter, M. E. (1985), *Competitive Advantage: Creating and Sustaining Superior Performance*. New York: Free Press

30 Ibid.

31 Ibid.

32 Ibid.

33 Lysons, K. and Farrington, B. (2006), *Purchasing and Supply Chain Management*. Harlow: Pearson Education

34 Fearne, A., Duffy, R. and Hughes, D. (2001), Concepts of collaboration: supply chain management in a global food industry, in Eastham, J., Sharples, L. and Ball, S. (eds), *Food Supply Chain Management*, Butterworth-Heinemann, pp. 55–89

35 Hutchins, D. (1999), *Just In Time*. Aldershot: Gower Publishing, Ltd.

36 Aghazadeh, S. M. (2003), "JIT inventory and competition in the global environment: a comparative study of American and Japanese values in auto industry", *Cross Cultural Management: An International Journal*, Volume 10, Issue 4, pp. 29–42

37 Atkinson, C. (2005), *Dell computers: a case study in low inventory* [online]. Retrieved from: www.inventorymanagementreview.org/2005/09/dell_computers_.html

38 Marsh, P., "Industry left high and dry", *Financial Times*, 12 April 2011

39 Goldman, S. L. and Nagel, R. N. (1993), "Management, technology and agility: the emergence of a new era in manufacturing", *International Journal of Technology Management*, Volume, 8 Issue 1–2, pp. 18–38

40 Reid, R. D. and Sanders, N. R. (2010), *Operations Management: An Integrated Approach*. New York: Wiley

41 Carter, J. R., Smeltzer, L. and Narasimhan, R. (1998), "The role of buyer and supplier relationships in integrating TQM through the supply chain", *European Journal of Purchasing & Supply Management*, Volume 4, Issue 4, pp. 223–234

Recommended reading

1. Van Weele, A. J., (2010). *Purchasing & supply chain management: analysis, strategy, planning and practice*. Cengage Learning EMEA.

2. Cousins, P., Lamming, R., Lawson, B. and Squire, B., (2008). *Strategic supply management: principles, theories and practice*. Pearson Education.

3. Lysons, K. and Farrington, B., (2006). *Purchasing and supply chain management*. Pearson Education.

CHAPTER 2

Understanding processes and procedures for successful working with stakeholders

By the end of this chapter, you will understand the processes and procedures for successful working with stakeholders.

Chapter overview

2.1 Analyse the purpose of organisational procedures and processes in sourcing goods and/or services

You will understand:
- Achieving value for money
- Supplier identification, assessment and selection
- Selection and awarding criteria

2.2 Compare team management techniques to ensure positive stakeholder relationships

You will understand:
- Positive relationships through positive contributions
- Overcoming resistance
- Identifying conflict and coping processes
- Cross-organisational teams
- Stages of team development – forming, storming, norming, performing

2.3 Compare the practical considerations of stakeholder management

You will understand:
- Accurate cost modelling
- Reduced impact of price fluctuations
- Early supplier involvement in product and/or service development
- Knowledge transfer and access to innovation
- Common metrics to drive change for both organisations
- Improving risk management and continuity of supply

> **2.4 Identify the process for terminating stakeholder relationships**
> You will understand:
> - Reasons for termination
> - The process of termination
> - Timing
> - Relationship impacts – amicable *v.* hostile
> - Legal considerations – finances, confidentiality, IPR, security, employee rights
> - Succession issues – continuity of supply

Connected stakeholder
This is a stakeholder that has a strong interest in a company's activities. This is due to its contractual or commercial relationship with the company. This definition includes suppliers

Introduction

This chapter focuses on working successfully with stakeholders. Stakeholders were defined in section 1.1 as 'people who have an active interest in or a concern about what is being procured'. Stakeholders can be internal, connected or external to a business.

Stakeholders may be interested in the specification, the tender process itself, the evaluation, the award and the subsequent contract management. They may also be interested in the outcomes of a procurement activity like financial savings, adding value, innovation or reduction of waste.

Some stakeholders will be important in all projects, whereas the involvement of others may change depending on what the business requirements are.

Internal stakeholders could include the following.

- **Internal end users** – the people and departments who will be using the product or service.

- **Contract managers** – the individuals or teams who will be responsible for the day-to-day management of the contract.

- **Legal** – a legal team may be involved in a procurement if the tender or contracting process is complicated.

- **Employees** – they can be affected by a procurement if it changes the way they carry out their role or transfers their job to a supplier organisation via outsourcing.

Connected stakeholders could include the following.

- **Suppliers** – the businesses that will be involved in the tender process, which may be existing suppliers or may be new suppliers.

- **Customers and clients** – these are important stakeholders, as the business will need to ensure that their requirements are met.

External stakeholders could include the following.

- **Competitors** – it is important to understand what is happening in the wider marketplace. What are your competitors doing?

- **Communities** – it is important to understand how a company and its procurement practices impact local communities in terms of the environment and economy.

- **Government and other public agencies** – these have greater importance in the public sector procurement environment.

This is not an exhaustive list, and it will change depending on the nature of each procurement or project.

2.1 Analyse the purpose of organisational procedures and processes in sourcing goods and/or services

Each organisation will have its own internal organisational procedures and processes for sourcing products and services. Some organisations, such as those operating in the public sector within the UK, will also have to abide by legislation including the Public Contracts Regulations (PCR) 2015. Procurement processes will provide guidelines and governance for stakeholders in terms of expected behaviours, such as threshold values (see below).

Achieving value for money

Achieving **value for money (VFM)** is one of the key goals of the procurement function. Traditionally procurement has been tasked with achieving the lowest possible price for inputs. But, achieving the lowest possible price will not always result in the best value for money. A company may purchase a cheaper product with the aim of reducing costs. But if this product is not as durable and has to be replaced more often, it does not offer value for money over the long-term. Although reducing cost is an important part of value for money, too much focus on this discourages a long-term perspective. KPMG points out that value drivers such as innovation, sustainability and legality require a long-term perspective.

A large part of an organisation's total spend comes from the external supplier chain. This demonstrates the importance of the procurement department and the value for money it brings to an organisation. That is one of the key reasons why procurement has developed into a strategic function in recent decades.

Value for money is often described as the 'three Es'; however, the National Audit Office (UK) notes that in some areas there is a fourth E.

- **Economy** – minimising costs for the business in terms of resources used or required inputs: spending less

- **Efficiency** – the relationship between the output from the product or service and the resources to produce it: spending well

- **Effectiveness** – the extent to which objectives are met: spending wisely

- **Equity** – the extent to which services are available, and reach, all of the people they are intended to: spending fairly. This is more applicable to public sector organisations such as government departments.

CIPS makes reference to some typical factors that are taken into account in defining value for money.

- **Fitness for purpose.** Does the product or service actually do what it is required to do?

- **Quality.** Does the product or service meet the quality levels that are needed? This will vary considerably from one procurement to another, depending on the nature of the requirement.

- **Total lifetime costs.** What is the total cost of purchasing the product or service? This will include elements such as maintenance and disposal costs.

A Z

Value for money (VFM)
The most advantageous combination of price and quality that makes a product or service fit for purpose and will achieve the buyer's required outcomes. This needs to be reviewed in terms of whole life costs

- **Risk.** Is the product or service a high-risk procurement?

- **Environmental and sustainability issues.** Ensuring that the production of the product or service does not have an adverse impact on the environment. This would include corporate social responsibility.

- Other factors contributing to the proposed solutions to the organisation's overall goals

Dimitri (2013)[1] referred to this as a multi-criteria approach, but you will notice that many of the criteria are non-monetary. These criteria should form part of the scoring and evaluation criteria used for procurements, which are listed below.

In recent years corporate social responsibility has also become a part of the value-for-money definition. This has been the case for both private and public sector organisations. Many organisations procuring the products and services have a social goal. They will look at the value the supplier can add. In this way value has a much wider meaning. A supplier may include the following added value elements in their tender submissions.

- Providing work experience opportunities for the long-term unemployed

- Providing education and training opportunities

- Apprenticeships

- Supplier staff undertaking voluntary work on specific projects

- Donations of products/materials for community projects

- Sponsorship of events

Remember
Value for money is not just about obtaining a product or service at the lowest price. It is often described as the four Es – economy, efficiency, effectiveness and equity.

Procurement professionals in both the public and private sectors want to ensure that any products and services purchased offer their organisations value for money. Value for money in the private sector is related to shareholder profit and business benefit. However, value for money in the public sector is related to ensuring that taxpayers' money is spent wisely. The definition of value-for-money will be different for every procurement undertaken. Dimitri (2013)[2] notes that value for money requires careful procurement design and planning as well as monitoring the contract once it has been awarded to ensure that the benefits actually occur.

Procurement procedures and processes

Procurement will have a number of procedures and processes in place in order to achieve value for money. These processes look at value for money in terms of applying competition, that is, obtaining a price from more than one supplier. Theoretically, the more competition the better. However, generally speaking, obtaining three different supplier bids is considered adequate competition. If you only have two bids and they are very different in terms of price, it can be difficult to assess whether a bid is abnormally low or high.

Below is a typical example of an internal procurement department's thresholds for buying products or services, although each company's threshold values will vary.

This information will be located in a company's procurement policy and should be communicated to all departments in the business.

- Under $5000 – one quote

- $5000–$10,000 – quote process, must have approached at least two suppliers for quotes

- $10,000 and above – competitive tendering of all contracts with a value over $10,000, must have approached at least three suppliers for quotes or tenders

- Approval for any single-source contract over $5000 where no competition has been applied must have a solid justification as to why competition has not been applied.

- Length of contract limited to three years to ensure that the market is reassessed regularly. Any contracts over this length may require additional approvals. For the majority of products and services that are located in the routine, bottleneck or leverage quadrants (see figure 1.4) this would be applicable. Where a product or service is considered to be strategic, the buyer may wish to enter into a partnership agreement, where a longer-term contract will be beneficial. Contract length should be reviewed on a case-by-case basis.

The evaluation and selection criteria can be used to contribute towards achieving value for money, by ensuring the most suitable supplier is awarded the contract based on price and other qualitative considerations.

Competition

Competition among suppliers is a key way of achieving value for money, and should always be applied unless there are justifiable reasons not to. We discussed Porter's Five Forces in section 1.3, and in some markets or for some requirements there may not be any viable alternatives to the current supplier. In the public sector there are legal rules in place around competition to support the creation of value-for-money, transparency and fairness. In the EU, once contracts hit a certain value, procurement departments are mandated to advertise contract opportunities across all of the member countries.

KPMG noted that a lack of compliance with procurement processes and procedures can result in benefits and value leaking from the buying organisation. This could happen in a variety of ways.

- Lack of contract coverage, e.g., no formal contracts with a supplier, or lack of agreed rates and terms and conditions. In this situation different parts of the business could be paying different prices for the same products and services. The organisation is not leveraging its volumes and it is losing out on potential discounts.

- Maverick buying activity. This occurs when the end user or the business makes purchases without adhering to the procurement process or using the contracts which are already in place. An example using the above values would be an end user purchasing a piece of machinery for $50,000 without undertaking a competitive process or getting a single-source approval. The supplier it selected may not have been the best value for money.

- If there is no formal specification the buying organisation may end up procuring a product or service that is not fit for purpose. Time and money may be wasted on trying to amend the product or service or re-procuring.

- Procurement activity is not assessed and managed in a consistent way. This could introduce risk, for example, where the buying organisation has agreed to supplier terms and conditions. Or risks may not have not been assessed, such as no check on supplier financial stability, insurances or health and safety.

Negotiation

> *Apply*
> Think about the procurement processes and procedures in the business that you work in. Do you think that they support the delivery of value for money?

Following on from competition in the market, another key way that procurement can achieve value for money is via negotiations. Zartman (2007)[3] said that the scope of negotiations has changed from predominantly price oriented to focusing on economic, sustainable, relational and reputation aspects. This is a result of procurement moving from a purely operational to a more strategic function. This is particularly the case when the buyer values the ongoing relationship with the supplier.

The procurement and supply cycle

We are now going to look at the procurement and supply cycle (figure 2.1). There are points all around the cycle where procurement can add value. The cycle shows generally the phases involved, from identification of a need right through to managing the asset that is the output of the procurement process. Over the course of this section we will discuss how procurement adds value at different stages of the cycle.

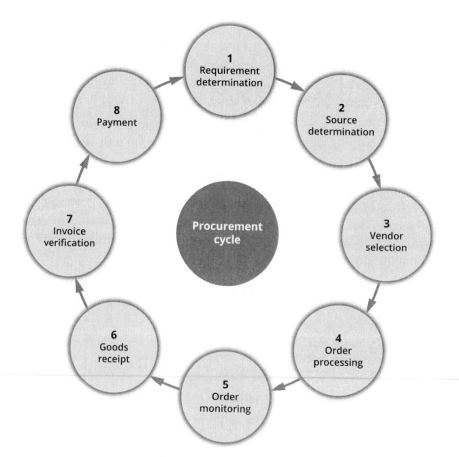

Figure 2.1 The simplified procurement cycle (Source: adapted from www.cips.org/en-gb/knowledge/procurement-cycle/. Copyright CIPS 2014. All rights reserved.)

Understand the need

The first stage is understanding the needs of internal customers and stakeholders. It is at this stage that specifications and KPIs are developed. Procurement can add value here in a number of ways.

- Consider the **make or buy** decision. Would manufacturing the product or offering the service using internal resources and staff be a viable option?

- Support the formation of a cross-departmental team to develop the specification. This is particularly relevant where the requirement will affect a large part of the organisation, or where it is strategic and/or of high value.

- Ensure that the requirement is not over-specified. Does the organisation need all of the activities included in a service?

- Review where branded products could be replaced by substitute non-branded products or materials to reduce costs.

- Encourage standardisation of common products and services across a company to benefit from leverage possibilities.

- Provide advice on whether a conformance or performance specification would be most suitable.

- Involve suppliers in this stage if this would be added value.

Make or buy
A decision about what products or services an organisation will manufacture or provide themselves in-house, and which will be purchased from outside sources

> *Remember*
> One of the key ways that procurement can ensure value for money is to apply competition to business requirements.

In order to ensure value for money for the buying organisation, internal end users will need to define what they consider to be value. KPMG stated that this should include a process of **value mapping**. This allows companies to think past cost cutting and allows them to look at value drivers that also contribute to revenue growth, improved use of assets and reduced risk. The end users define what value means and how this can be supported by supplier relationship management.

The process of achieving value for money for the buying organisation also involves removing waste from the supply chain. This can be done at the 'identify the need' stage as the organisation is reviewing exactly what it needs and no longer needs from the supplier. For example, a buying organisation may wish to reduce waste by reducing stock and moving to a JIT stock management process. This requirement would need to be detailed in the specification. There are seven wastes as defined by Taiichi Ohno.

Value mapping
A process in which value is created by reducing or eliminating waste and operational inefficiencies

1. (Excessive) transportation

2. Inventory (unnecessary stock holding)

3. (Unnecessary) motion

4. Waiting

5. Over-production

6. Over-processing

7. Defects

> *Remember*
>
> The mnemonic **TIMWOOD** can help you remember the seven wastes.
>
> **T**ransportation
> **I**nventory
> **M**otion
> **W**aiting
> **O**ver-production
> **O**ver-processing
> **D**efects

Review the market

Following development of the specification, a market review will need to be undertaken to assess the number of key suppliers in the marketplace and how the market operates. Market structure was discussed in section 1.3 when we reviewed Porter's Five Forces model. Understanding the market is key to understanding the level of competition. The level of competition will affect the sourcing strategy and sourcing process selected. This process may also involve some portfolio analysis.

Develop strategy

Procurement can also add value by taking a more strategic approach to the procurement of products and services and developing strategies for sourcing. This is often done via category management. By taking a more strategic approach procurement can add value by leveraging expertise and knowledge in the following ways.

- Spend reviews across various areas provide a fuller overview than reviewing spend on a contract-by-contract basis.

- Following on from spend reviews procurement can aggregate demand and consolidate spend, which can result in reduced costs.

- Supplier relationship management and improved risk management plans can be developed.

- Specialist category and supplier knowledge regarding the market and potential sources of supply can be developed.

Steps 4 to 8 of the procurement and supply cycle in figure 2.1 are discussed below in the section on identification, assessment and selection.

Contract management

Value creation and well-developed supplier relationship management practices go hand in hand. Developing supplier relationships is a key part of contract management. Supplier relationships can result in value for money in a number of different ways.

- Being able to identify and use an appropriate approach to deal with supplier issues

- Innovation developed as part of collaborative projects with strategic suppliers

- Reduction of waste

- Resilience and risk reduction

To ensure that a procurement department is achieving value for money an audit should be undertaken. CIPS said that this type of audit is completed to assess whether the organisation is gaining value from the processes and procedures that are in place. The results of these audits can then be used to refine the procurement process.

> *Remember*
> Procurement can add value at all stages of the procurement life cycle. The stages are: understand need, market review, develop strategy, supplier identification, develop documents, supplier selection, tender evaluation, contract award and contract management.

Supplier identification, assessment and selection

Supplier identification and selection are core operational tasks that a procurement department will undertake on a daily basis. These stages form the next part of the procurement life cycle model. There are various differences between the processes and procedures used by **private sector** and **public sector** buyers.

Supplier identification – private sector

Supplier identification involves a buyer looking at its external environment. After a buyer has developed a requirement, reviewed the market structure and developed a strategy, the process of supplier identification begins. There are a number of sources of information that a buyer can use to identify a suitable supplier.

- Internal stakeholders/user department knowledge
- Preferred supplier lists – what suppliers have been used by the business in the past?
- Internet searches
- Tradeshows, exhibitions and trade press
- Networking with other procurement professionals
- Advertising the requirement on e-procurement platforms
- Vendor engagement events
- Agents – this will be applicable when undertaking sourcing from low-cost countries such as China.

In some cases, the buyer will undertake vendor engagement events to make the supplier market aware of its requirements. This tends to be the case with large infrastructure projects. These events are useful to make a supplier aware of the key requirements and the tender process along with key timelines. This allows the supply market to start to consider the requirement in advance of the formal selection process. For instance, a supplier could start to discuss the requirement with potential subcontractors and build the necessary relationships.

Once a list of suppliers has been identified there are a number of key questions that a buyer should ask themself.

- How many suppliers in the marketplace are able to provide the product or service?

Private sector
Organisations that are owned by private individuals and enterprises

Public sector
Service organisations run by the government and usually funded by taxes

- Is this a single- or sole-source situation?
- What is the relative buyer and supplier power in the marketplace?
- How might the suppliers in the marketplace view the buyer? Do all of the suppliers have the same view?
- How will the make-up of the market affect the selection process?

Benchmarking
Comparing an element of one business, such as price, quality or service, against another

Following this a decision will be made regarding which suppliers to include in the process. The private sector buyer is free to invite as many suppliers to participate as it feels are relevant. Supplier identification may also be a time when a **benchmarking** exercise is undertaken to understand whether or not current prices are competitive in terms of market prices.

As discussed above, supplier identification includes pre-tender engagement activities. Response rates to tender processes will generally be better if you make contact with a supplier before you issue the tender to let them know that it will be issued. A supplier that has an understanding of the buyer and its requirements is more likely to respond than one that has received a tender request from an unknown buyer.

Remember
The number of suppliers that are identified in the marketplace will have a direct effect on the type of procurement processes and procedures used to select suppliers.

Supplier identification – public sector

Supplier identification in the public sector is a more transparent process than in the private sector. As mentioned above, when undertaking a procurement in the public sector in the EU, the buyer will be required to advertise the requirement in the Official Journal of the European Union (OJEU). This means that the requirement will be advertised across all the EU member countries.

Common procurement vocabulary (CPV) codes
Numerical classifications for products and services. The aim of these codes is to standardise the references used by buyers to describe the products and services that they are purchasing

When the buyer places the advert, it will need to select which **common procurement vocabulary (CPV) codes** match its requirements in order to facilitate the advertising process. There are a number of e-platforms that will allow a supplier to register for free to receive these adverts. When a supplier registers it includes in its profile the CPV codes for the products and services it supplies. When the advert is issued these portals match up the CPV codes in the buyer's advert with those that are in the supplier's profile, sending the supplier the relevant contract adverts. Two examples of these portals include Sell2Wales and Public Contracts Scotland. These portals can also act as directories for a buyer to identify a supplier for its requirements that are below the threshold values.

This will affect the supplier identification process and can result in far more tender returns, all of which will have to be fully evaluated. This is especially the case in areas where there are a high number of suppliers in the marketplace, such as stationery or construction services. If a public sector buyer is unsure about the level of competition in the marketplace it can issue a prior indicative notice (PIN), which informs the marketplace of the requirement, who the buyer is and when the tender is likely to be issued. This can be used to gauge the level of interest in the marketplace.

Public sector buyers are also able to undertake vendor engagement events, but these should be carried out before the contract is advertised. These are often advertised as part of the PIN process. The number of suppliers identified will inform the choice of process or the method used for supplier selection.

Supplier assessment stage, pre-qualification and selection

Once the potential suppliers in the marketplace have been identified the buyer will move on to the supplier assessment and selection process. This is part of stage 6 of the procurement cycle. This involves the following.

- Developing request for information (RFI) documents and criteria
- Evaluating suppliers against this criteria, only suppliers that meet the buyer's minimum requirements will be short-listed and will progress to the next stage (RFP)
- Evaluate tenders

When drafting the documents, procurement will have to decide which method of procurement best fits the marketplace and the requirement. Again, this differs between the public and private sector, and as a result these are discussed separately.

Supplier assessment stage, pre-qualification and selection – private sector

In the private sector the method of supplier assessment and selection will be governed by the internal policies and procedures around threshold values. This will let the buyer know the level of competition they are required to undertake in order to meet these procedures. A buyer may be required to obtain at least three quotes or tenders for all contracts worth over £10,000. In addition to this, the buyer will need to make sure that it adheres to any other assessment requirements such as risk assessments. Risk assessments will cover all aspects of potential risk including financial, commercial, and health and safety. Therefore, the first thing a buyer will need to do is establish whether to undertake a competitive process. Supplier assessment and selection will form part of this process.

The ways in which competitive bidding and competition can result in value for money were discussed above. Dobler and Burt (1996)[4] established a list of criteria for when competitive bidding should be used for supplier assessment and selection and when it should not. Where competitive bidding is inappropriate buyers will need to use negotiation (see later in this section). In the private sector it is possible to sole source if competition is not thought to be the best method of selection, but this will usually require internal sign-off with a sound justification.

When to use competitive bidding	When not to use competitive bidding
When the item or service is of sufficient value	When it's not possible to obtain firm prices
When there is a clear specification so that competitive bids can be evaluated side by side	When the specification is likely to change
When competition exists between a number of good quality suppliers	When price is not the main driver
When there is enough time for the process to be completed properly	When set-up cost and time is prohibitive

Table 2.1 When competitive bidding should be used based on Dobler and Burt (1996)

Although there are benefits to competitive tendering there are also a number of drawbacks.

- It takes time for the buyer to develop and issue the tender documents and evaluate the responses, and also for the supplier to respond.

- Bidders may be discouraged if they think that the buyer has no intention of switching suppliers and the buyer is using the process to benchmark its incumbent supplier. Suppliers may think this is the case if the buyer already has a longstanding incumbent supplier.

- Contract awards may be a one-off. In other words, regular competitive tenders do not result in deepening buyer–supplier relationships. Before competitive tendering a buyer will need to consider what type of relationship it wishes to develop with the supplier of the products and services.

The key method of supplier assessment and selection in the private sector is the use of a request for information.

- **Request for information (RFI).** The aim of this process is to create a shortlist of suppliers that will be invited to the next stage of the process. This is part of the pre-qualification stage. This process will be used in cases where the number of suppliers in the marketplace who can fulfil the requirement is high, the full extent of supplier capability is unknown and/or the requirement is not fully developed. This process also assists buyers to understand the types of suppliers that are in the marketplace.

Depending on the requirement and the number of suppliers in the marketplace, a procurement team may choose to undertake an RFI followed by an request for proposal (RFP), or it may choose to go straight to RFP stage. The following information is typically requested at the RFI stage.

- Information on previous contracts that are relevant to the buyer requirements – this is likely to include references. This will give the buyer a good indication of the supplier's capacity and competence.

- Financial information – profit and loss accounts

- Insurances – public, employer's and product liability

- Certificates such as ISO accreditations: ISO 9001, ISO 14001 or ISO 18001 – this will be dependent on the requirement

- Supplier acceptance of the buyer's standard payment terms and contractual terms and conditions

- Minimum levels of health and safety standards

At the RFI stage these will generally be applied as pass/fail criteria. For example, if the supplier does not have the relevant industry accreditations they would be removed from the process.

> *Check*
> What are the benefits and drawbacks for the buyer and the supplier of undertaking a competitive tender process?

Supplier assessment stage, pre-qualification and selection – public sector

Although public sector buyers still have a need to assess whether bidders meet the minimum requirements during the selection process, it is important to outline the differences between the supplier identification and selection processes in the public sector and in the private sector. Supplier selection in the public sector is far more regulated. At the time of writing, the latest change to the Public Contracts and Procurement Regulations occurred in 2015. There are four key principles of procurement in the EU.

2.1 L02

- Transparency in the process of procurement

- Equality of treatment of suppliers

- Non-discrimination – the requirement is advertised to suppliers in all of the EU countries

- Proportionality – the procurement process must be proportionate to the value of the contract

Due to the imposed threshold values and the resulting EU-wide advertising requirement, competition in the assessment and selection process is ensured. The threshold values are reviewed every two years. There are different threshold values for service contracts compared to works (construction) contracts. The threshold value for works (construction) contracts is significantly higher than that for services. These threshold values relate to the total value over the life of the contract.

The key procedure used to assess, pre-qualify and select suppliers in the public sector is the **restricted tender process**. This is a two-stage process. It involves an initial **pre-qualification questionnaire (PQQ)** to create a shortlist of suppliers. These suppliers will then be invited to the next stage of the process, the invitation to tender (ITT), if they meet the minimum requirements of the buying organisation.

This process will be used in cases where the number of suppliers in the marketplace who can fulfil the requirement is high or unknown, the full extent of supplier capability is unknown and/or the requirement is not fully developed. This is similar to running an RFI process.

An electronic PQQ must be issued to a supplier for a minimum of 30 days. A buyer must adhere to these timescales in order for its procurement to be considered legal.

Pre-qualification questionnaire (PQQ)
A document sent to potential suppliers asking for information necessary to support their qualification as an approved supplier

> *Remember*
> Both requests for information (RFIs) and pre-qualification questionnaires (PQQs) can be used for the selection stage of a tender process to ensure that short-listed bidders meet the requirements of the buying organisation.

Award stage – selection and awarding criteria

Following on from a pre-selection process such as an RFI or a PQQ, selection and awarding criteria are used by a buyer as a way of determining which is the best supplier to meet their requirement and enter into a contract with. Selection and awarding criteria should be carefully considered alongside the development of the specification. If they are not, then the buyer could end up with an outcome that does not meet its needs and is not fit for purpose. This links back to the concept of value for money. The buyer will need to select award criteria that will ensure the winning bidder provides the best value for money for the stakeholder's needs.

Selection and awarding criteria – private sector

Following on from short-listing suppliers at the selection stage, in order to be able to evaluate which supplier best suits the requirement, the buyer will issue a request for proposal. This is described in more detail below.

- Request for proposal (RFP). This process will be used in cases where there are fewer suppliers in the marketplace or shortlisting has already been undertaken and the requirement is well developed. Where an RFI has been used as part of the selection process it will be followed by an RFP.

At the RFP stage, several pieces of information are also required in order for the buyer to be able to make their decision regarding awards. This will include the following.

- Detailed information on how the supplier will produce the products or deliver the service, including method statements
- Risk assessments
- Full pricing information

The buyer will need to decide how this information will be evaluated. Each of the criteria should be allocated a percentage weighting. The suppliers will then be scored on each criteria in relation to whether or not they meet the requirements. End users and other relevant internal stakeholders should be fully involved in the development of tender selection, awarding criteria and in the full procurement process. This will ensure that the results meet the needs of the business and therefore provides a better outcome.

Awarding criteria used at the RFP stage will generally be made up of a mixture of price and quality. When buying routine and transactional items such as stationery, price will have a bigger weighting than quality. When buying services that impact people directly, such as adult social care, the weighting of the quality of the service will be higher than the price weighting. However, in the private sector you may often come across cases where the evaluation is done solely on price especially for lower value products and services.

A tender evaluation panel should be developed to evaluate the RFIs/RFPs. This should be a cross-functional team and ideally have representatives from key stakeholder groups as well as a representative from procurement to oversee the activity. The panel should remain the same throughout the evaluation process.

The RFP process may also include a scored presentation stage. This stage will include the top-scoring suppliers from the previous stages of the process, perhaps the top two or three. Bidders are then able to discuss their proposal in more detail and buyers are able to answer questions about the proposal. This scored presentation stage should have its own weighed scoring criteria.

Following the RFP stage, depending on the nature of the product or service, there may be additional stages to this process including an e-auction. Reverse e-auctions were defined in section 1.2. E-auctions are an effective means of increasing value.

Reverse e-auctions are typically carried out on the purchase of products like stationery and IT consumables, items that are located in the leverage quadrant of the Kraljic model. They are particularly useful if a number of tenders are close together in terms of their price submission and levels of quality. A supplier should be informed at the start of the tender process if the organisation intends to use an e-auction to finalise the award process. It could be that a buyer decides to include the three highest-scoring suppliers in an e-auction.

If an e-auction is not appropriate there are likely to be rounds of **negotiations** with a small number of bidders in order to extract further value from the deal and assess which supplier should be selected. Win-lose, lose-lose and win-win outcomes of negotiations were discussed in section 1.1. In situations where there is only a single-source of supply that has been previously pre-qualified, a buyer may move straight to the negotiation phase of the process. If this process results in a win-win outcome, a negotiation will also provide a good foundation for building a relationship with the supplier.

2.1 L02

Negotiation
A negotiation between a buyer and supplier is a discussion with the aim of reaching agreement, usually on the price of a product or service

> *Remember*
> Key procurement procedures used in the private sector for supplier selection include request for information (RFI), request for proposal (RFP), e-auctions and rounds of negotiations.

Selection and awarding criteria – public sector

Following on from the PQQ selection stage of a public sector procurement process, there are five key procurement processes and procedures that buyers can use in EU public sector procurements in order to assess and award contracts to suppliers. The type or process used will depend on the nature of the requirement. This is discussed further below.

- **Open tender process.** This is a one-stage process. It is similar to an RFP and is referred to as an invitation to tender (ITT). This process will be used in cases where there are fewer suppliers in the marketplace so shortlisting is not required and/or the requirement is well developed. It is important to remember that this process has no PQQ (selection) stage.

- **Restricted tender process (Part 2).** Following on from issuing an PQQ and selecting suppliers from a short-list, a buyer will then issue these suppliers a request for proposal (RFP). This more detailed stage of the process will evaluate how the suppliers intend to deliver the requirement.

- **Competitive procedure with negotiation.** This procedure can include a PQQ stage. Following this, shortlisted bidders are invited to submit a tender. Following the initial submission there may be subsequent rounds of tenders followed by negotiation. No negotiation is permitted following submission of the final tender. This process is time consuming and resource intensive.

- **Competitive dialogue.** This process is used when the buyer has a complex requirement and several phases of negotiation are required. Therefore, neither the open nor the restricted procedure is suitable. The use of this procedure must be justified. A PQQ will be undertaken first and then the stages of negotiation will be entered into with the shortlisted bidders. It is likely that the specification and the terms and conditions will be updated during these phases. Following this process, the bidders will submit final tenders. Further negotiation is permitted with the winning bidder(s) provided certain safeguards are observed. This process is time consuming and resource intensive.

- **Innovative partnership procedure.** This process allows for the research, development and purchase of a product or service within a single procurement. The final purchase must correspond to pre-agreed levels of performance and maximum costs. Following responses to the initial advert the buyer uses a negotiated approach to invite the suppliers to submit ideas to develop the required innovative products or services for which no suitable product is currently available. No negotiation is permitted following submission of the final tender. This process is time consuming and resource intensive.

There are minimum timescales for each of the procedures listed above.

As stated above, there is only one procedure where negotiation can take place after submission of the final tender – the competitive dialogue procedure. This contrasts with the private sector tender process which is often followed by negotiation in order to extract as much value as possible from the deal.

There is also another option in the public sector that has not yet been discussed. A public sector buyer could procure from a pre-established framework set up by another buyer or procurement collaboration. In these cases the selection stage has already been completed and the buyer will only need to undertake the award stage invitation to tender (ITT).

In order to procure from a pre-established framework the buying organisation must have been named in the original contract notice (advert). In Wales, a leading country in public procurement, there is a National Procurement Service (NPS). This service sets up collaborative frameworks for spend that are common and relative across public sector bodies, such as legal services and IT hardware. Buyers can then run a further competition (award stage) under the framework, which is much quicker and simpler than running a full open market competitive tender process. By purchasing like this, the public sector in Wales is able to leverage its large spend across multiple organisations to deliver better value for money.

In the public sector the use of MEAT (most economically advantageous tender) evaluation criteria helps procurement to achieve the goal of obtaining value for money. MEAT evaluation criteria are a mix of price and quality criteria.

Selection and awarding criteria (public sector)
Table 2.2 provides an example of MEAT awarding criteria. The procurement is for an out-of-hours call centre provision (5:00pm – 8:00am). In this example the level 1 price/quality breakdown is 40%/60% (which totals 100%), demonstrating that the quality of the service is more important than the cost. The level 2 criteria are then broken down into sub-criteria for price (which add up to 100%) and quality (which add up to 100%). When evaluating, a score will be given for each sub-criterion; the scores will then be weighted and added together to give a total weighted score for each supplier. The supplier with the highest overall score will be awarded the business.

Case study

Selection and awarding criteria (example)	
Level 1 criteria	**Level 2 sub-criteria**
Price – 40%	Cost of service delivery – 90%
	Cost of consultancy – 10%
Quality – 60%	Previous experience – 30%
	Customer service levels – 40%
	Management of service – 20%
	Innovation – 10%

Table 2.2 Selection and awarding criteria

The contract notices (adverts) that are issued by public sector bodies in the EU that are over the threshold values should clearly detail to a supplier the selection and awarding criteria. The notice must also detail the percentage weighting allocated to each of these criteria and sub-criteria. The method of scoring must be detailed along with a description of the type of answer that would achieve each score. The buyer is only allowed to consider the information provided as part of the tender process despite what they may already know about the supplier.

As well as detailing the weightings, the buyer will also have to be clear on any calculations used; for example, the formula used to calculate the price score will need to be detailed. Any formula used to calculate financial ratios such as the acid test ratio will need to be fully detailed to each supplier. A supplier can use this information to help it decide whether or not to bid, as it will be able to calculate whether it will be able to achieve a high score. These financial elements should be evaluated with the support of the finance team.

A cross-functional evaluation panel should also be developed. The same panel members must be present to evaluate all supplier responses. A justified reason for each score that is given must be detailed. If a buyer is found to have deviated from the stated selection and evaluation criteria, then suppliers are entitled to challenge the outcome of the procurement.

When a supplier is told whether it has been successful it must also be told its score against each of the criteria in comparison to the winning bidder's score. A supplier that has submitted tenders as part of a public sector process also has the right to receive detailed feedback on its submissions. This is not the case in the private sector procurement process.

Once a contract has been awarded, contract management also has a key part to play in ensuring that an organisation achieves value for money captured as part of the pre-award phase of the process. For example, if the new contract includes a saving as a result of a reduced cost, the costs over the lifetime of the contract should be tracked to ensure that prices are not creeping up. This includes performance management. This part of the process will include building appropriate relationships with suppliers. This is true in both the private and public sectors. However, it is often said that it is more difficult for a buyer to build relationships with a supplier in the public sector because of the competitive tender process that is undertaken every few years. The maximum contract length of a framework agreement in the public sector in the EU is four years.

Check
What are the key elements of supplier identification, selection and evaluation?

Remember
Key stakeholders should be involved when developing the evaluation and award criteria. This is the case in both the public and private sectors and will ensure that procurement achieves value for money.

2.2 Compare team management techniques to ensure positive stakeholder relationships

There are a number of techniques that procurement teams can use to ensure positive stakeholder relationships. Building these relationships can result in better procurement outcomes. Hillman and Keim (2010)[5] said that building better relationships with primary stakeholders, such as employees, customers, suppliers and communities could lead to increased shareholder wealth by developing competitive advantage.

Building these relationships is about understanding the objectives and requirements of individuals and groups. By trying to understand their position it may be possible to tailor communications and avoid unnecessary delays and conflict.

Positive relationships through positive contributions

One of the best ways to build positive relationships with business stakeholders is to ensure that they feel their interests have been considered and they are kept informed regarding initial objectives, the project plan, progress, outcomes, etc. In order to do this for a procurement activity or a project it is important to first identify who your stakeholders are.

As discussed in the introduction to this chapter it is highly likely that for each procurement the stakeholder group will be different due to changes in requirements. This is another reason why it is important to identify your stakeholders. This can be done via a brainstorming exercise. Once a list of potential stakeholders has been identified they can be mapped. In order to do this a stakeholder mapping exercise needs to be undertaken based on the stakeholders' level of power or interest.

There are a number of benefits to undertaking stakeholder mapping.

- It allows identification of key stakeholders (key players) who will need to be closely involved in the process. The requirements and expectations of these stakeholders will shape the project/procurement or process.

- It allows identification of the stakeholders that need a higher level of communication due to their level of power and interest.

- It allows us to start to think about how each stakeholder type should be managed and which should be prioritised. Each type of stakeholder needs to be managed in the right way. This is a key factor that contributes towards positive relationships, e.g., if a key stakeholder is not managed correctly it may later become an obstacle to progress.

- When positive relationships are created and actively managed, the outcomes of a project or procurement are likely to be better. This is because the stakeholder perspective will provide the buyer with useful information and insights.

Mendelow (1991)[6] developed a very helpful tool which can be used to map stakeholders and provide an insight into how these stakeholders should be managed. The model is a two-by-two model that results in four quadrants (see figure 2.2).

- The horizontal axis looks at the stakeholder's level of interest. How interested is the stakeholder in the requirement, the procurement process and the outcome? How likely is it to use its power to influence?

- The vertical access looks at the power a stakeholder has to influence. Is the stakeholder powerful?

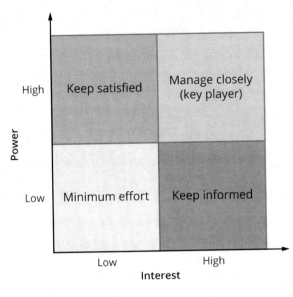

Figure 2.2 Stakeholder matrix based on Mendelow's theory

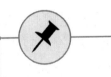

> *Remember*
> It is important to first identify who the stakeholders of a project/procurement are and then to map them based on their level of power/influence. The extent of their power and interest will affect how the buyer communicates with each stakeholder group.

The outcome of the model can be used to understand which stakeholders may be resistant to a particular strategy or project and which stakeholders will be supporters. It is important to identify and understand both of these groups. By understanding this it is possible to consider the practices and policies that could be used to gain support and engagement from stakeholders.

The procurement example below puts the model in figure 2.2 in context. In the example, a contract is currently in place for the purchasing of supermarket uniforms, but the business has decided to re-tender as it feels that the current price is too high.

Some stakeholders should be managed with **minimal effort**.

- These stakeholders are low in power and their level of interest is also low.

- Meeting their needs will take minimal effort. Resources and time will not be spent on this area.

- Lack of interest and power may make them more open to influence and they are more likely than others to accept the situation.

- An example of this stakeholder is a laundry service provider that currently cleans uniforms. It has a small interest due to its contract is to clean the uniforms, but they might be interested if the type of clothing were to change but would not be concerned with who the uniform supplier was.

There are some stakeholders to **keep informed**.

- These stakeholders are interested but they lack power. However, these stakeholders can increase in power when they join together.
- This group may try to gain power by joining with the stakeholders who are either key players or there to keep satisfied.
- They will need to be kept informed regularly of plans, outcomes and changes via a range of communication methods.
- An example of this type of stakeholder is the staff who will wear the uniforms, who will want a uniform that they are comfortable in. This group would also include the current supplier. They should be kept informed when procurement issues the tender and should be told about the outcome.

There are some stakeholders to **keep satisfied**.

- These stakeholders are high in power but have a low level of interest. If they become dissatisfied their level of interest may increase.
- Procurement needs to avoid them gaining too much interest and becoming key players; this can be achieved by keeping them satisfied.
- Examples of this type of stakeholder are the HR department and the managers of the affected staff.

Some stakeholders are **key players**.

- These stakeholders are high in power and their level of interest is also high. They can be seen as the opposite of the stakeholders who require minimal effort.
- These stakeholders will need to be involved early in the process and should participate in key decision-making in order to secure their support.
- They should be regularly updated with regard to progress, otherwise they could delay or stop progress altogether.
- An example of this stakeholder is the head of the marketing and branding department, as the look of the uniform needs to be consistent with the brand image of the supermarket.

Remember that stakeholder mapping should be done for each requirement or category of requirements. A stakeholder that is a key player for one procurement activity could be classed as a minimal effort stakeholder for another. If the procurement process that stakeholders were mapped for is extended over a long period of time, then the mapping should be updated regularly. This is because stakeholders, their relative interests and levels of power can change overtime, sometimes suddenly. Public sector organisations such as governments, due to the nature of their operation, purpose and goals, tend to have significantly more stakeholders than private sector companies. Therefore, the mapping and management of stakeholders are likely to be more complex.

However, there are some limitations to Mendelow's model.

- The model does not consider whether the stakeholder is a supporter of the project or against it.
- When mapping stakeholders their level of interest may be underestimated, which is a very subjective concept. This could result in under-engaged stakeholders slowing down progress or approval of the procurement project.
- The concept of power may be misunderstood.
- The mapping exercise may result in the selection of strategies that are biased to one type of stakeholder group.
- As with many of the models we have discussed, it only provides a snapshot in time.

Once the stakeholders have been mapped the team can develop a communication plan for each stakeholder group. The plan will outline the method of communication for each group as well as how frequently they will be communicated with. This is a key part of stakeholder relationship management. There are a number of benefits that can be achieved by developing positive relationships with stakeholders.

- Involving stakeholders makes them more likely to support a project/procurement. This is discussed more below.

- Support from stakeholders that have high levels of power and interest can mobilise resources and support for the project/procurement and can also reduce resistance.

- Stakeholders will often make important contributions via their expert input to a project, for example in terms of specification building. These contributions will be supported if there are positive relationships with stakeholders and they are involved from the start of the project.

- Fewer project delays caused by resistance lead to less waste.

> *Check*
> What are the four quadrants of the Mendelow model? Draw a quick sketch of the model.

Overcoming resistance

Having undertaken the process of identifying who the stakeholders might be and then mapping them in terms of power and interest, it is necessary to consider whether they support or resist the project/procurement. Overcoming resistance is also strongly linked to change management.

In order to assess this a similar model to the Mendelow model can be used (figure 2.3). The model has two axes. The vertical axis representing influence or power remains. The horizontal axis of the Mendelow model is replaced by the stakeholder's stance on the project: does it support the project or is it a resistor? The Mendelow model and this model should be considered together in order to get a fuller picture of the stakeholder environment.

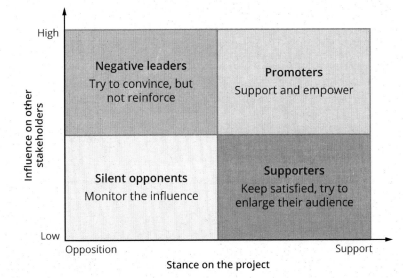

Figure 2.3 Overcoming resistance (Source: adapted from https://www.slideshare.net/ flemangin/csr-and-stakeholders-defintions-maps-configurations-and-strategies, based on Anderson, Bryson & Crosby (1999): Leadership for the Common Good, University of Minnesota, Saint Paul, MN)

In terms of procurement, it is necessary to ask ourselves how we get resistant stakeholder groups on board with the procurement department's objectives. Procurement would not be able to change the power or influence of a stakeholder, but it could change the stakeholder's stance on the project. How could it be moved from being a negative leader to a promoter, or from being a silent opponent to a supporter?

One of the most common examples of this debate is when an end user wants to continue using a supplier that a buying organisation has always used, but the buyer wants to undertake a competitive process to assess whether the supplier is really the best option for the buying organisation. Competition could reduce costs and improve quality, but the stakeholder wants to carry on using the current supplier. Resistance and the resulting conflict can cause delays and wastes resources. (Conflict is discussed in more detail below.) As indicated by the model, the biggest threat in terms of resistance comes from stakeholders that have a negative stance/view of the project and high influence.

The aim is to convert those on the left side of the model and move them to the right. This can be done by persuading them of the merits of the project, showing them the benefits and addressing the reasons they are resisting the project. In order to be successful at converting these stakeholders, a buyer should find out the type of information that would influence their decision and how they might wish to receive this information. Even if the buyer is unable to convert the resistors, by identifying them early it can anticipate their actions and put plans together to manage them.

As well as identifying the resistors it is equally beneficial to identify the promoters of a project, those with high levels of support and influence. For procurement projects that will result in significant organisational change, it is beneficial to identify a high-powered/senior project sponsor from those located in this area of the model (the promoters quadrant). These stakeholders can help to change the mindset of the resistors. They should be kept informed in order to retain their support. An example of a project that would result in such organisational change is an e-procurement system development and roll-out.

Remember
Projects and procurements may meet with resistance.
This resistance may be due to the fact that the objectives of the procurement process conflict with another department's objectives, or the resistance may be on a personal level. It is important to understand why stakeholders are resistant in order to be able to move them to a position where they accept the change and perhaps even support it.

Overcoming resistance relates to the soft skills of the buyer. Soft skills include emotional intelligence, empathy, influencing and relationship-building skills. Building relationships with key stakeholders in order to engage them is an important aspect of managing a successful procurement process. A key aspect to overcoming resistance is to put yourself in the place of the stakeholder. Why might they resist the process or project that you are trying to undertake? To overcome resistance, procurement needs to try and understand what the drivers for resistance are. There are a number of reasons why a stakeholder may resist a procurement project.

- Fear of change or uncertainty, e.g., a user group might fear the effect that using a new supplier could have on quality. This could be managed by involving stakeholders in the planning and supplier identification process and ensuring that they are kept informed.

- Loss of control, e.g., procurement stops user buying and moves all buying processes into the central procurement team. This could be managed by ensuring that the users are involved in the specification development and evaluation process.

An individual goes through various phases when resisting change. This is shown by the Kübler-Ross model. This model was originally developed in the 1960s to show the grief process that a person can pass through. However, it has now been widely applied to the process that a person goes through when they are experiencing change. People will pass through the curve at different speeds and not everyone will experience all stages.

It is common for the model to be split into three stages, as shown in table 2.3.

Stage	Common feelings/thoughts	Potential impact on procurement/project
1 Shock and denial	Happy with status quo Threatened Fear of failure	May avoid communication/ taking part in forward planning
2 Anger and depression	Suspicion Scepticism Frustration Isolation	Fixation on small issues which could delay progress
3 Acceptance and integration	New opportunities Relief that the change has passed Impatient regarding completion Acceptance Trust	Need to increase communications

Table 2.3 Kübler-Ross change curve

At stage 1 communication is key. It is very important to state what the change is, what the outcomes are and provide reassurance. During stage 2, a buyer should provide information on the change curve to show that emotions are typical and shared. At stage 3, people should be given tasks and responsibilities such as supporting specification development. Understanding what stage of the curve a person/group is at can help procurement to decide on appropriate communication methods, the support required and when to implement final changes.

> *Apply*
> Search on the Internet for the Kübler-Ross change curve model, read through the stages. Can you think of an example where you have gone through an experience of change? How could the stages outlined in the model have been applied?

Conflict
A disagreement, or difference of opinions or principles

Identifying conflict and coping processes

Conflict in the business environment is common; no two individuals or functions have the same needs and expectations. Due to the nature of procurement projects the procurement team will often have to resolve conflicts between stakeholders. Stakeholders may be in conflict with the project/procurement or each other. An example of this could be that the sales and marketing department may want to maximise the amount that a customer is able to customise the end product and be able to offer delivery on demand, while the finance function wants to reduce costs for the company. Conflict could also exist within the purchasing team between those who have different ideas about the best way to undertake a procurement activity.

A small amount of conflict can be beneficial, as it can serve to challenge the status quo and bring new ideas into the open. When it arises, conflict needs to be carefully managed. A significant amount of time and resources can be wasted on dealing with conflicting situations.

To begin with, a buyer will need to identity where conflict may occur. A useful model for doing this is Kurt Lewin's (1951)[7] force field analysis. This analysis aims to identify the driving forces for a project or procurement activity as well as the restraining forces. Change is a state of imbalance between the driving and restraining forces. At any time there are forces for change pushing towards a preferred state. There are also restraining forces for maintaining the current situation. The example above about procuring new uniforms for supermarket staff is used here to develop the model.

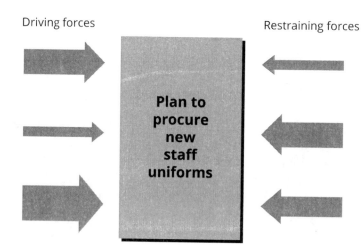

Figure 2.4 Force field analysis model

The model uses directional arrows to map the forces for and against change. The arrows are different sizes, as each competing or restraining force will have a different strength. The forces can also be given numerical values to demonstrate this. The left side of the model shows the driving forces for change, in this case for procuring new uniforms for the staff. In the example this could include the need to reduce the cost of staff uniforms, quality issues with the current supplier or a need to have uniforms that better represent the brand of the supermarket. On the right side are the restraining forces, the forces against procuring new uniforms. In the example this could include management from the marketing department not wanting to change the style of the uniforms due to concerns around brand identity.

> *Apply*
> Undertake a force field analysis exercise for a procurement project that you are currently working on.

By identifying the driving and restraining forces the procurement team will be able to identify where conflict may arise and the resources that may be required to reduce it. In this example, staff concern is a potential restraining force. This restraining force could be reduced by ensuring that staff are involved from the start of the project, for example, in writing the specifications for the new uniforms and in the supplier evaluation process.

The **Thomas-Kilmann model** (also known as the Thomas-Kilmann instrument) introduces different conflict management styles to cope with identified or emerging conflict (figure 2.5). This also links with the negotiation techniques that were discussed in section 1.1 in win-lose, lose-lose and win-win situations. The model looks at an individual's behaviour along the following two dimensions.

- **Concern for self (vertical axis).** This is the extent to which a person will try to satisfy their own needs first. This may also be referred to as assertiveness.

- **Concern for others (horizontal axis).** This is the extent to which a person tries to satisfy others' concerns. This may also be referred to as co-operativeness.

These two dimensions result in five different methods of responding to conflict. Different styles will be appropriate in different situations.

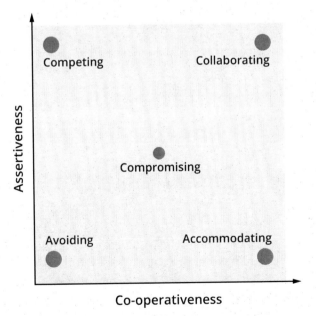

Figure 2.5 Thomas-Kilmann conflict model (Source: Copyright © 2009–2018 by Kilmann Diagnostics. All rights reserved. Original figure and text is available at: www.kilmanndiagnostics.com/overview-thomas-kilmann-conflict-mode-instrument-tki)

The five methods can be described as follows.

- **Avoiding** will be used when there is low concern for oneself and for others. This method does not deal with the conflict situation and therefore further conflict may arise at a later date. Examples of avoidance could include postponing an issue or withdrawing from a threatening situation. This may be appropriate for small issues; however, the underlying conflict does not get resolved.

- **Competing** will be used when there is high concern for oneself and low concern for others. A person's own interests are pursued at the expense of someone else's. Power is often used to secure the best outcome for the individual. This is linked to assertive forms of behaviour and is uncooperative. It can also leave the other party feeling defeated. If a procurement activity or project involves stakeholders that display competing behaviours these will have to be managed carefully to avoid the project being used to meet only their needs.

- **Accommodating** will be used where there is low concern for oneself but high concern for others. This is the opposite of competing behaviour, and there is an element of self-sacrifice. As discussed in chapter 1, there are some cases where maintaining the relationship with a stakeholder will be more important than the issue itself, i.e. this is used with very important internal stakeholders.

- **Collaborating** will be used where there is high concern both for oneself and for others. It is the opposite of avoiding. It is an example of 'expanding the pie', i.e. looking at options which will bring value for both parties or looking for a solution that is acceptable for everyone involved. Doing this requires a detailed understanding of the needs and wants of both parties and it can be time consuming to reach a conclusion that all parties are happy with, i.e. this could be used on very important contracts.

- **Compromising** occupies the middle of the model. It has elements of both assertiveness and co-operative behaviour. Generally, compromising will involve reaching a middle ground. This can result in an outcome that does not fully meet the objectives of either party and that does not offer the organisation the best value for money.

There is no single best style for coping with conflict; the method used will depend on the situation.

> *Remember*
> There are five methods that can be used to cope with conflict situations. These are avoiding, compromising, accommodating, competing and collaborating.

Cross-organisational teams
Teams that involve individuals from different departments that work together towards a common goal. A group of people working on a defined project that come from different functions/departments of the company. It can also include members that are from outside the company, such as suppliers

Cross-organisational teams

Cross-organisational teams are also commonly referred to as cross-functional teams. They are typically used in sourcing projects, new product development and commodity management (Leenders et al., 2001[8]). Cross-organisational teams can be a good way of developing positive stakeholder relationships with other functions of the business as well as with suppliers. Procurement staff are likely to be regularly involved in cross-organisational teams as the procurement department supports the whole business.

Creating cross-organisational teams brings together people with different skillsets, and this can serve to increase the outcomes from a project or a procurement activity. This leverages organisational resources and utilises expertise, which can result in outcomes that create more value. This approach is especially beneficial if the requirement is complex and likely to affect multiple internal departments, such as the procurement of a new IT system. Other examples of cross-organisational decisions include new product development, founding a new production facility and establishing a new business (Monczka et al., 2010[9]).Therefore, these types of teams will generally only work on strategic, high-value, high-risk projects and procurements.

These improved outcomes could include the points below.

- More comprehensive and accurate specifications resulting in reduced costs

- Innovation/creation of synergies by combining individuals and functions

- Improved risk management by viewing risk on a more holistic, organisation-wide basis

- Knowledge sharing/problem solving and development of team members

This process also links in with the five rights of procurement. If a cross-organisational team is developed, procurement will have access to more information on what the business considers to be the right quantity, quality, time, place and price. The work of Monczka et al. (2010)[10] also notes that cross-organisational supply management can reduce communication barriers between functions and organisations because members are in direct contact with each other. This also supports the development of positive relationships.

A good example of a cross-organisational team is one set up for the procurement of a new product or service that would affect many parts of an organisation, such as a new IT system. Such a team would need to include the following key points.

- End users of the system will use the new system in their daily work.

- The IT department must ensure the system will integrate with current systems.

- The procurement team should source and establish a contract with a supplier to deliver the system.

- The finance team needs to ensure that the project stays on budget.

- The legal team needs to be on hand to support any queries on data protection, cyber security, etc.

It is important for cross-organisational team members to have strong team-building abilities and excellent communication skills (van Weele, 2010[11]). Team formation and development is discussed further below. Working together as a team will build trust between stakeholders, which can result in better working relationships and improved procurement outcomes.

In a cross-organisational team the purpose of the team and roles and responsibilities must be clearly defined. This could be achieved by creating a team or project charter. All of the objectives for the procurement or project must be agreed in advance. Progress towards achieving the objectives should then be tracked and assessed to understand whether or not the procurement project has met its objectives, such as reduced costs or improved quality. This approach was supported by the work of Monczka et al. (2010).[12]

This type of working will also be required for some of the relationships that were identified as part of the relationship spectrum in section 1.1. This will be the case in particular for the more collaborative relationships such as strategic alliance, partnership, joint venture and co-destiny. These are all located on the right-hand side of the model and due to the nature of these relationships will require a high degree of co-ordination and contract between the companies involved. Van Weele (2010)[13] also noted that cross-organisational teams can include supplier members who offer value in terms of joint problem solving. This would apply to the more collaborative forms of relationship such as strategic alliances, partnerships, joint ventures and co-destiny situations. A typical example of a cross-organisational team that would include suppliers is a contract management team or a team set up to develop a joint product offering.

Cross-organisational teams

In Japan, buyer–supplier relationships are often built around the 'keiretsu' – a group of companies integrated around a manufacturer which is usually the focal company. The companies do not necessarily need to own or be part of each other. Typical of a Japanese horizontal *keiretsu* is Mitsubishi. The Bank of Tokyo-Mitsubishi sits at the top of the *keiretsu*. Mitsubishi Motors and Mitsubishi Trust and Banking are also part of the core group, followed by Meiji Mutual Life Insurance Company, which provides insurance to all members of the *keiretsu*. Mitsubishi Shoji is the trading company for the Mitsubishi *keiretsu*.

Case study

CIPS noted that the development of cross-organisational teams for the purpose of procurement projects was one of the development stages of procurement and supply management. It is about looking beyond achieving cost savings alone and looking at alternative ways of adding value and removing waste from the process. However, there are potential disadvantages of working in this way. There are high requirements and expectations of the people involved in the process. The costs of team interactions could be greater than the benefits realised (Monczka et al., 2010[14]). Teams can display 'groupthink', where the desire for group agreement and consensus reduces the problem-solving ability of the team.

Remember

Cross-organisational teams are generally used to manage large, strategic procurements or projects. The project will benefit from the synergies created by the group, which may even involve suppliers.

Cross-organisational teams are also likely to benefit from technologies for information sharing, such as intranets and video-conferencing. This is especially useful if the different functions are located geographically far away from each other and the teams set up are virtual.

Check

An organisation is planning on sourcing and implementing a new IT system. A cross-organisational team is being formed to manage the process. Who would you include in the team, and why?

Stages of team development – forming, storming, norming, performing

According to Tuckman's (1965)[15] team and group development model, there are four key stages to team development. The model itself (figure 2.6) was based on research that Tuckman carried out on team dynamics. Tuckman believed that these stages are inevitable in order for a team to grow to the point where it is functioning effectively and producing high-quality results (Abundi, 2010[16]). He believed the model applied to the development of all teams regardless of their members, purpose or culture. The total length of time that it takes a team to progress through all the stages will vary, as will the length of time spent at each stage. Team managers need to be able to recognise and understand the reasons behind group behaviour at each stage.

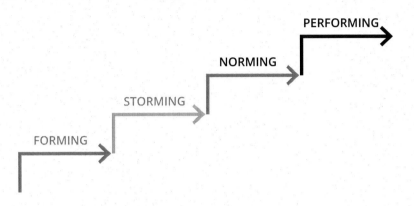

Figure 2.6 Tuckman's team and group development model

You will probably recognise some of the stages of this model (figure 2.6) from personal experience. The discussion below relates to the creation of a new procurement team for a food manufacturer. It assumes that the team is completely new, with none of its members having worked together before. They are also new to their individual roles within the team, and the team manager is also the procurement manager for the organisation. However, in reality a team is more likely to evolve gradually overtime as new members join and others leave.

Forming

The first stage is forming. This is the stage when the team first comes together. This may not happen all at once as it is unlikely that all team members will join on the same day. Therefore, the forming stage is a staggered process. The team will meet each other for the first time and will learn about each other. This stage is characterised by uncertainty. The members will learn each other's preferences for interaction, their skills and key competencies. At this stage it may be beneficial to undertake some team building activities. The focus here is on becoming familiar with each other and the new roles rather than undertaking the work itself.

Decisions will need to be made regarding how the team and the work will be organised. Each person will be learning about their role and how this fits into the wider business. Some may have experience of the food manufacturing industry, whereas for others it will be new. At this point it is important for the team manager to be clear about the objectives that the team needs to achieve and also to help the team establish how it will work together.

Storming

Storming is the second stage. During this stage there is a lot of change. Team members will compete with each other for status and acceptance of their ideas. As a result, team performance may decline at this stage of team development. There may also be conflict in the team as this is also the stage where the more dominant members of the group will emerge. (See 'Identifying conflict and coping processes' earlier in this section.)

The team manager will need to support the team through this period, as some teams can find it difficult to move beyond this point. Then the team starts working towards the goals and objectives that it has been set, for example to generate savings of 10% or reduce the supplier base. It learns how to solve problems together and starts working together as a proper team.

Norming

Norming is the third stage. It is at this point that team performance begins to improve, as members of the team start to work together more effectively. Working together as a team seems more natural and members may even value the differences between them. The team members have started to trust each other and will actively request each other's input, recognising each other's key strengths and working together towards a common goal.

At this point the team has agreed on the ways of working together, the processes and tools that will be used, how it will share information and resolve conflict. The team members are taking on more responsibility and the team manager is less involved and acts more as a coach and mentor.

Performing

At this fourth stage the team is performing and delivering benefits, meeting its objectives and goals by working together. The team is functioning at a high level and is motivated. Not all teams will reach this level; some will stop at the norming phase.

The team can now agree about change without conflict or the involvement of the team manager. The team is working effectively as a group and does not require the level of oversight that was needed at the other stages. However, it is possible even at this stage for a team to revert back to an earlier phase. For example, if a new member joins the team it may revert back to the forming stage. Therefore, throughout its life, as people join or leave a team it will move around the different stages of the model.

In 1977, Tuckman working with Jensen added a fifth stage: 'adjourning'. This stage refers to when the team is completing the current project and the members will move on to new projects and form new teams. This can result in feelings of sadness for the team members, and this stage therefore focuses more on the wellbeing of its members. There should be time for capturing the lessons learned and the knowledge from the project as well as for celebrating success. The process for team formation will then begin again as the members join new teams and project groups.

> *Remember*
> Tuckman's model of team development has five stages – forming, storming, norming, performing and adjourning. These team development stages will also apply to the development of cross-functional teams.

Teams that are not working together effectively will display a number of negative characteristics.

- Poor communication between members of the team and with other teams

- Lack of clarity on job roles and responsibilities

- Blaming other members of the team for failure
- Lack of focus on achieving objectives and goals
- Not meeting deadlines
- Producing low-quality work
- Team members competing with each other and often working alone
- Conflict
- Low levels of motivation
- Low levels of trust

Summary

In this section we have looked at how procurement works with the stakeholders. These stakeholders for example, could be an end user or a supplier. Procurement professionals build relationships with these stakeholders in order to enable them to run procurement processes that meet the needs of the stakeholders and the objectives of the wider company. This process is also likely to involve recognising conflict and stakeholder resistance. The buyer will need to manage these behaviours by taking appropriate action in order to add value to the process.

2.3 Compare the practical considerations of stakeholder management

There are a number of practical considerations with regard to stakeholder management. We have already discussed how to manage resistance and conflict. In this section we will look at different tasks such as cost modelling and early supplier involvement (ESI). These are tasks undertaken by procurement that require stakeholder input in order to add value to the process. These considerations will bring a number of benefits for a buying organisation. However, they will also require resources and the careful management of relationships with both internal stakeholders and connected stakeholders, such as suppliers.

Accurate cost modelling

Before discussing **cost modelling** it is important to differentiate between the terms 'cost' and 'price'. As defined by CIPS,[17] cost is 'the total sum involved, including all expenditure associated with ownership and use of a product or service, including price'. A supplier's costs will be made up of a number of elements including but not limited to raw materials, labour, overheads and profit margin. Whereas price should be a true reflection of the cost, in reality it is not the case. Price is just the amount paid to a supplier for a given product or service.

Cost modelling can be used to identify overpriced elements, and elements of the product or service that have a higher profit margin. Cost modelling is a key skill that buyers should develop in order to make their procurements more successful.

Cost modelling
A process that buyers use to understand all of the costs that make up a supplier's price. The model is used to understand how the cost is broken down across the production of a product or service

As its use spreads through the organisation, cost modelling will move from being a skill to a core capability that provides value for the business. Before beginning the process of cost modelling a procurement team will need to have segmented its spend (see section 1.2).

Cost modelling will generally be undertaken based on spend located in the strategic quadrant of the Kraljic model (figure 1.4) as it is these suppliers that would be targeted for developing a partnership relationship. It should be noted that not all procurement activities require cost modelling, especially those that can achieve value for money via competitive tendering and strong procurement processes.

In order to achieve accurate cost modelling the procurement team will require help from internal stakeholders, including the users of the product or service and the finance department. A cross-organisational team of internal stakeholders should be developed to take the cost modelling project forward. Cost models can also be developed in collaboration with a supplier as part of partnership-style supplier–buyer relationships. The quality of the model is improved by capturing the knowledge of a supplier. A model that has been developed collaboratively has a greater chance of being fully applied (Ask and Laseter, 1998[18]).

A number of benefits can be achieved by developing accurate cost modelling.

- It allows buyers to understand what makes up a supplier's costs, which ultimately result in the price it charges the buying organisation. This information allows the buying organisation to reduce the price it pays and therefore increase its profitability. This can be achieved by targeting the negotiations at areas of the price where a supplier has higher profit margins and more flexibility to reduce its price.

- Having undertaken cost modelling, the buyer understands the supplier's pricing strategy.

- Having a better understanding of the supplier's costs increases the power of the buyer to negotiate. As well as reducing price, it may be able to gain added value elements, for example free staff training.

- Accurate cost modelling can also be used as a baseline to calculate savings achieved, which contribute directly to a company's bottom line.

- Data from cost modelling provides a more accurate information base than is available where cost modelling has not been undertaken. This information can then be used to develop procurement strategies that will result in cost savings for the buying organisation.

Cost modelling – developing procurement strategies
Through cost modelling a buyer may come to understand that one of the main cost drivers for a product or service is the cost of labour. In this example we will imagine that the supplier has a low profit margin on the labour cost and is paying staff the minimum wage. (In the UK there is a legal requirement to pay a minimum wage.) Therefore, if the buyer is unable to negotiate on the majority of the supplier's cost base, the buying organisation may take the decision to look at low-cost country sourcing where the cost of labour will make the product cheaper, even taking into consideration the cost of transportation of the finished products. The buyer may develop a procurement strategy of low-cost country sourcing in areas such as China and India.

Case study

Ask and Laseter (1998)[19] note that there are five key principles to ensuring accurate and robust cost models.

- Capture cost drivers, not just elements of cost. As discussed, elements of cost include materials, labour, etc. Buyers also need to look at what drives these costs. In terms of labour cost, drivers could be productivity or the national minimum wage. This helps the buyer to model different scenarios, for example, increasing labour productivity or sourcing from an area with lower salary costs. This provides the buyer with more information so that it can better advise the business.

- Build commodity-specific models to look at cost drivers. Differences in products will cause different cost drivers to emerge among commodities.

- Consider the impact of the total cost of ownership. This gives far more detailed information than looking at the costs alone.

- Start with a simple model and only add complexity if it is required. Start with only the most important cost elements and drivers. This will vary dramatically depending on the nature of the products or services being modelled.

- Triangulate around data to improve accuracy. This can be achieved by using multiple data sources, for example, using the cost structures from multiple suppliers and industry data.

Cost modelling also links in with cost engineering. Once you have established a cost model you can review where there may be waste that can be removed.

2.3 LO2

Triangulation
A statistical concept based on understanding whether data is valid or not by reviewing information from multiple data sources. Data is considered to be valid if it is verified by two or more reliable sources of information

---

Check
What are the benefits for the business of cost modelling?

Reduced impact of price fluctuations

Price fluctuations can have a big impact on an organisation, particularly its profitability. Commodity products such as oil, grain and precious metals are most at risk from price increases.

Price fluctuations can occur for a number of reasons.

- A product becomes scarce and demand outstrips supply. For example, a supply chain capacity may be disrupted by a new buyer entering the market or by a buyer increasing the volume it purchases. In markets where China has increased its volumes of purchases this has caused demand issues.

- Increases in import duties or exchange rates increase product prices. At the time of writing, in 2018, the USA has imposed high import duties on the price of steel and aluminium produced in the EU and imported by the USA.

- Political instability. This could include changes in government, election periods in non-democratic countries, and military coups.

As mentioned, supply and demand changes are another reason why prices could fluctuate. Price elasticity was discussed briefly in section 1.3. When demand for a product or service is largely unaffected by an increase in price, the product or service is said to be **price inelastic**. This situation is likely in markets where there are few competitors and buyers do not challenge prices. In contrast, a product or service where a slight change in price brings about significant changes in demand is said to be price elastic. This tends to happen in markets where there are a large number of substitute products and buyers are easily able to switch, e.g., stationery or cleaning products.

If price increases are very high they may limit the ability of a business to make a profit and remain competitive in the marketplace. If this continues over the long-term it could result in a company going out of business.

Deloitte noted that the frequency and/or magnitude of extreme price changes has increased. It was suggested that the reason for this is the effect of globalisation, which tends to amplify the speed and magnitude of price shocks. However, by working with stakeholders, procurement can reduce the potential impact of price fluctuations.

> *Remember*
> Price fluctuations can have a big impact on a business. They should be monitored and managed in order to reduce risk for the business.

By understanding which of the products or services it purchases are the most vulnerable to price increases, a buyer can highlight potential risk areas. These areas can then be actively monitored and plans and processes can be put in place to mitigate any potential price increase. The longer and more complex a buyer's supply chain, the more risk there is of price fluctuations.

A buyer can reduce the impact of price fluctuations by working with key stakeholders. In order to do this successfully the buyer will need to build a collaborative working relationship with the supplier. This relationship should be based on 'expanding the pie' by creating win-win strategies. By working with a supplier, a buyer will have a better forward view of when price fluctuations might occur, and they can work together to minimise the impact of these for both parties. Where there is no buyer–supplier relationship the supplier may simply pass on the price increase to the buyer.

Working with a supplier could involve several techniques.

- Monitoring elements in the market across the whole value network of suppliers that could increase costs, e.g., each component part included in a finished product. This should involve accurate forecasting of how prices in the market linked to the elements that make up the supplier's product or service are likely to behave over both the short and the long-term. If the supplier is reviewing trends and is involved in a partnership relationship with a buyer, they are likely to make the buyer aware of this as soon as they know.

- Forward buying. The buyer will purchase a greater quantity than is currently needed in order to secure the goods at today's price, thereby avoiding price increases.

- Working with a supplier once potential increases in the supplier's prices are anticipated to help it mitigate increases from its supply chain.

- Working with a supplier on supply chain efficiency projects to remove waste and reduce costs elsewhere if increases are unavoidable.

- Preparing strategies to deal with increases, e.g., if it is evident that import duties are going to substantially increase, a buyer could begin to look at alternative national sources of supply within its own country, thereby avoiding the tariffs.

A buyer may also be able to gain valuable information from internal stakeholders on price fluctuations. If the buying organisation has an analytics and reporting team, this team may also track the commodity markets and interest rates. Other ways that a buyer could reduce the impact of price fluctuations include hedging.

Forward buying
This involves buying a quantity greater than the volume currently required in order to avoid future price increases

Hedging
A hedge is deal that a buyer can undertake to try to mitigate the effect of price increases. It involves buying similar quantities of the same product in two separate markets at the same time on the basis that a price increase in one market will be offset by a price decrease in the other market

Financial hedges can help to avoid significant unexpected price increases. The finance team would be able to support the buyer with this.

2.3 L02

Once a buyer has become aware of any likely price increases it will need to inform its internal stakeholders. The end users, for example, will need to know about any likely price increases, as they will need to plan for this in their budgets. Similarly, if price increases cannot be avoided the finance team will need to be involved in any changes to internal budgets.

There is also a need to consider how price fluctuations will affect the customers of the buying organisation – the buyer's external stakeholders. Are the goods or services that the customers are buying price elastic or price inelastic? If demand is price inelastic the buying organisation may be able to pass on price fluctuations to its own customers.

> *Apply*
> Consider the current procurements and contracts that you, or another company you are familiar with, are working on. Do you think that any of these may be subject to price fluctuations? Why might this be the case?

Early supplier involvement in product and/or service development

Early supplier involvement (ESI) is a process that involves a company's preferred supplier in the development of new products and services. This practice has strong roots in the Japanese car industry (Johnsen, 2009[20]). It remains common in the automotive industry and in consumer electronics (Leenders et al., 2001[21]). There is also evidence of this process being used in the construction sector.

The process involves the buyer and the supplier developing cross-organisational teams in order to develop and co-ordinate these new products and services. (See section 2.2 for more on cross-organisational teams.) These cross-organisational teams will involve internal, connected and external stakeholders. For example, an end user of the supplier's product would be an important internal stakeholder. The supplier would be the connected stakeholder and the buyer's end customer could also be included in these discussions as an external stakeholder.

The aim of the process is to create a superior end product or a service with a greater value than the buying organisation could have created alone. In order to obtain the most value from the process, suppliers should be involved at the specification development stage. This additional value should enable the organisation to either charge a higher unit price for the end product or service, sell additional volume, or both. In some cases the buyer may be totally dependent on a supplier's input to bring a product to market. Internal end users would still need to be closely involved in the specification development stage, working with the supplier on changes and improvements. This process of early supplier involvement can serve to add further value to the value chain.

Only a supplier that is considered to be strategic and is located on the right-hand side of the relationship spectrum model (see chapter 1) would be involved in such processes. Ideally these will be suppliers that have long-term relationships with the buyer, developed over a number of years. Johnsen (2009)[22] noted that relationship-specific factors, which are often underestimated, are in fact critical success factors in early supplier involvement practices.

A Z

Early supplier involvement (ESI)
A type of collaboration between a buyer and supplier in which the buying organisation involves the supplier in the product or service development process

In order to ensure the contribution to the process, the buyer needs to select a supplier that views the buyer as either a 'development' or 'core' customer. Van Weele (2010)[23] noted that the process of ESI leads to more long-term and collaborative relationships between suppliers and supply chain partners. So, the process itself will also have benefits for the buyer's SRM plans. Internal stakeholders such as end users will also be able to support the buyer to select a suitable supplier to be involved in ESI activities.

Handfield et al. (1999)[24] developed the model shown in figure 2.7. This illustrates ESI as a sliding scale, from no supplier involvement in new product development on the left to full involvement on the right. The arrow at the bottom demonstrates that as the supplier is more involved in the process its level of responsibility also increases.

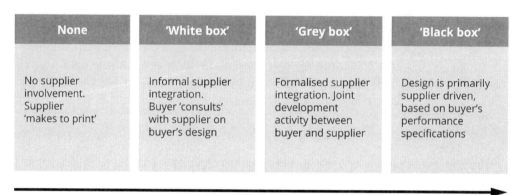

None	'White box'	'Grey box'	'Black box'
No supplier involvement. Supplier 'makes to print'	Informal supplier integration. Buyer 'consults' with supplier on buyer's design	Formalised supplier integration. Joint development activity between buyer and supplier	Design is primarily supplier driven, based on buyer's performance specifications

Increasing supplier responsibility

Figure 2.7 ESI model (Source: Reprinted from Petersen, K. J., Handfield, R.B. and Ragatz, G.L., 2005. Supplier integration into new product development: coordinating product, process and supply chain design. Journal of operations management, 23(3-4), pp.371-388, with permission from Elsevier)

Before ESI begins, to mitigate any risks the buyer should ensure that the relationship is covered by a contract in order to set out the ground rules. This should start with a non-disclosure agreement (NDA) between the buyer and supplier to protect any confidential and commercially sensitive information and stop it getting to any of the buyer's competitors. The contract with the supplier should detail several points.

- It should set out the key roles and responsibilities of both parties.

- It should specify how the supplier will be paid for any product design/ development work. Where the buyer and supplier are in a partnership relationship and joint product development has been undertaken this discussion may also include how any profits that arise from the sale of the product will be shared.

- It should clarify ownership of **intellectual property** rights (IPR).

Intellectual property
Products or services created as a result of an individual's ideas

> *Remember*
> Early supplier involvement is a form of supplier relationship management undertaken with strategic suppliers. The involvement of the supplier in processes such as new product development should result in increased value for the buyer.

However, supplier development does not always have to be about the joint creation of a new product or service. An ESI project could be about improving a supplier's current way of working, like supporting a supplier to adopt a buyer's ordering system. It could also involve looking at ways in which waste in the supply chain could be reduced or eliminated. There are a number of benefits for a buying organisation if it involves its suppliers in the ESI programmes.

- The supplier may be able to bring additional knowledge and innovation to the product design stage of the process, which could result in cost savings.

- The overall quality of the product can be improved.

- Performance can be improved (Mikkola and Skjøtt-Larsen, 2006)[25]. Suppliers can draw on their own supply chains and relationships. This may serve to support upstream risk management (Zsidisin and Smith, 2005[26]).

- Product development costs can be reduced (Bonaccorsi and Lipparini, 1994[27]; Leenders et al. 2001[28]; Mikkola and Skjøtt-Larsen, 2006[29]).

- Involving a supplier could increase the speed that a company is able to get a product to market (Mikkola and Skjøtt-Larsen, 2006[30]). This could enable it to capitalise on sales before other suppliers enter the market, thus offering a competitive advantage.

- ESI can serve to further enhance the supplier relationship as the supplier feels itself to be a valued business partner through being involved in such projects. This could encourage the supplier to come forward with further ideas for improvements.

However, there are also a number of disadvantages and risks.

- There are often issues with communication between the buyer and supplier as well as issues with managing the relationships (Mikkola and Skjøtt-Larsen, 2006[31]).

- If the relationship breaks down there could be issues producing the product or service in the future. Mikkola and Skjøtt-Larsen[32] noted that this was a particular issue if the buyer relied on a sole supplier for the development of a core product or service.

- It is necessary to carefully select the suppliers that are invited to participate in ESI projects. Time and resources could be wasted on supplier development if the wrong supplier is included.

Knowledge transfer and access to innovation

As discussed previously, businesses seek to secure competitive advantage in order to increase their profitability. To support the process of gaining competitive advantage, a buyer will need to gain additional knowledge of products, services and marketplace developments, as well as obtaining access to innovation. To achieve this, a buyer will typically target the key suppliers with which they have the most collaborative relationships. Without the safety of a collaborative relationship a supplier is likely to be unwilling to share such information with the buyer. However, a buyer can also gain a great deal of knowledge and innovation by engaging with its own internal stakeholders.

A buyer can encourage innovation and knowledge transfer from a supplier through the use of outcome-based/performance specifications (see chapter 1). Procurement should work closely with internal stakeholders/users to develop specifications that allow the marketplace to be innovative. This is important, as although procurement will often have a good level of market knowledge it will never know all of the possible supplier solutions that could be used to achieve an outcome.

Supply Management magazine (2018)[33] discussed how procurement should act as an enabler for innovation and not get too tied up in excessive processes.

It also noted the enabling aspects of the procurement department, including its in-depth market knowledge and its connection to the whole business via its network of internal stakeholders. There is a need for procurement to create an environment where a supplier is actively able to share its ideas and transfer knowledge. This could be done in specific forums or it could be more ad-hoc. *Supply Management* (2018)[34] also stated that although innovation discussions are often carried out with large, key suppliers, innovation often comes from smaller start-up suppliers.

As well as good buyer–supplier relationships, this process also requires effective two-way communication. Knowledge transfer is a two-way process, and the supplier can also gain valuable information from knowledge transfer from the buyer. Bönte and Wiethaus (2005)[35] noted that a buyer's technical knowledge may increase the efficiency of its supplier.

There are a number of benefits of knowledge transfer and innovation for the buyer.

- Cost savings, profitability and competitive advantage for being the first company to bring an innovative product or service to the marketplace

- The development of relationships with suppliers that may result in more transfer of knowledge and innovation beyond the original project

- Improvements to current products and services in the company's portfolio

- The opportunity for procurement to demonstrate the value that it can bring to the wider business

- The development of cultural changes internally that promote the development of innovation and knowledge sharing

However, there are also a number of risks.

- The management of intellectual property rights (IPR) is a risk, as information that provides the buyer with a competitive advantage could be leaked to competitors that the supplier works with. This risk is increased if new products or services have been created jointly with the supplier as a result of knowledge transfer.

- Bönte and Wiethaus (2005)[36] noted that knowledge disclosure bears the risk of benefiting one's own competitors due to opportunistic knowledge transmission through the common supplier.

Gaining access to knowledge and innovation involves taking risks. However, is there an inherent conflict between procurement and innovation due to the existence of processes and procedures? To support the process of knowledge transfer and access to innovation for the buying organisation, procurement needs to balance risk management with risk-taking (*Supply Management*, 2018[37]).

Procurement needs to be mindful of the length of time procurement processes can take. Natoff (2010)[38] believes there has to be a culture of 'controlled risk taking' and experimentation, and that procurement should create the conditions for this within its teams. *Supply Management* noted that for procurement to support this process, the department needs to become more innovative (*Supply Management*, 2018[39]).

Check
What are the benefits and drawbacks for the buyer of knowledge transfer with suppliers?

Case study

Knowledge transfer and innovation

In a strategy to support market share, Mastercard needed to improve its speed to market. There was a need to work closely with small companies developing innovative products. Mastercard needed to on board them quickly so that it did not lose their interest. To speed up the process a streamlined contract was developed with the legal team's support. In less than a year this process resulted in the on-boarding of 12 suppliers. The benefits of this include making the process more efficient so procurement staff can focus on more value-adding activity as well as faster access to innovative companies that may have worked with competitors.

(Source: Supply Management, 2018[40])

Dynamic purchasing system (DPS)
As its name suggests, this is dynamic. Therefore, a supplier can be on-boarded onto the system or removed at any point during its life. A supplier will be required to pass a pre-qualification questionnaire (PQQ) and, once approved, it can submit a tender for any requirements within the scope it has been short-listed for. A DPS can be for any length of time, unlike frameworks which have a maximum length of four years

For a buyer that works in the regulated public sector environment it can be difficult to see how knowledge transfer and innovation could be achieved while continuing to work within the regulations. However, this can also be undertaken in the public sector via the innovative partnership procurement procedure. Alternatively, a buyer could develop a **dynamic purchasing system** to enable it to have access to a new supplier as it enters the marketplace. Uyarra et al. (2014)[41] noted, however, that suppliers perceived that there were several barriers including the following.

- Lack of interaction with procuring organisations
- Over-specified tenders, as opposed to the use of outcome-based specifications
- Low competencies of procurers
- Poor management of risk during the procurement process

It is very important to share information with internal stakeholders. Transferring knowledge internally also helps the buyer to support its internal customer better, as it gains a better understanding of the requirement. This process of sharing can be undertaken via cross-organisational team development.

Remember
There are both benefits and drawbacks to knowledge transfer with suppliers. Buyers will be required to take a risk-based approach when undertaking this process.

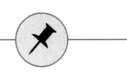

Common metrics to drive change for both organisations

Metrics is another term used to describe key performance indicators (KPIs). In order to derive additional value from key relationships buyers and suppliers need to turn their attention towards improving their performance jointly. This is a move away from traditional metrics, which focus solely on the performance of the supplier or solely on the buyer's internal performance. Developing common metrics is especially important as companies become more interconnected, forming supply chains and networks. Cai et al. (2008)[42] noted that it was important for buyers to measure the performance within the company as well as between the companies that are interacting with each other in the supply chain.

The scope of performance measurement can be widened, moving from being internally focused to also including suppliers. This mutual approach will allow both the buyer and the supplier to better allocate resources to the relationships and act appropriately. The approach would need the involvement and commitment of senior sponsors in both the supplier and buyer businesses in order to be successful.

Due to the investment of time and resources required, this type of approach would only be used with a key and strategic supplier. In order for this approach to be successful both parties would need to have a joint goal that they want to achieve together, such as increasing profitability or reducing waste in the supply chain. If a supplier and buyer have a mutual understanding of each other's long-term goals this will help to reduce uncertainty and the probability of working in opposite directions, therefore reducing the potential for wasted resources.

As well as looking at common metrics relating to traditional KPIs such as cost and delivery, a buyer and supplier can also measure the performance of their relationships with the aim of creating positive changes. O'Toole and Donaldson (2002)[43] noted that relationships have positive links to performance if viewed from a mutual perspective. A relationship-based KPI is different from traditional KPIs. Relationship-based KPIs are qualitative measures whereas traditional KPIs tend to be quantitative measures. These KPIs are not direct measures of outcome, but they all affect the outcome in one way or another (Damlin, 2012[44]).

Damlin et al. list six qualitative KPIs that can be used as common metrics to measure the buyer and supplier relationship.

1. **Trust.** As dependency in relationships between a buyer and a supplier increases, trust becomes more important. Stuart, Verville and Taskin (2012)[45] stated that a supplier that does not have mutual trust between the members of its supply chain will find it hard to compete with a supplier that does have trust between its members.

2. **Power.** This arises due to dependencies. If the supplier is dependent on the buyer, this creates buyer power; if the buyer is dependent on the supplier, this creates supplier power.

3. **Transparency and information sharing.** This relates to the information exchanged between the buyer and supplier. Hsu et al. (2008)[46] noted that this information sharing can either be at a tactical or a strategic level. High levels of transparency will involve the buying organisation and the supplier's organisation sharing information on their future vision, corporate plan and objectives. This can help the parties to work more effectively together to drive value.

4. **Communication.** This is the glue that holds the supply chain together and reduces the risk of conflict and issues developing (Mohr and Nevin, 1990[47]). Communication also links with transparency and information sharing.

5. **Commitment.** This is the willingness of the parties to the contract to put effort into the relationship (Mohr and Spekman, 1994[48]). Several academics note that this is key to buyer–supplier relationships and therefore it is important to measure.

6. **Co-operation.** Crotts et al. (2001)[49] define co-operation as either similar or complementary actions that are taken by both parties within an interdependent buyer–supplier relationship in order to reach mutual objectives. Co-operation is needed across supply chains for them to be successful.

Qualitative measures
Measurements of non-numerical data that tends to be based on thoughts and feelings, for example, how satisfied the end customer is with the product manufactured by the supplier and buyer

Quantitative measures
Measurements of numerical data, for example, the percentage of deliveries from the supplier that arrive on time and in full

Trust
A belief that one party is acting in the best interests of another party

> *Remember*
> When developing KPIs for a strategic supplier, a buyer should look beyond the traditional types of KPI. KPIs relating to the relationship between the buyer and supplier should also be developed and measured in order to add further value.

These relationship-based KPIs are difficult to measure compared to more traditional, numerical KPIs. However, Damlin et al. (2013)[50] suggest they should be measured on a scale from one to five, with one being the lowest value and five the greatest. For example, a buyer and supplier who consider trust between them to be high may score a five for trust, but may consider communication to need improvement and therefore give it a score of two.

A cyclical process should be used to manage these common buyer–supplier metrics (see figure 2.8). The first stage in the process is the define stage. This should be done in collaboration with the supplier. Both companies can gain something from working on this together, such as developing trust and working relationships, etc. The required KPIs can be identified and defined, and they can be ranked in order of importance.

The next stage is to measure each of the KPIs. Both the buyer and the supplier should give their measure separately to start with in order to get an independent view. They may both have very different ideas – a buyer may believe trust to be high whereas a supplier could perceive trust to be low. Ideally this should be done cross-organisationally by each party to give a more holistic view. It might be that the buyer wishes to involve production, stores, procurement and finance. Rarely will all departments of the buying organisation have the same view of a supplier and of the relationship between buyer and supplier.

The results should then be analysed to give an overview of the relationship from both parties. Following this the buyer and supplier need to define what should be done to improve the relationship in the future in order to drive value for both businesses. This process to decide where improvements need to be made should be co-operative. The final stage is to control and sustain the results. Has the ideal state been reached or does the cycle need to be undertaken again?

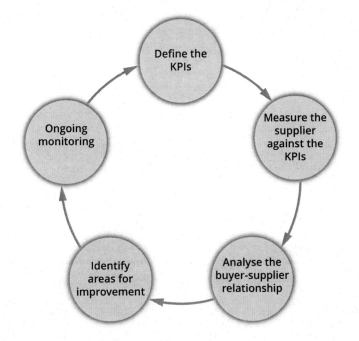

Figure 2.8 Managing metrics

Damlin et al. (2012)[51] noted a large number of benefits of looking at common relationship measures and metrics.

- Enabling the buyer and supplier (including the supply chain if present) to be more competitive in the marketplace

- Lower transaction costs, such as trust leading to the development of vendor-managed inventory and the need for less extensive contracts

- Reduction of opportunistic behaviours from both parties, which should improve information flows

- Improved customer relationships and reputation

- Improved profitability

- Improvements in quality

- Reduced conflict

Improving risk management and continuity of supply

Risk management (see chapter 1) is a key concern for procurement, as risk to the business is present throughout the procurement process. Risk around continuity of supply can be particularly high. Continuity of supply refers to the buying organisation having access to the correct levels of materials and products from its supplier so that it can undertake its own production. A lack of supply could result in costly downtime, late deliveries to customers and a detrimental effect on the buying organisation's reputation in the marketplace.

The Kraljic model was considered in chapter 1. Continuity of supply is most crucial for those products and services that are located in the bottleneck quadrant of the model (figure 1.4). In 2000 one of the main Philips factories caught fire. This stopped supply to Ericsson for its mobile phones. This resulted in an estimated loss for Ericsson of $400 million and eventually led to the company leaving the mobile phone market (Rice and Caniato, 2003[52]). Although this is an extreme example, it highlights how important continuity of supply is. To improve risk management and ensure continuity of supply, procurement teams need to undertake **business continuity planning (BCP)**. BCP should be undertaken as a cross-organisational exercise involving various internal stakeholders and the supplier.

Risk management and continuity of supply have become more important over recent decades as the amount of products and services procured from external suppliers increases. Supply chains are increasingly susceptible to unplanned, unanticipated disruption. This is due to the fact that integration techniques such as just in time and Lean supply have made supply chains more fragile (Zsidisin et al., 2005[53]).

With increasing globalisation, the world is now a more connected place and what happens in one country can have an impact thousands of miles away. Events that have affected global supply chains include the terrorist attacks of 11 September 2001 and the Japanese tsunami of 2011. These are often referred to in contracts as **force majeure** events – events where the supplier is unable to provide the products or services.

Gilbert and Gips (2000)[54] saw a business continuity system as consisting of four key stages.

Business continuity planning (BCP)
A process that a company uses to develop a plan to enable it to recover from a disruption in the shortest possible time

Force majeure (French for 'superior force')
An exclusion clause excluding the party from liability due to 'acts of God'

2.3 LO2

- **Risk identification**. This can be achieved via a risk mapping exercise (see below). This should also include supplier performance and market, and the wider external environment. Sharing information with suppliers and internally with stakeholders will support this process.

- **Risk assessment**. Review risks in terms of the likelihood of occurrence and the impact on the business if risks did occur. Refer back to section 1.2, which provides a detailed explanation of how to do this.

- **Risk ranking**. Use the risk assessment scores to rank and prioritise the risks. High risks should be given top priority.

- **Risk management**. This will involve either risk taking, accepting the risk and attempting to mitigate against it, or risk transferring. Risk transferring involves passing the risk onto someone else, usually either the supplier or the customer. This can be done via the clauses included in contracts.

In order to fully understand risks around supply continuity the first step for procurement is to map the supply chain. This forms part of the risk assessment stage as detailed above.

Kildow (2011)[55] notes that the following are key areas to review.

- Ascertain which suppliers are critical suppliers this will also include any critical subcontractors if the supply chain has more than one tier. Are any of these suppliers classified as high risk? For example, are any located in an area at high risk of natural disasters? Do any of them have a poor history of financial performance?

- Are there any single points of failure, like sole- or single-source agreements? This may be a key concern for buyers that have rationalised their supply bases in recent years. Stamatis (2012)[56] argues that **supply base rationalisation** has increased supply chain risk considerably since buyers are dependent on fewer suppliers.

- Are there any internal dependencies to keep the supply chain functioning, such as IT systems?

Supply base rationalisation
When a buyer reduces the number of suppliers it has for a product or service. This is normally done as part of an exercise to cut costs. Buying from just one supplier will allow the buyer to leverage its spend and should result in reduced prices

> *Remember*
> Business continuity planning should include risk identification, risk assessment, risk ranking and risk management.

Procurement should include key suppliers and internal stakeholders when devising its business continuity plans. This was supported by CIPS, especially with regard to involving offshore suppliers. CIPS noted the importance of looking beyond first-tier suppliers and further into the web of supply when building and maintaining business continuity plans. Research from Hallikas et al. (2005)[57] suggested that as mutual dependency increased between buyers and suppliers, so should collaborative risk management and joint learning.

A buyer can work with both its suppliers and internal stakeholders to improve risk management and continuity of supply in a variety of different ways.

- Include key internal stakeholders in supplier qualification and evaluation, for example, by involving finance in reviews of a supplier's accounts. This could include Dun & Bradstreet credit checks and reviews of the supplier's profit and loss accounts, as well as getting health and safety information reviewed by a health and safety professional. If any concerns arise, these should be documented in risk assessments and approved at the relevant levels of authority.

- Risk could be reduced for core products and services by using a dual-sourcing or multiple-sourcing approach. If one supplier is unable to supply the products or services the other supplier(s) can flex up to deliver the additional volume. In order for this to be successful, volume will have to be carefully managed to keep the second (or third) supplier interested and willing to provide support during difficult periods.

- A buyer could create a relationship with its key suppliers in which they are able to provide early warning of potential issues rather than hiding them until it is too late to resolve them. In order to do this the buyer–supplier relationship will need to be characterised by trust and open two-way communications.

- Stock could be held by either the supplier or a third party to minimise the impact of force majeure events. However, there will be a cost to the buyer for holding additional stock. This cost must be weighed up against the cost if a stockout event were to occur.

- Buyers could enter into **escrow agreements**. An escrow involves a third party holding documents or information for two other parties. Although continuity of supply is generally associated with the supply of raw materials or products it can also relate to services such as software. In the case of a software escrow agreement the supplier deposits the source code with a third party. This ensures that the buyer has access to software maintenance even if the software developer goes out of business.

Formal contract management processes can also be used to improve risk management. If contract management is undertaken on a regular basis the process may unearth issues before they affect supply continuity. These issues can then be managed or the risk mitigated.

There are many advantages of risk mitigation and securing continuity.

- At its very basic levels it ensures the survival of the business.

- It minimises financial losses from production stops and loss of customers to competitors.

- It minimises loss of good reputation in the marketplace. Reputation can take years to build up but can be destroyed very quickly.

- It supports the process of supplier relationship management.

- It encourages an environment of monitoring and planning, which displays good business practice.

Equally there are some limitations.

- Some risks may remain unknown until they have happened.

- Risk management can be costly and resource consuming, and many potential risks may never materialise. For example, cost and resource are required to find and qualify a second source of supply.

2.4 Identify the process for terminating stakeholder relationships

Up until now we have discussed stakeholder relationships in terms of how they are managed and the benefits and drawbacks they can bring for the buying organisation. The process of terminating these stakeholder relationships will now be covered. The stakeholder relationship that will most commonly be terminated is the relationship with suppliers.

Like personal relationships, there will come a point when the buying organisation and the supplier end their relationship. There are numerous reasons why this may happen which are discussed further below. The process of termination should be planned and managed to minimise disruption and exposure to risk for the business. It is possible that either the buyer or the supplier may seek to terminate the relationship. To date, a lot more research has been undertaken on the development of supplier relationships than on the termination of these relationships.

Reasons for termination

There are various reasons why a buyer–supplier relationship may come to an end (see section 1.1). To recap, here are the most common reasons for termination.

- The contract comes to a natural end and there is no longer a requirement to purchase that product or service. Once both the parties have performed their part of the contract it will terminate by performance.

- The contract has reached the end date specified in the terms and conditions. If the contract is not formally extended it will come to a natural end.

- The contract is re-tendered and another supplier can provide a more competitive offer. As such the contract with the current supplier ends and a contract with a new supplier begins. This practice is common where a buyer regularly undertakes competitive tender processes, for example, in public sector organisations.

- The buyer may be undertaking a process of supply base rationalisation (see section 2.3). Therefore, "although relationship endings are usually equated with failure it can also be a planned strategy by which a company changes its relationship portfolio as it responds to changing market circumstances" (Alajoutsijärvi et al., 2000[58]; Havila and Wilkinson, 2002[59] and Vaaland, 2004[60]). A smaller supplier base will allow the buyer to leverage its volume and will also bring relationship management efficiencies.

- The supplier suddenly increases prices with no justifiable reason, e.g., the supplier may have underpriced the tender and may now be trying to recoup some of its losses or may consider the buyer to be an exploitable customer (see section 1.2, supplier preferencing model).

- The contract with the supplier is terminated due to a material breach, such as poor performance. If a supplier is consistently under-performing then a buyer may wish to end the agreement. Default clauses will state what defaults will trigger either party's right to terminate the contract. This can result in conflict situations and legal proceedings involving arbitration, mediation or a court. In some cases this might have been amplified by a lack of performance and contract management.

- The supplier is involved in activities that could damage the reputation of the buyer by association. An example of this would include a supplier breaching human rights via the use of child labour or unsafe working environments. This could be covered under default clauses.

- The supplier becomes insolvent. This can also be classed as a material breach of contract. This would enable the buyer to formally end the relationship and seek an alternative supplier. This may come as a surprise if the buyer has

Contract frustration
As a result of an unforeseen incident beyond either party's control, the obligations of the contract become impossible to perform. UK law states that when contract frustration occurs the contract can be terminated. This can be avoided by adding a force majeure clause naming the possible events. Those events are now classed as foreseen

not carried out adequate due diligence on the supplier before entering into a contract. If the supplier is critical and the buyer and supplier have a close relationship, the buyer may take steps to support the supplier.

- The supplier merges with or is acquired by another company. Depending on how the buyer views this company (which could be a competitor) the buyer may wish to terminate the contract. Most contracts will allow for termination if there is a change of ownership.

- The supplier may terminate the relationship because it no longer wishes to deal with the buyer as a customer, for example, if the business is not profitable. This would be a situation where the supplier views the buyer as a nuisance (see the supplier preferencing model in section 1.2). The supplier may prefer to target more attractive and profitable customers in order to grow its business.

- In rare circumstances a contract can terminate due to contract frustration. There is case law to support this type of termination (MacMillan 2008[61]).

> *Remember*
> There are multiple reasons why buyer–supplier relationships terminate. Termination may be triggered by either the buyer or the supplier. Common reasons include the contract coming to a natural end, the contract no longer offering value for money for the buyer, or one of the parties committing a material breach of contract.

There are a number of reasons why the supplier may choose to terminate the contract; however, termination by the buyer is generally more common. Supplier preferencing was discussed in section 1.2. There are instances where a supplier may view a buyer as a nuisance, perhaps if the buyer is expensive to service and there is little profit in the relationship. In these situations, the supplier may seek to terminate the relationship. In this case it may be possible for the buyer to salvage the relationship, if this is desirable, by negotiating with the supplier regarding how they can become a more attractive customer. For example, they could offer the supplier increased volumes of business.

The process of termination

A buyer and supplier will rarely enter into a contract planning for it to come to an end unexpectedly. Before deciding to terminate a contract early, the buyer will need to carefully review all threats to the business that could result from doing so. There are likely to be both financial and operational risks of terminating contracts. An example of these risks could be the buyer not being able to deliver to its own customers and as a result not being paid on time.

This process of managing contract termination should involve all key stakeholders in order to give the buyer a fuller, more accurate picture. There may be key operational considerations that the buyer is not aware of. Key stakeholders that should be involved include the operations, sales, legal and finance teams. The operations and sales teams will be aware of the volume of supplies needed over the coming weeks. The legal team will be able to advise on any potential negative effects of termination such as early termination fees, and the finance team will be able to review how this might affect the buyer's financial situation. Figure 2.9 is a high-level overview of the steps to terminate a contract from the buyer's perspective.

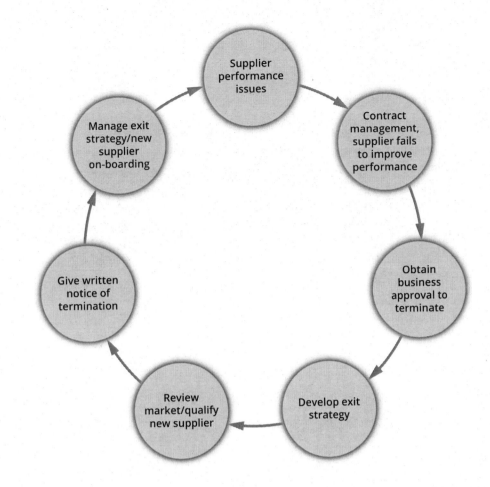

Figure 2.9 Supplier termination process

Identifying performance issues and contract management

The first step on the model (figure 2.9) is identifying performance issues with a supplier. The second is the use of contract management. In terms of poor performance, termination will generally be a last resort for the buying organisation. If contract management has been undertaken, poor performance should be highlighted to suppliers at performance reviews. Following the meeting the supplier should be given clear actions that need to be undertaken within a given timeframe. This gives the supplier an opportunity to rectify the situation, and the buyer to continue with the relationship. If the supplier is not aware that the buyer is unhappy with its performance the situation will not improve. However, if performance and contract management has been undertaken and the supplier still fails to improve, the buyer will have little choice but to start the process of contract termination.

Obtain business approval to terminate

If the supplier has instigated termination and the buyer wants to continue the relationship, the period prior to official termination may involve a negotiation period. As mentioned above, if the supplier is strategic to the buyer it may try to make itself a more attractive customer. This could be done by increasing the volume of business with the supplier or reducing the payment terms. If the negotiation stage fails, the relationship will continue to termination. If the buyer is terminating the relationship, depending on the value of the contract, the type of relationship and whether or not the supplier is considered strategic, the buyer may have to develop a business case in order for senior management to approve the termination. The requirement for this process will vary between organisations.

Develop exit strategy

The buyer will need to ensure that there is a detailed exit plan so that there is minimum disruption for the business' day-to-day operations. Managing the exit of a supplier is as much a project as on-boarding a supplier. As with any project that an organisation would undertake, resources must be allocated to it in order for it to succeed. There should be external and internal support, key milestones and objectives that should be developed and payment profiles agreed. The exit plan needs to take into account TUPE (transfer of undertakings protection of employment) provisions if the contract has a TUPE liability (see below). It should also consider the onboarding of the new supplier.

There are also other practical considerations for the buyer.

- What will happen to any stock currently on supplier premises?
- What will happen to any assets or equipment that belong to the supplier or have joint ownership?
- What about any outstanding work the supplier is required to complete?
- What about outstanding payments to the supplier?

Review market and qualify new supplier

Before formally exiting the relationship with the incumbent supplier the buyer must locate and qualify a new source of supply. This will ensure that operations continue and there will be continuity of supply. This process will be easier if there are several alternative suppliers in the marketplace. (See section 1.1 for a discussion on identification, selection and assessment of suppliers.)

Give written notice of termination

Most contracts will detail that termination must be made in writing, although other methods such as fax may be acceptable. Termination clauses normally have a given notice period, which is generally 90 days but could be as little as 30 days. The length of the notice period will also affect the process of termination. The shorter the notice period the less time the buyer will have to mobilise a new supplier. In the absence of a formal written contract English law states that a 'reasonable' period of notice should be given. What is classed as reasonable will depend on the circumstances of the relationship. If the buyer fails to give full notice in the proper format the supplier could claim that the buyer has breached the contract terms.

Communicating the termination is an important step of the process. The method used for this will again depend on the existing buyer–supplier relationship. However, the method should be considered carefully and managed to try to ensure that the termination period will be as amicable as possible.

Manage exit and new supplier on-boarding

As noted above, the exiting of a supplier also requires the buyer to manage the on-boarding of a new supplier. A contract will have to be developed and signed, and realistically there is likely to be a cross-over period involving both the exiting supplier and the new supplier. The buyer will need to build relationships

with this new supplier in order to support the delivery of the contract going forward. This process may also involve a TUPE transfer of staff (see below).

The process of termination itself will vary depending on the nature of the contract. The buyer will need to review where on the Kraljic model the product or service is located, e.g., there will be more risk for the buyer if it is terminating a strategic contract (high value/high risk) or if it terminates a bottleneck contract (high risk/low value). Risk will be lower if it terminates a contract with a supplier it considers to be routine (low value/low risk) or leverage (high value/low risk).

Although the process of termination itself will be detailed in the contract, how the relationship is terminated will vary depending on the reason for terminating the contract and whether it was the buyer or the supplier that terminated the relationship. In the case of the buyer terminating the relationship, it is vital that the buyer has documented the supplier's shortcomings in terms of delivery and contract breaches. If the supplier terminates the relationship, the buyer will have less control over the situation.

The process of termination will be more complex if the contract is poorly constructed and vague. In these cases it will not be clear what each party's responsibilities are. If the contract was terminated due to performance issues, then this is also a good time for the buyer to review the contract as part of its continuous improvement processes. This review should include what worked well and what caused issues, such as whether the KPIs need to be improved. This information from lessons learned can then be used to ensure that the next contract is more successful.

> *Remember*
> Exiting a supplier relationship should be a well-managed process to ensure that continuity of supply or service is maintained, a new supplier is successfully on-boarded and conflict is kept to a minimum.

Relationship impacts – amicable *v.* hostile

The impact on the relationship and whether it is an amicable or hostile termination will depend on the reasons for termination. The potential reasons for terminating buyer–supplier relationships were discussed above. If the relationship has ended because the service has been carried out or products required have been delivered or because the contract has expired, the relationship is more likely to remain amicable. This is due to the potential for doing business together in the future. If on the other hand the contract was terminated because either party committed a material breach of contract there is far more likely to be a negative impact on the relationship.

There is a link here with power relationships between the buyer and supplier. If the relationship was terminated before the contract came to a natural end, the party that terminated the contract will have the power in the relationship. Hostility is likely to be increased if the buyer is a core customer to the supplier, and through termination the supplier is likely to lose a significant portion of its turnover.

Whether the relationship will be amicable or hostile during termination also depends on what the relationship has been like throughout the contract term.

Mediation
This involves a neutral third party which encourages the buyer and supplier not just to think about their legal rights under the contract but also their commercial interests. Mediation attempts to get both parties to reach a compromise

Arbitration
The settling of a dispute between buyer and supplier by an impartial third party. This party may be named in the contract. The buyer and supplier agree to accept the third party's decision

Evergreen contracts
These are contracts with no end date. Like an evergreen tree that never loses its leaves, an evergreen contract is never-ending

Auto-renewal clauses
Clauses in a contract which state that if the buyer does not give sufficient notice, for example 90 days' written notice, then the contract will auto-renew for another period. These clauses are common in software licences

Consider the relationship spectrum that was discussed in section 1.1. If the buyer and supplier have always had an adversarial or arm's-length relationship, this is likely to continue throughout the termination process.

It is always better to end the buyer–supplier relationship amicably as the buyer may need to work with the supplier in the future. This is more important in markets where the potential pool of suppliers is small. Former suppliers may also be viewed as a less risky alternative to new, untested suppliers (Hadjikhani, 1996[62]). The buyer will also have to continue to work with the supplier organisation during the termination period, and this process will be smoother if the relationship is still amicable. The length of this period will vary depending on the contract clauses.

Emotions can be intense during contract termination especially if the buyer and the supplier have had a long relationship or either party feels that it has been wronged in some way. It might be that the buyer failed to pay the supplier or the supplier was providing a poor service to the buyer. Ensuring that evidence for material breaches is used as justification is essential. Contract terminations should not be undertaken based on feelings. If the process is well-managed the buyer is likely to be able to avoid a hostile situation.

If the result of termination is the development of a hostile buyer–supplier relationship it is likely that the buyer will have to manage conflict (see section 2.2). Conflict and hostility may result in the parties having to enter into mediation, arbitration or in the worst case having the case settled by a judge in court. Both mediation and arbitration are forms of alternative dispute resolution (ADR). They involve trying to resolve issues via negotiation rather than through litigation. Some professional bodies have their own mediators and arbitrators that organisations can use. This is common in the construction industry. Both processes can be time consuming for the buyer and the supplier, but they are likely to be significantly less costly than litigation.

Where contract termination results in hostile behaviour from the supplier it is likely that the transition of services will be more difficult. The supplier may withhold valuable service information or the quality of service may decline further. In these cases, it may be necessary to change the approach and focus on relationship building to ensure the supplier agrees to perform its contractual obligations.

Legal considerations – finances, confidentiality, IPR, security, employee rights

To ensure that the organisation has options to end the relationship a buyer must be certain that a contract has adequate termination provisions. For this reason most organisations will avoid entering into evergreen contracts or contracts with auto-renewal clauses. It is also an advantage to the buyer if they can include a 'termination for convenience' clause. This means that the buyer can terminate for any reason, at any time during the contract. However, the buyer would still be bound to undertake its obligations under the contract, such as giving the supplier a full notice period and paying for all of the work completed up until the end of the notice period.

Many key terms in a contract, such as those surrounding confidentiality and IPR, will survive the termination of an agreement. This means that even when the contract has ended, the buyer's confidential data and IPR will still be protected.

A well put together contract should also have detailed provisions covering the responsibilities of both the buyer and the supplier on termination, in relation to finance, confidentiality, IPR, security and employee rights, amongst others.

Finances

Before initiating the process of termination, the buyer needs to ensure that early termination will not result in any financial penalties. This should be clearly detailed in the terms and conditions. There are more likely to be financial penalties for early termination if the contract is governed by the terms and conditions of the supplier.

If the supplier has committed a material breach of the contract the buyer may be entitled to some financial remedies, perhaps if the supplier has performed poorly. In the case of an IT support contract, if a supplier has not resolved a critical system failure within the required period of time the buyer may be entitled to receive service credits from the supplier.

There will generally be a cost associated with terminating a supplier contract, for instance, the cost associated with the transition period if two suppliers are operating in parallel, or the cost associated with a new supplier delivering at a slower pace while it mobilises. There may also be reputational costs if the buyer has supply issues following termination and cannot meet the requirements of its own customers.

The effect that termination has on finances will also depend on how closely the buyer and supplier were linked and how much financial information they shared with each other. If the supplier was operating on an open book basis then on termination the buyer will be required to destroy any information relating to this in line with confidentiality provisions. Lastly, the buyer will also have to consider final payments made to the supplier.

Service credits
A contract mechanism for performance management. If a supplier fails to meet the standard set in the service credits the buyer has the right to deduct set amounts of money from the payments owed to the supplier

> *Remember*
> There can be financial penalties if contracts with suppliers are terminated early. Buyers should ensure that they have all the required information on termination so that they are able to make an informed decision.

Confidentiality

After a contract has been terminated a buyer will want to ensure that the confidential information it shared with the supplier will continue to be protected. This information could include details of a buyer's production process or technical product. If any of this information was released into the marketplace it could seriously affect a buyer's competitive advantage and therefore its future profitability. This is particularly the case in technological and creative industries.

All contracts should contain confidentiality provisions. These will often include indemnity arrangements, so that if a party breaches these terms there will be financial penalties. Confidentiality provisions usually survive a contract termination for a fixed period of time.

If during the course of the business relationship the parties have entered into a non-disclosure agreement (NDA) this can offer both buyers and suppliers additional protections. If an NDA is issued by the buyer to the supplier, it will protect the buyer's data. Or the NDA can be two-way, in which case both the buyer's and the supplier's confidential data is protected.

Non-disclosure agreement (NDA)
A non-disclosure agreement means that if a party to the agreement discloses confidential information there will be a penalty for doing so. The penalty is usually financial

The exit plan should clearly detail how any confidential data belonging to the buyer should be transferred back to them once the contract ends. The parties also need to agree on an acceptable method for the supplier to destroy all remaining proprietary information belonging to the buyer that is not transferred. This also links to the area of IPR (see below).

> *Check*
> If there is conflict following a contract termination, what methods of alternative dispute resolution could a buyer use to resolve the conflict?

IPR

IPR stands for intellectual property rights. IPR and its use following termination should be clearly detailed in the contract terms and conditions. CIPS noted that there are four main types of IPR that are likely to be encountered in procurement and supply contracts.

- **Patents**. They protect inventive, functional design ideas.

- **Copyrights**. These protect original works of expression.

- **Trade secrets**. Valuable information on technology that is regarded as confidential and/or providing competitive advantage.

- **Trademarks**. These are marks and symbols that distinguish the products and services of a provider from those of other companies.

What happens to IPR once a contract has been terminated depends on who owns the IPR – the buyer or the supplier. This will be more complex if the buyer and the supplier have developed joint IPR during the contract period. If the contract states that the IPR is to be jointly owned it should also detail what rights each of the parties has to exploit the jointly owned deliverables. For example, it might state whether the parties can exploit these deliverables independently or whether they can only do so with unanimous agreement.

It may be the case that a buyer and supplier have separate IPR agreements in addition to their standard contract. These IPR agreements may grant the user a licence to use the IPR. For example, a supplier may own all newly created IPR and may license it back to the buyer as part of the agreement. Even though the contract between them has terminated the buyer may still need to contract with the supplier in order to obtain a licence for the IPR.

Security

In this context security relates to the security of data after a contract has been terminated. If there are no data security clauses in a contract the buyer will have no way of requiring the supplier to return the data or dispose of it in a manner that does not affect the security of the buying organisation. Contracts may specify a period when this must be done by the supplier.

It is good practice for a buyer to have a contract with each of its suppliers, but this does not always happen. In the UK in 2018 the new General Data Protection Regulation (GDPR) replaced the Data Protection Act 1998. This change in the law makes it mandatory for a buyer (data controller) to have a formal contract in place with all suppliers that process personal data on their behalf (processor). This must require the processor to delete or return all personal data once the contract has ended.

Employee rights

The main area of importance around employee rights in the UK is TUPE 2006 legislation. TUPE stands for Transfer of Undertakings (Protection of Employment). This piece of legislation was later amended by the Collective Redundancies and Transfer of Undertakings (Protection of Employment) (Amendment) Regulations 2014. TUPE was defined and discussed in section 1.1.

TUPE is a complex piece of legislation that aims to protect the rights of employees when the organisation they work for transfers them to a new employer. These rules apply equally to both the public sector and the private sector. One of the main elements of TUPE is deciding when it applies. ACAS (the Advisory, Conciliation and Arbitration Service) states that TUPE applies in the following situations when the identity of the employer changes.

- **Outsourcing**. A supplier takes over activities from a buying organisation.

- **Re-tendering**. A new supplier takes over activities from another supplier. The service that is being transferred must be fundamentally the same for TUPE to apply. This is very common in the public sector due to the requirement to apply competition to all contracts over the threshold values once the contract term has ended.

- **Insourcing**. A buying organisation takes over activities from a supplier and brings them back in-house.

If TUPE does apply to an employee when they transfer to the new company, they will do so with all of their terms and conditions of employment intact. This means that the new employer must give them as a minimum the same rate of pay, the same employee benefits and the same amount of annual leave, for example.

> *Remember*
> Before undertaking any procurement, a buyer will need to review whether or not TUPE applies. If TUPE does apply this could affect the costs of the tendering supplier and the length of the mobilisation period for the new supplier.

During the TUPE process both the outgoing employer and the incoming employer have a duty to inform and consult with the employees regarding the process of the transfer. This might include providing information on any changes to the staff structure or whether there will be any redundancies. For example, the company that the employees are transferring to may already have someone in the equivalent role or they may believe that they can deliver the service with fewer staff members. Dealing with these issues can be the most challenging part of TUPE.

In public sector procurements there is a requirement to provide the TUPE data on the potential transition to employees up-front as part of the procurement documents. Depending on the complexity of the contract and the TUPE process there may be a need for independent legal support.

Case study

TUPE

A buyer undertakes a competitive tender process for the supply of catering services in its on-site canteen. No changes are made to the way the service is provided. The current supplier (Catering for You) employs four full-time staff, working five days a week. Following the tender process, a new supplier (Lunchtime Ltd) is awarded the contract. It was able to offer the service at a cheaper price.

As the nature of the services has not changed, the four full-time staff who were employed by Catering for You will be TUPE transferred and will undertake the same work for Lunchtime Ltd. After transfer, their pay, working hours, and terms and conditions will remain the same.

Apply
Review the recent procurements that your organisation or an organisation you are familiar with has undertaken. Did any of these involve a TUPE transfer?

Succession issues – continuity of supply

Continuity of supply was discussed in section 2.3. Continuity of supply issues will be more applicable to contracts that are terminated prematurely due to the deviation from the original contract end date. As mentioned above, buyers should ensure that the business will be able to secure continuity of supply from another supplier before terminating agreements with the current supplier. This will involve identifying an alternative supplier, qualifying it and undertaking all of the necessary due diligence as well as negotiating terms and conditions. This can be a time consuming process, and the buyer needs to ensure that it has enough time to undertake all of these activities.

Following this the buyer along with other internal stakeholders such as the operations team will need to manage the transition period between the current and new supplier. This will be more complex and time consuming if there is a TUPE transfer of staff involved.

As discussed above, an exit strategy should be agreed with all key stakeholders before the start of the contract. This should support the continuity of supply during the termination period. The exit strategy should detail some particular points in terms of continuity of supply.

- An obligation for the current supplier to continue delivering the services at the same level of quality for the transition period. This will ensure business as usual for the buying organisation and its stakeholders.

- An obligation for the supplier to continue to abide by all the terms and conditions of the contract. For example, it will continue to deliver on time and meet all other required key performance indicators.

- A requirement for the supplier to provide access for the buyer to all the necessary information that will be required to keep delivering the service after the transition period. This information could include data, procedures or error logs. Without this the buyer may be unable to deliver the service.

- A requirement for a parallel service for a given period of time while the new supplier gets the service up and running. The buyer should include a right to extend this period if there could be many transition issues. There will be a period of learning and bedding in for the new supplier. This will be similar to the forming stage of Tuckman's model (see figure 2.6). There will be a cost to the buyer for this as it will have to pay two suppliers. This cost should be built into the budgets.

- A requirement for the supplier to keep the same team performing the services during the transition period. This will ensure levels of quality remain, as well as a smooth transition period. It will also avoid the supplier transferring its best staff to other projects before the contract has formally ended.

Buyers can include a specific business continuity clause in contracts with suppliers that are providing products and services which are critical to business continuity. This clarifies the buyer's expectations around the supplier's roles and responsibilities during this period.

Chapter Summary

This chapter has looked at the different types of stakeholder that a buyer might encounter and how to successfully work with these stakeholders. To begin with, it looked at the different processes and procedures involved in buying products and services. Following this, how to successfully manage teams of stakeholders was considered. This is a key skill for all buyers. This involved looking at some key models including the Mendelow model, Tuckman's model of team formation and the Thomas-Kilmann model for managing conflict. The more practical considerations of stakeholder management were also discussed. Finally, there was a discussion of the reasons why supplier relationships might come to an end and how this process can best be managed to avoid disruption to the business.

End of Chapter Assessment

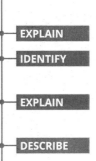

1. Explain what is used to describe value for money. **EXPLAIN**

2. Identify how many conflict management styles there are in the Thomas-Kilmann model and explain links with negotiation techniques. **IDENTIFY**

3. Risk identification is a key stage of business continuity planning. Explain how this can be achieved. **EXPLAIN**

4. Describe a valid reason for terminating a contract. **DESCRIBE**

References

1 Dimitri, N. (2013), "'Best value for money' in procurement", *Journal of Public Procurement*, Volume 13, Issue 2, pp. 149–175

2 Ibid.

3 Zartman, I. W. (2007), *Negotiation and Conflict Management: Essays on Theory and Practice*. Abingdon: Routledge

4 Dobler, D. W. and Burt, D. N. (1996), *Purchasing and Supply Management: Text and Cases*. New York: McGraw-Hill

5 Hillman, A. J. and Keim, G. D. (2001), "Shareholder value, stakeholder management, and social issues: what's the bottom line?", *Strategic Management Journal*, Volume 22, Issue 2, pp. 125–139

6 Mendelow, A. L. (1991), *Mendelow's Power-interest Grid*. Ohio: Kent State

7 Lewin, K. (1951), *Field Theory in Social Science*. New York: Harper and Row

8 Leenders, M. R., Fearon, H. E., Flynn, A. and Johnson, P. F. (2001), *Purchasing and Supply Management*. New York: McGraw-Hill College

9 Monczka, R. M., Handfield, R. B., Giunipero, L. C., Patterson, J. L. and Waters, D. (2010), *Purchasing and Supply Chain Management*. Andover: Cengage Learning EMEA

10 Ibid.

11 Van Weele, A. J. (2010), *Purchasing & Supply Chain Management: Analysis, Strategy, Planning and Practice*. Andover: Cengage Learning EMEA

12 Monczka, R. M., Handfield, R. B., Giunipero, L. C., Patterson, J. L. and Waters, D. (2010), *Purchasing and Supply Chain Management*. Andover: Cengage Learning EMEA

13 Van Weele, A. J. (2010), *Purchasing & Supply Chain Management: Analysis, Strategy, Planning and Practice*. Andover: Cengage Learning EMEA

14 Monczka, R. M., Handfield, R. B., Giunipero, L. C., Patterson, J. L. and Waters, D. (2010), *Purchasing and Supply Chain Management*. Andover: Cengage Learning EMEA

15 Tuckman, B. W. (1965), "Developmental sequence in small groups", *Psychological bulletin*, Volume 63, Issue 6, p. 384

16 Abundi, G. (2010), *The five stages of project team development* [online]. Retrieved from: www.pmhut.com/the-five-stages-of-project-team-development

17 CIPS, Glossary ('cost' definition) – www.CIPS.org

18 Ask, J. A. and Laseter, T. M. (1998), "Cost modeling: A foundation purchasing skill", *Strategy and Business*, Issue 10, pp. 10–20

19 Ibid.

20 Johnsen, T. E. (2009), "Supplier involvement in new product development and innovation: Taking stock and looking to the future", *Journal of Purchasing and Supply Management*, Volume 15, Issue 3, pp. 187–197

21 Leenders, M. R., Fearon, H. E., Flynn, A. and Johnson, P. F. (2001), *Purchasing and Supply Management*. New York: McGraw-Hill College

22 Johnsen, T. E. (2009), "Supplier involvement in new product development and innovation: Taking stock and looking to the future", *Journal of Purchasing and Supply Management*, Volume 15, Issue 3, pp. 187–197

23 Van Weele, A. J. (2010), *Purchasing & Supply Chain Management: Analysis, Strategy, Planning and Practice*. Andover: Cengage Learning EMEA

24 Handfield, R. B., Ragatz, G. L., Petersen, K. J. and Monczka, R. M. (1999), "Involving suppliers in new product development", *California Management Review*, Volume 42, Issue 1, pp. 59–82

25 Mikkola, J. H. and Skjøtt-Larsen, T. (2006), "Platform management: Implication for new product development and supply chain management", *European Business Review*, Volume 18, Issue 3, pp. 214–230

26 Zsidisin, G. A. and Smith, M. E. (2005), "Managing supply risk with early supplier involvement: a case study and research propositions", *Journal of Supply Chain Management*, Volume 41, Issue 4, pp. 44–57

27 Bonaccorsi, A. and Lipparini, A. (1994), "Strategic partnerships in new product development: an Italian case study", *Journal of Product Innovation Management: An International Publication of the Product Development & Management Association*, Volume 11, Issue 2, pp. 134–145

28 Leenders, M. R., Fearon, H. E., Flynn, A. and Johnson, P. F. (2001), *Purchasing and Supply Management*. New York: McGraw-Hill College

29 Mikkola, J. H. and Skjøtt-Larsen, T. (2006), "Platform management: Implication for new product development and supply chain management", *European Business Review*, Volume 18, Issue 3, pp. 214–230

30 Ibid.

31 Ibid.

32 Ibid.

33 Jacobs, K. (2018), *How procurement can enable innovation* [online]. Retrieved from: www.cips.org/en-gb/supply-management/analysis/2018/february/How-procurement-can-enable-innovation/

34 Ibid.

35 Bönte, W. and Wiethaus, L. (2005), "Knowledge transfer in buyer – supplier relationships – When it (not) occurs", *RWI Discussion Paper*, Volume 34

36 Ibid.

37 Jacobs, K. (2018), *How procurement can enable innovation* [online]. Retrieved from: www.cips.org/en-gb/supply-management/analysis/2018/february/How-procurement-can-enable-innovation/

38 Ibid.

39 Ibid.

40 Ibid.

41 Uyarra, E., Edler, J., Garcia-Estevez, J., Georghiou, L. and Yeow, J. (2014), "Barriers to innovation through public procurement: A supplier perspective", *Technovation*, Volume 34, Issue 10, pp. 631–645

42 Cai, X. Q., Chen, J., Xiao, Y. B. and Xu, X. L. (2008), "Product selection, machine time allocation, and scheduling decisions for manufacturing perishable products subject to a deadline", *Computers & Operations Research*, Volume 35, Issue 5, pp. 1671–1683

43 O'Toole, T. and Donaldson, B. (2002), "Relationship performance dimensions of buyer–supplier exchanges", *European Journal of Purchasing & Supply Management*, Volume 8, Issue 4, pp. 197–207

44 Damlin, A., Dietersdóttir, K., Fornander, D., Brykt, J. M., Polyantseva, E. and Sundquist, D. (2012), *Measuring Buyer – Supplier Relationship Performance*. Gothenburg: Chalmers

45 Ian Stuart, F., Verville, J. and Taskin, N. (2012), "Trust in buyer – supplier relationships: Supplier competency, interpersonal relationships and performance outcomes", *Journal of Enterprise Information Management*, Volume 25, Issue 4, pp. 392–412

46 Hsu, C. C., Kannan, V. R., Tan, K. C. and Keong Leong, G. (2008), "Information sharing, buyer – supplier relationships, and firm performance: a multi-region analysis", *International Journal of Physical Distribution & Logistics Management*, Volume 38, Issue 4, pp. 296–310

47 Mohr, J. and Nevin, J. R. (1990), "Communication strategies in marketing channels: A theoretical perspective", *The Journal of Marketing*, pp. 36–51

48 Mohr, J. and Spekman, R. (1994), "Characteristics of partnership success: partnership attributes, communication behavior, and conflict resolution techniques", *Strategic Management Journal*, Volume 15, Issue 2, pp. 135–152

49 Crotts, J. C., Coppage, C. M. A. and Andibo, A. (2001), "Trust – commitment model of buyer – supplier relationships", *Journal of Hospitality & Tourism Research*, Volume 25, Issue 2, pp. 195–208

50 Damlin, A., Dietersdóttir, K., Fornander, D., Brykt, J. M., Polyantseva, E. and Sundquist, D. (2012), *Measuring Buyer – Supplier Relationship Performance*. Gothenburg: Chalmers

51 Ibid.

52 Rice, J. B. and Caniato, F. (2003), "Building a secure and resilient supply network", *Supply Chain Management Review*, Volume 7, Issue 5, pp. 22–30

53 Zsidisin, G. A., Melnyk, S. A. and Ragatz, G. L. (2005), "An institutional theory perspective of business continuity planning for purchasing and supply management", *International Journal of Production Research*, Volume 43, Issue 16, pp. 3401–3420

54 Gilbert, G. A. and Gips, M. A. (2000), "Supply-side contingency planning", *Security Management*, Volume 44, Issue 3, p. 70

55 Kildow, B. A. (2011), *A Supply Chain Management Guide to Business Continuity*. New York: Amacom

56 Stamatis, D. (2011), *10 Essentials for High Performance Quality in the 21st Century*. Boca Raton: CRC Press

57 Hallikas, J., Puumalainen, K., Vesterinen, T. and Virolainen, V. M. (2005), "Risk-based classification of supplier relationships", *Journal of Purchasing and Supply Management*, Volume 11, Issue 2–3, pp. 72–82

58 Alajoutsijärvi, K., Möller, K. and Tähtinen, J. (2000), "Beautiful exit: how to leave your business partner", *European Journal of Marketing*, Volume 34, Issue 11/12, pp. 1270–1290

59 Havila, V. and Wilkinson, I. F. (2002), "The principle of the conservation of business relationship energy: or many kinds of new beginnings", *Industrial Marketing Management*, Volume 31, Issue 3, pp. 191–203

60 Vaaland, T. I. (2004), "Improving project collaboration: start with the conflicts", *International Journal of Project Management*, Volume 22, Issue 6, pp. 447–454

61 MacMillan, C. (2008), Taylor v Caldwell (1863), in: Mitchell, C. and Mitchell, P. (eds.) *Landmark Cases in the Law of Contract*, Oxford: Hart Publishing, pp. 167–203

62 Hadjikhani, A. (1996), "Project marketing and the management of discontinuity", *International Business Review*, Volume 5, Issue 3, pp. 319–336

Recommended reading

ACAS, Transfer of undertakings (TUPE). [online] Retrieved from: www.acas.org.uk/index.aspx?articleid=1655 [Accessed on 25 February 2019]

Mendelow, A. L., (1991). *Mendelow's Power-interest grid. Ohio: Kent State*.

Monczka, R. M., Handfield, R. B., Giunipero, L. C, Patterson, J. L., and Waters, D. (2010). *Purchasing and Supply Chain Management*, Hampshire, C engage learning EMEA

Leenders, M. R., Fearon, H. E., Flynn, A. and Johnson, P. F., 2001. *Purchasing and supply management*. McGraw-Hill College

CHAPTER 3
Understanding the concept of partnering

Learning outcome

By the end of this chapter, you will understand the concept of partnering.

Chapter overview

3.1 Analyse the concept of partnering and where it is a suitable approach

You will understand:
- The three types of partnering
- Partnering *v.* 'traditional' contracting agreement
- The drivers for partnership sourcing
- Advantages for purchaser and supplier
- High spend
- High risk
- Technically complicated supplies
- New services
- Fast-changing technology
- Restricted markets

3.2 Appraise the process of partnership implementation

You will understand:
- How to identify items potentially suitable for partnership sourcing
- 'Sell' the philosophy to senior management and other functions of the organisation
- Define the standards that potential partners will be expected to meet
- Establish joint commitment to the partnership
- Reviews and audits

3.3 Identify the reasons why partnerships fail

You will understand:
- Poor communication
- Lack of senior management support and trust
- Lack of commitment by one or both parties
- Poor planning
- Lack of value-added benefit
- Changes in the market
- Corporate cultural differences
- Logistics and distance barriers

Partnership relationship
A commitment between a buying organisation and a supplier entering into a long-term, collaborative relationship based on trust and mutually agreed objectives and goals for the benefit of both parties

Introduction

In this final chapter the development of partnership relationships between a buyer and supplier will be explored. Partnership relationships were discussed briefly in chapter 1 when the relationship spectrum was studied. Partnerships are a highly collaborative form of relationship, located on the right-hand side of the spectrum. Refer back to section 1.1 if you need to refresh your memory on this topic.

As discussed previously, a buyer will have a wide range of different types of relationships with its suppliers depending on the nature of the product or service being procured. Also how they are viewed by the supplier and the structure of the external marketplace. Developing partnership relationships takes more time and resources than developing transactional relationships. Therefore, a buyer will have fewer partnership relationships than other transactional relationship types, such as arm's-length relationships.

Before entering into a partnership both partners will undertake a period of due diligence to ensure that the partnership relationship is a good choice for both companies. This will be undertaken at the most senior levels of both the buyer and supplier companies.

Due diligence will involve reviews of the other partner's financial situation and performance and whether there is synergy between the companies' visions, missions and objectives. It is also likely to include a review of the softer aspects of the business including culture and management style to see whether or not these are likely to be compatible. If this is not undertaken fully, the buyer could partner with the wrong supplier, which could result in the failure of the partnership and wasted resources and effort. The reasons for partnership failure are discussed in more detail in section 3.3.

3.1 Analyse the concept of partnering and where it is a suitable approach

The procurement and supply department will have many different types of commercial relationships within their suppy chains. Some will be collaborative and some will be adversarial. A small number of these relationships will be buyer–supplier partnerships. It is important to remember that partnership relationships will not be suitable for all supply situations. This will be looked at in more detail later in the section.

It is necessary to point out here that a public sector buyer working under the EU procurement regulations is unable to enter into formal partnership relationships with any supplier. This is due to the regulatory environment, which requires a buyer to competitively tender requirements that are over the EU threshold values. This happens every four years in the case of framework contracts, for example. However, a public sector buyer is able to develop collaborative relationships over the fixed lifetime of the contract.

The three types of partnering

There are three types of partnership relationship that a buyer and a supplier could choose to enter into as outlined in the model developed by Lambert et al., (1996).[1]

This model is detailed in table 3.1, along with a description of each of the three types of partnership and a practical example.

When deciding to enter into a partnership a buyer and supplier must carefully consider which type of partnership would best suit their situation.

The decision about which type of partnership to undertake will be based on the strength and number of partnership drivers and facilitators that both parties have. The more drivers and facilitators that are in existence, the more likely they are to have a more integrated type 3 partnership. Partnership drivers are discussed in more detail later in this section.

It is important to recognise that although it is possible to migrate from a type 1 partnership to a type 2 partnership this is not usually the case. With partnership a higher number of partnership drivers and facilitators is not necessarily better, it is more important that we have the correct level of partnership. For example, a type 3 partnership is resourced at much higher levels which may include relationships at CEO levels between the parties and the sharing of corporate strategies.

Type	Partnership description	Practical example
1	The organisations recognise each other as partners and co-ordinate activities and planning on a limited basis. The partnership has a short-term focus and involves only one function within each organisation. Partnerships of this type are less time intensive to develop.	The buyer and supplier set up a partnership to improve an aspect of their relationship, such as delivery over the next year. Procurement is involved from the buyer side and operations from the supplier side.
2	Both companies progress beyond co-ordination of activities to integration. The partnership has a long-term focus and a number of functions within both companies are involved.	The buyer and supplier have decided to invest in the same ordering and delivery system to improve integration. The scope of the partnership now spans several years. From the buyer side procurement, operations and stores are involved. From the supplier side sales and operations are involved. A cross-organisational team has been developed to manage progress.
3	The companies share a significant level of operational integration. The buyer and supplier view each other as an extension of each other's firm. No end date is set for the partnership.	The buyer and supplier now have additional integrated systems and have developed just in time (JIT) delivery and stock holding. The supplier is viewed and treated as a key partner and is involved in product development.

Table 3.1 The three types of partnership (Source: adapted from Lambert et al., 1996[2])

> ❝ *Of the relationships which are partnerships the largest percentage will be type one with only a limited amount of type two. Type three partnerships should be reserved for those suppliers or customers who are critical to an organisation's long-term success.* ❞

(Source: Lambert et al., 1996[3])

Apply
Think about the partnership relationships that your company or a company you are familiar with has with its suppliers. Do you consider these to be true partnerships?

Lambert et al. (1996)[4] noted that an organisation will enter into a limited number of type 3 partnership relationships. This is due to the large amount of resources and time involved in developing these type 3 partnership relationships.

Very often, senior members of a company consider a relationship they have with a supplier to be a partnership. Lambert's research demonstrated that many of these relationships were not partnerships but were instead long-term contracts with price and volume guarantees for the supplier. Just because both parties are achieving the desired outcomes and benefits from a relationship does not mean that the buyer and supplier have a partnership relationship. Lambert et al. stated that it is important to remember that a partnership relationship is not necessary in order to achieve business success for both the buyer and supplier. A buyer and supplier can jointly develop new products/services, reduce costs and waste, and increase performance without developing a partnership-style relationship.

Remember
There are three types of partnership relationship: type 1, type 2 and type 3 (Lambert et al., 1996[5]). These are based on how closely integrated the companies are, the number of functions involved in the relationship and the planned length of the relationship. Type 3 has the highest degree of integration between the buyer and supplier, and as a result will require more resources and time to maintain the relationship.

Partnering versus 'traditional' contracting agreements

'Traditional' relationships are those located on the left-hand side of the relationship spectrum. They include adversarial and arm's-length relationships. They are traditional in the sense that the buyer is simply contracting with the supplier to receive a product or service rather than adding value, for example by improving processes or reducing waste. There are a number of characteristics that differentiate between having a partnership relationship with a supplier and having a traditional contracting relationship.

- Early supplier involvement (ESI)

- No tender process or win-lose negotiations

- Shared costs and benefits
- Greater levels of information sharing and transparency
- Joint performance measurement and KPIs
- No defined end period
- Less contractual

ESI versus buyer-developed specifications

In a traditional contract situation, a buyer will develop a specification for the required products and services by working with internal user departments. The supplier will not be involved in this process. This specification will then be used as part of the competitive tender process. However, with partnership sourcing the supplier will be involved at a much earlier point, usually at the specification development stage. Some products or services are likely to be jointly developed by the buyer and supplier. This is an example of early supplier involvement (ESI) which was discussed in section 2.3.

No tender process or adversarial negotiations

Generally, before a traditional contract is entered into with the supplier, it will have been involved in a competitive tender process which involves supplier selection, evaluation and negotiation. The supplier's offering is compared against those of other suppliers in the marketplace. This process was discussed in detail in section 2.1. However, with partnership sourcing the supplier is generally not 'selected'; instead, the relationship evolves overtime as the partner becomes more involved in the buyer's business.

In terms of fulfilling the ongoing requirements of the buyer, where a partnership relationship exists, the buyer will not go to competitive tender for each different scope of work. CIPS notes that buyers will exclude other suppliers and suppliers will exclude other buyers, with the two partners focusing on each other and their objectives rather than on the supply market. However, the buyer will need to continually benchmark the prices from the partnership supplier to ensure that it is still getting value for money.

Following a formal tender process, negotiation is often undertaken with suppliers, which may result in a win-lose situation. However, in the case of partnerships these discussions will be based on a win-win situation. This is due to the fact that for both partners, maintaining the relationship will be more important than the short-term benefit they could gain from adversarial, win-lose styles of negotiation.

Shared costs and benefits

Partnership will involve the sharing of both the costs and the benefits of the products and services that are being produced as part of the buyer–supplier partnership. Sharing of costs could help with joint investment in research and development or the supplier absorbing the costs of development.

Sharing the benefits could include both partners seeing an increase in profits or a reduction in waste due to the synergies gained from working together. Shared benefits could also include both the buyer and supplier reducing their stock holding costs by sharing information on production. Sharing benefits encourages a supplier to develop innovative ideas. In contrast, under a traditional contract, especially one where a supplier is being squeezed on its profit margin, any cost-saving ideas will be kept for the benefit of the supplier's profitability.

Greater information sharing and transparency

Partnership sourcing will also involve sharing information with the partner organisation beyond the realms of what would be shared under a traditional contract. This would include information that gives the buying organisation a competitive advantage in the marketplace, such as market intelligence. This is especially the case when compared to a 'traditional' adversarial buyer–supplier relationship located on the left-hand side of the supplier relationship spectrum.

Information sharing may involve the process of open book costing (see section 1.4). These elements are likely to be the key to the buyer and supplier's competitive advantage in the marketplace. However, in traditional sourcing relationships the supplier and the buyer will be wary about sharing information with each other, e.g., in traditional contracting the buyer is only able to estimate the supplier's costs. They may do this by undertaking cost modelling.

Joint performance measurement

As part of a traditional contract and contract management process a buyer will measure the success of a supplier by including key performance indicators in the contract. These will measure operational elements such as percentage of deliveries on time and in full, or the number of non-compliant products in a delivery. Only the supplier's performance is measured. However, with a partnership agreement aspects of both the buyer and supplier's performance will be measured and shared between the parties. These will rocognise shared goals and objectives and help drive and deliver improved performance. This may also include measuring the health of the partnership relationship as well as the operational success of the partnership (see section 2.3).

No defined end period

Partnership relationships, especially type 3, are long-term, without a defined end period. Traditional contracting agreements will typically last from one to three years, having a defined term. As a result of the increased length of the relationship, partnerships tend to focus on long-term objectives, with the partners being a key part of each other's future plans, whereas more traditional contracting agreements focus on short- to medium-term objectives.

Less contractual

Generally, where a partnership relationship is in place rather than a traditional contracting relationship, the terms and conditions covering the agreement will be less extensive. In the spirit of partnership there is less need to specify treatment for failure in performance as it is in the best interests of the buyer and supplier to make the partnership a success. However, there will still be a requirement to agree objectives and KPIs.

Lambert et al. (1996)[6] said that the strongest partnerships tend to have shorter and less specific contracts or in some cases no formal contract at all, just a one- to two-page partnership agreement. McDonald's and Coca-Cola have a partnership that is based on trust; there is no written contract and there are likely to be more mutually beneficial terms.

3.1 L03

> *Remember*
> Several characteristics distinguish a partnership relationship from a traditional contract.
>
> - Joint product development rather than a buyer-developed specification
> - No tender process or win-lose negotiations
> - Shared costs and benefits
> - Greater level of information sharing and transparency
> - Joint performance measurement
> - No defined end period
> - Less contractual

The drivers for partnership sourcing

There may be a number of drivers/motivators for both the buyer and the supplier to enter into a partnership relationship. It is highly likely that these drivers will be closely linked with the strategy of the procurement function and the wider strategy of the buyer's whole business, as well as the strategy of the supplier. Ideally both partners will have drivers for developing a partnership relationship.

According to Lambert et al. (1996)[7] both the buyer and supplier must believe that they will receive significant benefits that would not be possible without a partnership. There may be one main driver for development of a partnership relationship, or a combination of drivers.

The drivers are unlikely to be the same for both the buyer and supplier but they need to be strong for both parties (Lambert et al.)[8]. Possible drivers include the following.

- Working together will generate synergies which are likely to result in reduced costs and increased profitability. A focus on long-term collaboration will leverage the value-adding potential in supply chain relationships. Both reduced costs and increased profitability are likely to secure the future survival of a company.

- **Product life cycles** have reduced in recent decades. This is especially the case for technological products, such as mobile phones. This has created the need for businesses to develop products more quickly. This can be assisted by creating partnerships and involving supply partners early in the process or developing products jointly.

- Changes in the marketplace or unstable markets may result in buyers and suppliers needing to work together more closely in order to survive, for example in markets where the costs of inputs are increasing.

- There may be a need to improve performance to satisfy the ultimate customer in the supply chain.

- The desire to reduce stock-holding and to move towards world-class standards of supply chain management such as just in time (JIT) or Lean production. Both of these strategies require close working relationships with the supply chain due to the dependencies that they create.

Product life cycle
A period of time which involves developing a product from scratch, bringing the product to the marketplace, sales in the market and the eventual decline and removal of the product from the marketplace. The model has four key stages: introduction, growth, maturity and decline

- There may be a need to reduce waste in the supply chain. Partners can work together to identify wastes, such as unnecessary or duplicated activity, bottlenecks, delays, errors, rejects and unnecessary inventory. This links to the first point: by decreasing waste, partners are likely to increase value.

- Partnerships may be required for access to the market. Foreign or restricted marketplaces might require a buyer to partner with a local supplier, for instance.

- A buyer needs to source customised/highly complex products or services. Sourcing these products and services will require a different type of relationship than sourcing common and repetitive items.

- Whole supply chains are now competing with each other as they are networked. When companies are members of these competing supply chains the companies that manage key relationships the best will have better results.

- A partnership can increase security of supply. When supplies are scarce a supplier is likely to ensure that its partners are supplied as a priority.

- The supplier strategy is to further develop its relationship with the buyer, moving it from a 'development' to a 'core' customer (supplier preferencing). Suppliers may well approach the buyer to develop a partnership relationship.

The drivers from the perspective of both the buyer and the supplier are based around the perceived benefits that they will gain from engaging in a partnership-style relationship. These benefits include reduced costs, reduced waste, higher sales and increased profitability. These are discussed in more detail below. In addition to this companies are unable to possess all of the competencies required to produce their products or services themselves. Therefore, partnerships between a buyer and supplier are becoming more and more essential (Serem et al., 2015[9]).

From the list above, you will notice that some of the drivers will be a result of what is happening in the external marketplace. A buyer and supplier will both need to be aware of their external environment. The external environment can be better understood by undertaking a STEEPLE analysis (see section 1.3).

> *Remember*
> Both the buyer and the supplier will have at least one main driver for entering into a partnership relationship. In reality there are likely to be multiple drivers of different strengths for both the buyer and the supplier.

Lambert et al. (1996)[10] developed the partnership model illustrated in figure 3.1 to understand the drivers and facilitators of partnership relationships. The model should be used by both buyer and supplier. Firstly, it should be used internally by each party to look at the drivers for partnership and whether or not entering into a partnership relationship would be appropriate and beneficial. Once both the buyer and the supplier have decided internally that a partnership would have potential benefits for their company, they must present the drivers to each other, decide on which drivers can be accepted as joint goals and jointly review the facilitators such as cultural compatibility. Based on the drivers and facilitators, an agreement must be reached on the type of partnership and how it will be implemented. The model can also be used to assess relationships to see whether they need to be changed or developed, or whether they are performing well as they are.

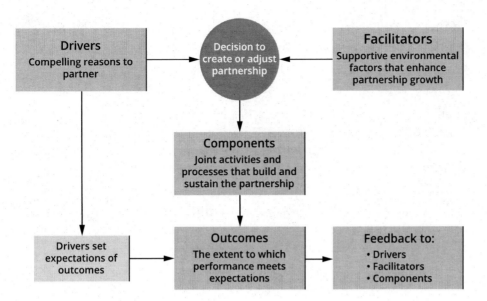

Figure 3.1 The partnership model (Source: Douglas M. Lambert, Margaret A. Emmelhainz, and John T. Gardner, "Developing and Implementing Supply Chain Partnerships," The International Journal of Logistics Management, Vol. 7, No. 2 (1996), pp. 1–17. Copyright by Douglas M. Lambert. For more information about The Partnership Model and how it has been used to structure relationships with corporations globally see: www.drdouglaslambert.com)

> *Check*
> List three drivers that a buyer or supplier may have for entering into a partnership relationship.

Advantages for purchaser and supplier

Coming together to form a partnership-style relationship will bring a number of advantages for both the buyer and the supplier. It is these drivers and advantages that encourage a buyer and supplier to commit the resources required to build a partnership. Lambert et al. (1996)[11] noted that a well-managed partnership can bring benefits similar to those found as a result of the creation of a joint venture or **vertical integration** without the pains of ownership. These advantages of partnership need to be sustainable for both the buyer and the supplier over the long-term. There are joint advantages of partnership as well as advantages that are more related to either the buyer or supplier.

The joint advantages of partnership include the following.

- Working together and collaborating is likely to result in synergies which could bring reduced costs and increased profitability for both partners.

- Investment costs, such as new machinery and research and development can be shared by both partners.

- Partnership can lead to improved competitive advantage and/or increased market share. These are both likely to generate increased profits.

> ❝*In the global economy, a well-developed ability to create and sustain fruitful collaborations gives companies a significant competitive leg up.*❞
>
> *(Source: Kanter, 1994[12])*

Vertical integration
When a buyer owns companies within its supply chain. There could be forward vertical integration where a buyer owns a distributor, or backward vertical integration where a buyer owns one of its suppliers of raw materials

- Partnering may allow either partner to enter different markets due to the previous experience of the other partner.

- Risk may be reduced through risk sharing and improved risk management practices, as risks are managed jointly.

- Information and knowledge sharing will enable both the buyer and the supplier to have better market knowledge. This will also reduce risks. Knowledge sharing should be a two-way process that allows both companies to learn and develop from the partnership. This area would also include the ability to undertake joint problem solving.

- A buyer and supplier can share resources, such as staff knowledge and skills, and machinery. Brownell and Reynolds (2002)[13] note that organisations becoming more Lean has increased their need to partner with suppliers.

- Entering into a partnership may significantly speed up innovation and new product/service development, due to the pooling of staff, knowledge and finance resources. This can reduce the time it takes to get a product or service to market, which would also offer the partners a competitive advantage over their rivals.

- By working in a more collaborative way the buyer and supplier may be able to identify waste in the supply chain. Reducing waste will add value and also reduce costs.

Partnership advantages for the buyer include the following.

- As partnership relationships are generally long-term, the buyer is likely to be able to gain price stability from the supplier. This will aid in planning and financial management. There is also likely to be greater transparency regarding supplier costs, especially if open book costing is undertaken (see section 1.4).

- Cost savings may be made as a result of supply base rationalisation (previously the buyer may have had more than one supplier providing the products) and leveraging volume with the supplier.

- There may be greater continuity of supply. If there is a shortage of supplies in the marketplace a supplier is likely to service its preferred customer first. This is likely to be the customer that it is most integrated with. Developing a partnership relationship with a supplier is likely to make the buyer a preferred customer.

- The supplier should view the buyer as a 'core' customer (supplier preferencing) once they enter into a partnership relationship. This may result in improved service, such as increased responsiveness and quality.

- Improved services for the customer of the buying organisation. This could be achieved via "reduced inventory, shorter cycle times, and more timely and accurate information" (Lambert et al., 1996[14]).

Benefits of partnership

Global fast-food chain McDonald's discovered that by establishing partnership relationships with regional distributors which serve as the single distributor to all restaurants within a region, both delivery and ordering costs were reduced.

(Source: Lambert et al., 1996[15])

Case study

Partnership advantages related to the supplier include the following.

- The supplier will gain certainty of business, for example in terms of both volume and length of business, which will result in greater stability for the supplier.

- It may gain an increased volume of business if the buyer was previously dual-sourcing or multiple-sourcing its requirements and has now placed all of its volume with one supplier.

- It may have increased involvement in initiatives, such as supplier development or early supplier involvement (ESI) in new projects, which could result in additional business for the supplier.

> *Remember*
> There will be a number of advantages for a buyer and supplier entering into a partnership relationship. These joint advantages can include reduced costs, increased profit, improved competitive advantage, entry into different markets, reduced risk and sharing of knowledge and resources.

As well as advantages, partnership sourcing can bring disadvantages for both partners. Again, these disadvantages can be joint or related specifically to either the buyer or the supplier. The disadvantages will need to be managed carefully to ensure they do not outweigh the advantages.

The joint disadvantages include the following.

- If a partnership relationship breaks down or one partner fails, there could be serious repercussions for the remaining company due to the level of dependence that the partners have on each other.

- Partners can become locked into a relationship in which they are incompatible. This happens for various reasons and is discussed in more detail in section 3.3. The facilitator evaluation is designed to avoid this outcome.

- There is a risk that confidential information or IPR from the buyer or supplier will be leaked to the marketplace by the other partner which could seriously affect a company's competitive advantage. This should not happen in a true partnership.

- Planned benefits and advantages will not materialise unless the relationship is actively managed by both partners. This active management can be costly and resource intensive.

- Relationship management can be costly for both partners in terms of the resources that are required to maintain a partnership-style relationship which is one of the main reasons that 70% of supplier relationships will not be partnerships (Lambert).

- Being locked into one relationship reduces the flexibility of both the buyer and the supplier. Flexibility can be key for the success and survival of a company.

The disadvantages that only affect the buyer include the following.

- The supplier could become complacent overtime as it no longer has to compete for the buyer's business. For example, it will not have to participate in competitive tender processes. This could result in reductions in quality or cause price creep on the products and services. A true partnership, however, should be creating mutual value and benefits.

- The buyer is locked into a relationship, and as a result is unable to take advantage of offerings from other suppliers in the marketplace that might have become more competitive, or have access to newer technologies. This could affect the buyer's ability to compete in the marketplace, however, again this should not happen in a true partnership.

The disadvantages that only affect the supplier include the following.

- The supplier can become over-dependent on the buyer's business, focusing on the relationship at the expense of business development with other customers. It is worth noting that in the EU under the OJEU regulations this level of dependency would be less likely to materialise due to the nature of the process.

- CIPS discusses the risk of bad buyer behaviour, e.g., exploiting transparency of costings to force supplier's prices down. This shouldn't occur in a true partnership but we have to recognise that change and in particular management change might alter the relationship over time.

It is clear that partnership relationships have both advantages and disadvantages for the buyer and the supplier, which need to be carefully weighed up by both parties before a partnership relationship is developed. Once the relationship has been developed it needs to be actively manged and committed to by both partners. This active management will prevent a number of the disadvantages from arising.

High spend

A buyer will have different levels of spend with each individual supplier. It will have a high spend with some suppliers and is likely to have a lower spend with a wide range of suppliers. This high volume of low-value spend is referred to as **tail spend**. The buyer might focus relationship investment (such as a partnership style) on the 20% of suppliers that provide its highest-value products and services. This is an example of the Pareto principle (see section 1.2).

In terms of the value of 'high spend', this will also vary from one company to another depending on total overall spend. What is high spend for a small company may be considered low spend for a multi-national company located in several countries.

Looking at the Kraljic model (1983) which was studied in chapter 1 (see also figure 3.2), there were two quadrants that contained spend that was of a high financial risk. These were strategic products and services and leverage products and services. As part of segmenting its spend and developing a Kraljic model, a buyer will have identified its high-spend products and services and plotted them in these quadrants.

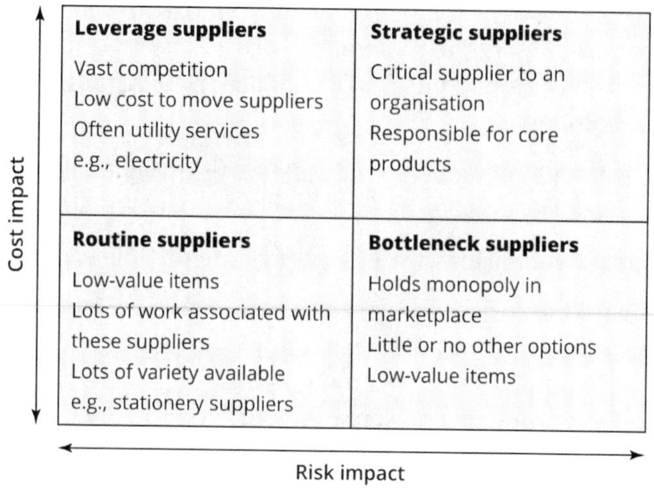

Leverage suppliers	**Strategic suppliers**
Vast competition Low cost to move suppliers Often utility services e.g., electricity	Critical supplier to an organisation Responsible for core products
Routine suppliers	**Bottleneck suppliers**
Low-value items Lots of work associated with these suppliers Lots of variety available e.g., stationery suppliers	Holds monopoly in marketplace Little or no other options Low-value items

Cost impact (vertical axis) — Risk impact (horizontal axis)

Figure 3.2 Based on The Kraljic matrix of different supplier types

Leverage products and services are those that a buyer can use to leverage its spending power by creating large contracts and testing the marketplace via a competitive tender process. Therefore, this type of high-spend product or service would not generally be suitable for a partnership relationship. The buyer is likely to gain benefits, such as cost savings and increased profitability, by undertaking competition without having to expend resources on developing a partnership.

Strategic products are those that have both high financial impact and high supply risk. Due to the increased supply risk as well as high financial risk, the buyer would benefit from developing a partnership-style relationship with a supplier. High supply risk is discussed in more detail below.

Where the buyer has a high value of spend with a high profit impact with the supplier (high financial risk), it will be beneficial to develop a partnership relationship. As already discussed, developing a partnership could lead to a number of synergies which may allow the buyer to make savings on the spend. If spend is high, even saving 1% or 2% could have a large impact on the profitability of a company. The buyer could use the high level of spend, and therefore potential financial benefits, to develop a business case to demonstrate to senior management and the wider business the value that a partnership with a high-spend supplier could bring.

McKinsey (2013)[16] notes that where there was collaboration between buyers and suppliers the EBIT (earnings before interest and taxation) growth rate was more than double that of those that did not collaborate. Due to the high percentage of spend that was made with these suppliers, the financial benefits of partnership development could be significant for both buyer and supplier. These financial benefits could include the following.

- Unit costs may be reduced for the buyer due to economies of scale achieved from placing all volume with one supplier.

- Costs may be reduced by removing waste from the supply chain.

- Profitability for the buyer may be increased as a result of the cost base being reduced and the selling price to consumers remaining the same.

- Value sharing models may be used. For example, if any cost savings are found they might be split 50/50 between the buyer and the supplier. Alternatively, the buyer and supplier may negotiate a predetermined benefit for the buyer each year, for example 3%, with the remainder of the savings staying with the supplier.

- Savings could also be made on stock holding if the partners developed Lean or just in time stock holding. This would improve the cash flow of the buying organisation.

We have already discussed that the costs of partnering can be high, "not least because of the time needed to explore, establish and manage the partner relationship" (The Partnering Initiative, 2018[17]). Therefore, partnerships generally should not be developed with tail-spend suppliers, unless they supply a high-risk product or service which is critical to the buying organisation.

> *Remember*
> A buyer may enter into a partnership relationship with a supplier that provides products or services that are high spend or have a high value for the organisation. In order to assess which suppliers would be in this category the buyer should undertake a segmentation analysis using the Kraljic model (see section 1.2).

High risk

Managing risk is vital for the survival of any company. For a buyer, managing supply risk is an important part of its day-to-day role. Each product or service in a buyer's portfolio will have different levels of supply risk. Some of the products and services such as stationery or office cleaning services will be very low risk. Others such as a critical component from a foreign supplier will have a much higher level of supply risk associated with them. High risk also links to business criticality and business continuity: which supplier is the buying organisation unable to function without? An example of this type of supplier would include one that operated all of a company's IT systems.

Thinking back to the Kraljic model, there were two quadrants that contained high supply risk products and services. These were the bottleneck and the strategic quadrants. Bottleneck items are those with a high level of supply risk but a lower financial risk, whereas strategic items are those that are both high risk and high value. Taking into account the discussion in the passage on high spend earlier in this section, generally partnerships will be developed with those suppliers that are located within the strategic quadrant of the Kraljic model.

Some products and services located in the bottleneck quadrant may be low in value but vital for the production process or delivery of services. However, bottleneck suppliers are not suitable for forming partnerships.

For high-risk products and services, supply chain continuity will be important. Issues of supply chain continuity are caused when risks occur, and a supplier is unable to deliver products or services within the required timeframe, or in some cases unable to deliver them at all. Therefore, it will be beneficial for supply chain continuity to enter into a partnership relationship with a supplier that can provide a product or a service that has a high risk around, for example, delivery.

Demand risk
The risk that the forecast demand levels may not be met by actual customer demand

Ryu, Park and Min (2007)[18] stated that companies that rely on partnerships are better able to adapt to unforeseen changes, noting that the presence of risks will increase the positive effects of buyer–supplier partnership quality. Srinivasan et al. (2011)[19] said that this was particularly the case for **demand risk**. Partnerships can also result in improvements to the flow of information and co-ordination. Having more and better quality information can also reduce supply risk for the buyer.

The benefit for buyers of developing partnership relationships for high-risk products and services is that partners can undertake a joint risk management approach, which may provide additional mitigation. Partners can also share the risks. However, partnership itself can also open the buyer up to risk. Ramsay (1996)[20] noted that partnership sourcing was a high-risk strategy. Some of these risks include the sharing of commercially sensitive information with the supplier, which could leak into the marketplace if it is not actively managed. There is also the issue that in many cases partnership sourcing will generally create a single-source relationship between the buyer and the supplier. This may leave a buyer without a supply source if, for example, the supplier goes into liquidation or is located in an area that experiences a natural disaster.

Skjøtt-Larsen et al. (2007)[21] identified several risks, including supplier complacency, opportunistic behaviours, the risk of being locked into a relationship with the wrong partner, and the difficulties of measuring the success of the partnership.

> *Remember*
> A buyer may enter into a partnership relationship with a supplier that provides products or services that are high spend or have a high value for the organisation. In order to assess which suppliers are in this category the buyer should undertake a segmentation analysis using the Kraljic model (see section 1.2).

3.1 LO3

Technically complicated supplies

Technically complicated supplies are generally those that are not 'off the shelf' but are specially developed or adapted for the buyer by the supplier. They are often technology based, and offer the buyer a competitive advantage in the marketplace.

These products and services are likely to be of high financial risk and also high supply risk, located in the strategic quadrant of the Kraljic model. They are therefore the type of product and service suitable for the development of partnership relationships. It is often argued that higher levels of integration or partnerships are required in the supply chain, especially for complex business conditions (van der Vaart and van Donk, 2008[22]) and complex products and components (Nazli Wasti et al. 2006[23] as cited in Srinivasan et al., 2011[24]).

When a product or service is technically complex there may only be a small number of suppliers in the marketplace that are able to provide the goods or service. This could be due to an inability to use a substitute product as a result of technical complexity. In addition to this the cost of switching suppliers is likely to be high. This could be for a number of reasons, including the cost to set up tooling and production for that particular product, as well as the level of knowledge that the supplier has developed. This knowledge will add value. These issues link back to the Porter's Five Forces model which was discussed in chapter 1 (see section 1.3).

Due to the likely small number of suppliers in the market and therefore the inability of the buyer to leverage its demand via a competitive tendering process, instead the buyer may be able to gain value from the relationship by developing a partnership. However, this is only likely to be successful with a supplier that views the buyer as a development or core customer (supplier preferencing). If the balance of power is firmly with the supplier, the buyer may be unable to develop a partnership relationship. The buyer will gain value by being able to access the specialist equipment and technology that the supplier has.

Lambert stated that partnership:

> ❝ *may also enhance the development and use of specialised equipment and processes between the parties, without fear of technology transfer to a competitor.* ❞

(Source: Lambert et al., 1996[25])

Improvements in technology and innovation are also key ways that both the buyer and the supplier can reduce costs and increase profitability.

The type of value that could be gained here would also include access to specialist knowledge and skills held by the supplier. The supplier is likely to have specialist (tacit) knowledge that would not be easily replicated by another supplier. These capabilities and this knowledge could enable the buyer to gain a competitive advantage in the marketplace.

It may not necessarily be the product or service that is technically complicated; it may instead be the supply chain. The product may come from a foreign supplier and the buyer may have to use a number of different types of logistics to get it to the end destination, for example air, sea and road freight. Creating a partnership with a supplier that is part of a technically complicated supply chain would have benefits: the logistics risk could be reduced by sharing up-to-date information on schedules and deliveries or operating integrated systems.

New services

New product development is sometimes referred to as NPD. With shorter product life cycles companies need to innovate constantly in order to survive. New products and services can be costly, high risk and resource intensive to develop for the buying organisation. Therefore, development of new services may be best supported by entering into a partnership relationship with a key supplier to share the costs and risks and enjoy access to additional resources. This will offer a number of benefits for both the buyer and the supplier.

Before entering into a partnership, a buyer must research the supplier and review whether or not it will have the capacity to meet projected quality, delivery and volume requirements. Ideally when developing new products and services, due to the risk, the buyer should partner with a supplier that will reduce this risk, for example, due to its innovative skills.

With regard to new product and service development, a partner supplier should be involved as early as possible in the development process in order to gain the maximum benefits from the partnership relationship. This refers to the concept of early supplier involvement (ESI, see chapter 2). Cross-organisational teams developed for NPD should include the partner supplier.

The buyer and supplier will have the benefit of being able to pool knowledge and resources on things such as research and development, staff, and data on consumer behaviour. As a result, they may be able to reduce the cost of a new service or product development and increase the speed at which they take the service or product to market. If, as a partnership, the buyer and supplier can take a new product or service to market before their competitors, they will be able to obtain a competitive advantage. Companies offering new products and services can charge a premium price. The partners will enjoy increased profitability while others are still developing their products and trying to launch them in the market.

Innovation will also be a key consideration when developing new products and services. Developing a partnership with a supplier may provide a buyer with access to additional innovation. The partnership relationship is likely to provide the supplier with assurances that the buyer is committed to the relationship. Therefore, sharing commercially sensitive information and knowledge will not result in opportunistic behaviour from the buyer that could negatively affect a supplier.

Partnering with suppliers will also be beneficial if the new product or service is being developed for a new market, i.e. one that the buying organisation is not currently selling into. This will be particularly relevant if the supplier has knowledge or experience of servicing these markets.

However, a downside includes the fact that where a product or service is created in partnership more stakeholders are involved in the process e.g., perhaps both parties design engineers and marketing personnel. This adds complexity to the stakeholder engagement and management process, which will need to be actively managed by the buyer. This process can be time intensive.

> *Remember*
> If a buyer is developing a new product or service, it may decide to partner with a supplier. The benefits of this include sharing costs and risks, as well as access to additional knowledge and innovation.

Fast-changing technology

In today's modern world technology changes quickly. Look at how often Apple releases a new model of the iPhone. What is cutting-edge today will have been replaced by a newer version of the product or service in a matter of months. These reduced product life cycles are due to competitive pressures and increasing consumer expectations. As a result of this, there may be circumstances where a buyer will have to act quickly to develop a partnership relationship. This process could be helped by undertaking the following proactive tasks.

- Periodic scanning of the marketplace to understand new supplier entrants and the products or services they offer.

- Undertaking research on what competitors in the buyer's marketplace are doing.

Developing partnerships can give a buying organisation access to innovation that offers a significant competitive advantage to the buyer. There are also profit advantages. New products and services that offer the latest technology can be sold at a premium price. In order to ensure these benefits are achieved the buyer must clearly inform the supplier of the innovation objectives of the partnership relationship. This is discussed in more detail in section 3.2.

We have already discussed that partnership can reduce product development time and increase the speed at which a buyer can launch a product in the market.

> *In the tech world, partnerships are often about getting to market fast, accessing talent and resources as an alternative to an aggressive hiring process.*
>
> (Source: Eben, 2018[26])

By entering into a partnership with a supplier, the buying organisation will be able to expand its knowledge and capabilities without developing them in-house, which would take significant time and delay product launch. A supplier can be a significant source of specialist technological knowledge and innovation.

Eben (2018)[27] noted that seeking a supplier that is a technology expert will also free up the buying organisation to focus on its own core competency areas.

When both the buyer and supplier are focusing on their core competencies, they are likely to create more value than if their focus were spread over multiple areas.

When developing partnerships with suppliers for innovation purposes, buyers need to consider their current capabilities. However, buyers should also think about the potential technical capabilities that the supplier will have in the future (Cousins et al., 2008)[28]. Being the supplier's partner of choice today could result in competitive advantage tomorrow.

Restricted markets

Restricted marketplace
A market where there are only a small number of capable and competent suppliers

A buyer may seek to develop a partnership with a supplier if the supplier is operating in a **restricted marketplace** that new suppliers are unlikely to enter. Marketplaces may be restricted for a number of reasons.

- High financial investment is required to enter the market; for example, the cost of production technology or equipment could be prohibitive.

- Some markets have low levels of profitability, and as a result, new suppliers are not tempted to enter the marketplace.

- In markets where brand loyalty is high, it would be difficult for a supplier to break into a marketplace and compete with strong, established brands.

- Some markets are heavily regulated by governments and legislation.

- In some markets, obtaining access to distribution channels is difficult due to pre-existing relationships.

- In some markets, existing companies collude in order to deter new entrants, for example by undertaking aggressive marketing strategies.

In a restricted marketplace there may be few competent and reliable suppliers. As a result the supplier is likely to have a high level of power. By developing a partnership relationship with a supplier operating in a restricted marketplace, the buyer will ensure continuity and security of supply now and in the future. The buyer is also likely to be able to negotiate more effectively with this high-powered supplier if they are partners. This is because the success of the relationship will be more important to both parties than short-term gain. We have already discussed continuity of supply and the benefits it can bring, including reduced risk, reduced costs and protection of the reputation of the buying organisation.

Before entering into a partnership with a supplier in a restricted marketplace the buyer will need to review how it is viewed by this supplier.

> *Check*
> Under what circumstances would a partnership-style relationship be considered a suitable approach for a buying organisation?

> *Remember*
> If a buyer is operating in a restricted marketplace it may decide to develop a partnership with its strategic suppliers, thereby ensuring continuity of supply and improving the buyer's negotiating position.

3.2 Appraise the process of partnership implementation

PwC (PricewaterhouseCoopers) (2013)[29] noted that many companies encounter difficulties in initiating, developing and managing partnership relationships. This section discusses key aspects of implementing a successful partnership, before we consider the reasons why partnerships fail in section 3.3.

Implementing a partnership relationship will take a significant amount of time and resources from both the buyer and the supplier. It is important that the implementation phase is well planned, co-ordinated and executed in order to ensure that the expected benefits of the partnership come to fruition. Implementation is just one phase of the relationship. Partnerships, like all buyer–supplier relationships, will also have a relationship life cycle (see figure 3.3) and need to be managed over time to fully optimise the relationship. It is worth noting that timescales can be variable and there are examples of companies such as Coke and McDonald's whose type 3 partnership has been very long term, now over 60 years.

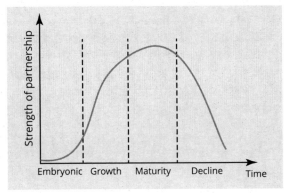

Figure 3.3 Partnership life cycle model

Different skills will be required from the buyer and the wider organisation as the relationship passes through the four stages of the life cycle model. Cousins et al. (2008)[30] stated that during the embryonic stage buyers would need to move the relationship past any implementation barriers. During the growth stage, more traditional management skills are needed, such as measurement, control and problem solving. In the third stage buyers will need to know how to develop the relationship going forward; this includes making the decision to divest.

Identify items potentially suitable for partnership sourcing

An important aspect of deciding which type of relationship we will want to have with our suppliers is recognising and deciding which items (products and services) in our organisation's portfolio would be suitable for partnership sourcing. As mentioned above, a company will source a wide range of products and services from external suppliers, but not all of these will be suitable for partnership sourcing.

Across all sectors of the economy the number of products and services procured from external suppliers has increased in recent decades. This is a result of buying organisations focusing on core competencies in order to create additional value and sourcing other non-core elements from external suppliers.

Choosing to source via a partnership relationship is in itself a procurement strategy. The strategy must be carefully considered alongside other strategies that could be used for the product or service, such as low-cost country sourcing or undertaking a competitive tender process. Cousins et al. (2008)[31] noted that it was important to consider relationships with suppliers at the item, product or service level because of the different experiences that different areas of the business might have with the same supplier.

According to CIPS, the products and services most suitable for partnership sourcing are the vital ones that match the following criteria.

- They are used in products and services that represent a company's unique selling proposition/point (USP).

- They represent the buying organisation's greatest opportunity for profit. This affects where on the Kraljic model the product or service would be plotted.

- The buying organisation's most important customers depend on them.

- In the case of a public sector organisation, the general public relies on the buying organisation to provide them.

Again, we will need to cast our mind back to the Kraljic model (see section 1.2). As noted in section 3.1, the items (products and services) that are best suited to partnership sourcing are those that are located in the strategic quadrant of the Kraljic model. These are the products and services that carry high financial risk and also high supply risk. Tevelson et al. (2013)[32] stated that across all industries around 85% of buyers segment their supply base in order to identify potential partners.

Any inability to source these strategic products and services could have serious repercussions for the buying organisation. Developing a partnership can reduce the risks of sourcing these strategic products and services. Changes in prices and therefore profit potential could also have serious impacts. Therefore, there are likely to be a number of drivers and advantages for sourcing such a product or service from a supplier.

As part of the analysis of which product should be sourced via a partnership relationship, a buyer also needs to consider the structure of the marketplace and the relative levels of power of the buyer and the supplier (see section 1.3 and the discussion of Porter's Five Forces model). In markets where supplier power is high there may be little incentive for a supplier to enter into a partnership agreement, but there is likely to be value for the buyer in creating a partnership.

This leads us to the next consideration: will the supplier want to enter into a partnership relationship with the buyer? As noted by Partnership Sourcing Ltd, there is a need to assess the other partner's management interest in developing a partnership relationship.

> *Trying to develop a partnership where one is not warranted will waste valuable resources while providing minimal return. Not having a partnership where one is appropriate squanders an opportunity for competitive advantage.*

(Source: Lambert et al., 1996[33])

In order to assess this the buyer will need to undertake supplier preferencing (see section 1.2). Ideally it would be best to consider a partnership development with suppliers that are located in the core quadrant. However, partnerships could also

Unique selling proposition/point (USP)
These are the elements of a product or service that differentiate the buying organisation's offering from that of its competitors. This could be a feature of a product or it could be related to cost or quality. USPs are a source of competitive advantage

be undertaken with suppliers that viewed the buyer as developmental. These two sets of suppliers are also likely to want to develop a partnership with the buyer.

To summarise, in order to select an item (product or service) suitable for partnership sourcing, the buyer should do the following.

- Review each of the products and services in its portfolio in terms of financial and supply risk.

- Use the above information to plot these items onto the Kraljic model. The buyer should then make a list of all the products and services located in the strategic quadrant.

- Following this the buyer should review which suppliers provide these strategic products and services. These suppliers need to be plotted onto a supplier preferencing model.

- Those suppliers located in the strategic quadrant should be targeted for developing partnership relationships. Suppliers in the development quadrant should be reviewed to see whether there would be benefits to developing partnerships with them.

There are unlikely to be many suppliers located in both the strategic quadrant of the Kraljic model and the core quadrant of the supplier preferencing model. If there is more than one supplier, the buyer will need to review which of the potential partnerships has the most drivers and benefits associated with it. The buyer can then prioritise which partnership should be developed first.

Once a supplier has identified a potential partner the process of **due diligence** will begin. This needs to be carefully managed with all information being reviewed thoroughly to ensure that the buyer does not waste resources developing a relationship with an unsuitable supplier. The buyer should satisfy itself that the supplier is financially stable and has the correct accreditations and insurance levels to undertake the work. It should also ensure that the supplier is not involved in an activity that could potentially damage the reputation of the buying organisation by association, such as poor human rights practices. This should all occur before the partnership model is used.

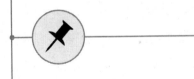

Due diligence
Undertaking a thorough appraisal or conducting an evaluation to establish all the facts prior to entering into an agreement

> *Remember*
> A buyer needs to carefully review all the products and services in its portfolio to identify the areas where developing a partnership would generate the most benefits and value, and would therefore be worth the time and resources required.

'Sell' the philosophy to senior management and other functions of the organisation

Once the buyer has identified a suitable partner supplier and undertaken the necessary due diligence, it will need to sell the partnership philosophy to senior management and the wider organisation. As noted by Partnership Sourcing Ltd there are three key elements to selling the philosophy of partnership sourcing.

- Selling the idea to senior management

- Selling the idea to the wider organisation

- Selling the idea to the potential partner (though this may not be required if the partner has approached the buyer about developing a closer working relationship)

Selling the philosophy to senior management

The first step is to convince senior management of the benefits and value of the partnership sourcing strategy.

> ❝*It is particularly necessary for the success of the partnership that top management and the functional departments' management are convinced of its benefits.*❞

(Source: Sima & Balam, 2014[34])

Business case
A justification for a proposed project or undertaking on the basis of its expected benefits

It is likely that selling the philosophy to senior management will involve the development of a formal **business case**. Cousins et al. (2008)[35] noted the importance of care, consideration and the development of a business case before a buyer adopts a different way of working with a supplier. The business case will need to detail all the potential options for working with the supplier market, such as developing a partnership, running a competitive tender for a single supplier or contracting with multiple suppliers. The advantages and disadvantages of each option will need to be detailed clearly.

Forbes states that:

> ❝*It is a significant challenge to construct a compelling business case to win over stakeholders and persuade a diffusion of interested parties across two organizations. The requisite skills run far beyond the procurement professional's traditional remit.*❞

(Source: Forbes, 2017[36])

As such, there will be a need for the buyer to have a number of soft skills including influencing, persuading and negotiating. The buyer may also need to consider reaching out to other functional areas for support with writing the business case.

The business case will outline the current situation, the drivers for partnership sourcing, and the expected benefits and advantages for the buying organisation. It may also include a high-level timeline of events/milestones that will need to be undertaken in order to implement the partnership relationship. To gain buy-in from senior management there must be clear business benefits for the buying organisation.

Apply
Review business cases that have been developed for projects within your organisation to familiarise yourself with the content and layout of a business case.

Selling the philosophy to functional areas

Once senior management have approved an idea, the buyer will need to sell the idea to the rest of the buying organisation. Gaining buy-in and winning the trust of stakeholders from all levels of the buying organisation will be crucial for success. Emmett and Crocker (2006)[37] noted that if the whole company does not buy into the importance of developing a supplier as a collaborative partner it will not happen, as the departments will not free up the resources required to develop a partnership.

It will be beneficial if a member of senior management can act as a **project champion** for the partnership project. Lambert et al. stated that:

> *partnership management requires a champion or change agent who will promote the partnership concept throughout the organisation.*

(Source: Lambert et al., 1996)[38]

Project champion
A person within an organisation that is implementing a project or business change who takes responsibility for ensuring the project or change is successful

It will be beneficial if this champion comes from the highest management levels of the business to demonstrate the importance of developing the partnership relationship.

Selling the philosophy to the rest of the organisation will require a stakeholder mapping exercise (see figures 3.4 and 2.2). The buyer will need to identify stakeholders that have high interest in the partnership philosophy but that also have a high level of power. These stakeholders are defined in Mendelow's model as key players. Procurement can then use these stakeholders' interest, influence and power to support them in selling the philosophy to the rest of the business. The project champion will also be key to this process, and to influencing other stakeholders to gain their support. This will be pertinent to other stakeholders with high levels of influence and power but low levels of interest in the project.

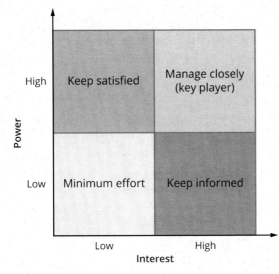
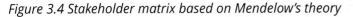

Figure 3.4 Stakeholder matrix based on Mendelow's theory

The stakeholder mapping exercise will also enable the buyer to identify any stakeholders who may oppose or resist the move towards developing a partnership relationship. Actions can then be put in place to communicate with these stakeholders in order to persuade them of the benefits of entering into a partnership relationship. These stakeholders need to be converted into supporters before they are able to mobilise support against the partnership relationship.

In order to get the identified key stakeholders to support the proposed procurement strategy, the buyer will need to use their influencing skills. Influencing is one of the soft procurement skills. In order to be able to effectively influence others the buyer will need to clearly understand the position of procurement and the stakeholders position. The buyer could be proposing strategy with numerous positive benefits for the business but unless the buyer can understand any potential negative impacts on stakeholders, then they will be unable to influence their opinions and decisions.

Once the key stakeholders have bought into the idea, the philosophy can be communicated to the functional areas and departments in a number of ways. The method used will depend on the stakeholder group the buyer is communicating with.

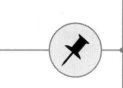

> *Remember*
> It will be key for the success of the partnership relationship to gain the support of senior management. The buyer should develop a business case in order to sell the partnership philosophy to the senior management team. Ideally a member of the senior management team should also act as a project champion.

In selling the philosophy to the wider company there will also be an element of change management. Kotter's eight-step change management model (figure 3.5) will be useful for buyers to follow when they are selling the philosophy to the rest of the business.

When the buyer is selling the philosophy, both to senior management and to the wider business, it needs to create a sense of urgency to start with. This sense of urgency will encourage people to take action and drive the partnership relationship process forward. The concept of supplier relationship management and the benefits it can bring need to be sold to the business. This could be done by demonstrating all of the benefits that the buying organisation is currently missing out on by not being in a partnership relationship with the supplier. Next, via stakeholder mapping, the buyer can identify its guiding coalition. The guiding coalition will be the staff in the business who will support and champion the strategy of developing a partnership relationship.

Following on from this, the buyer along with the champion and the supplier will need to develop a strategic vision and initiatives for the partnership project. This is discussed in more detail later in this section. As part of step 4, the buyer should enlist a volunteer army, who will be who the stakeholders identified as key players, and keep them informed in the stakeholder mapping exercise. Both of the 'key players' and 'keep informed' stakeholder groups would have high levels of interest in the partnership project.

Figure 3.5 Based on Kotter's eight-step change model (Source: adapted from www.kotterinc.com/8-steps-process-for-leading-change)

3.2 L03

Moving on to step 5, the buyer will need to enable action by removing any barriers to progress. By using stakeholder mapping and identifying which stakeholders may resist the partnership project, the buyer will be able to start thinking about the driving forces behind the reasons they oppose the strategy. It may also be helpful to undertake a forcefield analysis here. Once the buyer is aware of the driving forces behind any resistance, it can work to remove them. For example, if the operations department is unsupportive due to concerns over using a single supplier, the buyer could demonstrate to this team the risk management and supply continuity plans that will be put in place to manage this. It could also involve the operations department in this process.

Once the partnership project is underway, the buyer should aim to generate some small wins which can be used to build momentum to drive forward more complicated and time-consuming business changes. This may also serve to gain support from any stakeholders that still resist the partnership relationship. Following on from this the project will need to accelerate progress to get the buyer and supplier to the point where they are both benefiting from the new style of relationship. The change should then be instituted and embedded within both the buyer and supplier companies to ensure that the partnership relationship does not fail. (Partnership failure and its causes are discussed in detail in section 3.3.)

> *Check*
> What are the eight steps of Kotter's change model? Explain how these could apply to selling the philosophy of partnership to senior management and the wider business.

Selling the philosophy to the supplier

The buyer will also need to sell the partnership philosophy to the supplier. If the supplier views the buyer as a core or development customer, it is likely to welcome the chance to form a partnership and gain greater benefit from what is already a close business relationship. This is due to the supplier viewing the buyer as an appealing customer with high-value business.

Before moving to a partnership relationship, there is already likely to be a collaborative relationship in place due to the strategic nature of the products to the buyer. It could be that the buyer and supplier have already worked on joint projects and the supplier may have been involved at the development stage for new products or services (ESI). This close working relationship will serve to support implementation of a closer, partnership-style relationship.

Selling the philosophy of a partnership relationship to the supplier will be similar to selling the idea to the senior management in the buying organisation. The best way to sell the philosophy to the supplier is to clearly detail the business benefits of entering into a partnership with the buyer. As with the development of the business case, this will require a lot of groundwork and effort by the buyer in order to be able to demonstrate the joint model of tangible business benefits for buyer and supplier.

These early discussions with a supplier should be open and honest in order to set the tone for the forthcoming relationship. They should also be undertaken in person in order to start the process of developing closer relationships between the staff of the buyer and supplier.

In addition, the buyer will need to determine who the key stakeholders are in the supplier's business and undertake stakeholder mapping. The idea that the buyer identifies as a key player should first be presented to a senior member of the supplier organisation. This person will have high levels of power as well as high levels of interest in the partnership project. They will then be able to support selling the philosophy to the rest of the business.

The supplier will also need to sell the philosophy of partnership to its senior management team and the rest of the organisation. This will be key for the success of the project. If the supplier's internal organisation has not bought into the partnership philosophy, it is unlikely that the partnership will be a success. Both the buyer and supplier organisations need to fully support the project and dedicate time and resources to implementing the partnership.

As is the case with internal stakeholders the buyer will also need to use influencing skills in order to sell the idea to the supplier. Understanding the suppliers position may be a more difficult process than understanding an internal stakeholders position and therefore a buyer is likely to need stronger influencing skills here. The buyer will also need to spend more time understanding the position of the supplier than that of their internal stakeholder as they will have less information on the suppliers business and future plans.

Remember
In order to support the implementation of the partnership the buyer will need to ensure that it sells the philosophy to the wider business. In order to do this the buyer will need to undertake stakeholder mapping to highlight supporters, and those internal stakeholders who are likely to resist the partnership.

Define the standards that potential partners will be expected to meet

Before officially entering into a partnership relationship the buyer will need to determine its own standards and requirements for the relationship with the supplier. Due to the strategic nature of partnership sourcing these standards will link back to the procurement strategies of the buying organisation as well as to the wider business mission, strategy and objectives. These standards will also link to the drivers for entering into a partnership relationship.

Before the buyer can define the required standards it would like the supplier to achieve, the buyer will need to assess the current situation. The buyer will have to look honestly at both their own and the supplier's current performance, as well as the relationship between them. This review should look at what works well now and what could be improved in order to gain additional benefits and value for both partners. Note, going forward the type of partnership relationship will be determined jointly in a partnership meeting using the partnership model.

For a partnership relationship to be successful it is key that the supplier understands the standards that the buyer is aiming to achieve. Generally, the buyer will have decided to move to developing a partnership relationship in order to make a strategic change to the way it manages its supply. Sima and Balam (2014)[39] commented that such standards could include the factors listed below.

- Commitment to total quality management (TQM) and clearly defined quality management
- Ability to apply the just in time (JIT) method
- Ability to provide supplies locally and/or globally

- Willingness to take part in innovation programmes
- Flexibility management

Next to be looked at is how and why a buyer might define these factors as standards to be met by a partnership relationship, as well as how the partnership would support a move towards these standards.

Commitment to total quality management (TQM) and clearly defined quality management

The concept of **total quality management (TQM)** was discussed in section 1.4. The quality of the products or services provided by the supplier can have a substantial effect on the overall quality of an end product or service. Quality will be key for products and services located in the strategic quadrant of the Kraljic model and therefore for those suppliers identified for partnership sourcing.

TQM is a strategic business practice, and a partnership-style relationship with a supplier would be needed in order for it to be implemented. As noted by Carter et al. (1998)[40] TQM requires that companies have more formal mechanisms of interacting with suppliers, high levels of integration and co-operative approaches. All of these are key aspects of a partnership relationship. TQM also requires a relationship built on trust, which would make it unsuitable for more transactional or adversarial relationship types.

A buyer may request that the supplier commits to developing TQM over the life of the partnership, raising its quality standards to the level required by the buying organisation. To ensure that this happens the buyer and supplier should develop joint KPIs that link to this required standard. Development of TQM will require significant resource from both the buyer and the supplier, and so the supplier will need to be committed to this strategy.

Clearly defined quality management also links in with TQM. Therefore, as part of the partnership development the buyer and the supplier may jointly review and redevelop their quality management policies and procedures. By developing quality within a partnership relationship, the buyer will expect to obtain benefits, such as improved product quality, reduced cost of rework, reduced defects and waste, and improved customer satisfaction levels from the buyer's customers. This may also serve to improve the buyer's reputation in the marketplace and support it in winning new customers in the future.

Ability to apply the just in time method

The concept of the just in time (JIT) method of stock holding and production was discussed in section 1.4. JIT is based on low stock holding, with the supplier's products/services being delivered to the buyer just before they are required. Highly collaborative relationships, such as partnerships, are required to develop these systems. This is because JIT can increase the supply risk as the process is so Lean that there is no extra stock, meaning tolerance of mistakes is low.

- The buyer will need to minimise the risk of a 'stockout' situation. A stockout situation would be costly for the buyer in terms of production downtime. It could also affect its reputation if it were unable to deliver to its own customers on time. This may require that the supplier holds extra stock.

- Implementing the JIT method requires the integration of buyer and supplier systems. Integration of the two companies is a key part of partnership relationships, and the level of integration will increase as the partnership moves from type 1 through to type 3 (if required).

3.2 LO3

Total quality management (TQM)
Efforts of all departments within an organisation to improve processes, products and services

Working capital
Capital of a business that is used in its day-to-day trading operations, calculated as the current assets minus the current liabilities

Multi-national company (MNC)
A company that operates in more than one country, for example McDonald's

- Quality levels must also be high. There is no time to wait for additional stock to be delivered if quality is poor.

There are various benefits for the buyer partnering with a supplier to implement JIT. The main benefit will be to reduce stockholding, which will reduce costs and improve working capital levels.

Ability to provide supplies locally and/or globally

The ability to supply globally will only be relevant to a buyer working for multi-national companies (MNCs), which operate internationally with offices in several countries. For a buyer who is working for multi-national organisations there may be a requirement to rationalise the supplier base and work with one supply partner that can deliver both locally and globally.

Due to the high level of spend and the high risk that is likely to come with such a procurement strategy, the buyer would benefit from developing a collaborative partnership. Developing a partnership relationship will ensure continuity of supply, which is a key issue when there is a single-source of supply.

The main benefits for the buyer will include reduced cost through leveraging its spend with one supplier. Additional benefits include standardisation of quality across all operations and the requirement to only undertake SRM activities with one supplier instead of several that may be scattered around the word.

Remember
In order to ensure that the partnership meets expectations and targets as part of the implementation process, the buyer needs to clearly define the standards it expects from the supplier at the start of the partnership process.

Willingness to take part in innovation programmes

Innovation is a key reason why a buyer enters into a partnership relationship. This is likely to be a key standard that a buyer expects from a supply partner. Innovation could relate to the product or service itself or the production and delivery process. The buyer needs to set this standard here to demonstrate the level of information and knowledge sharing required as part of the partnership relationship in order to facilitate innovation.

By entering into a partnership, the buyer will expect to gain knowledge and skills from the supplier to enable it to make various improvements and innovations, for example, reduced time to market and improved product quality. A buyer needs to ensure that it innovates in order to compete within its own marketplace. Innovation will have benefits for the buyer, including reduced costs and increased profitability.

Flexibility management

Flexibility management refers to the supplier's ability to react flexibly to changes required by the buyer. These changes requested by the buyer are likely to be a result of changes in the buyer's external environment. Flexibility management links to the concept of 'agile' supply chains (see section 1.4). Agile supply relates to how fast a supplier is able to respond and adapt to changing business needs.

Agile working requires a close relationship between the buyer and the supplier in order to be successful. The buyer and supplier must have a collaborative-style relationship such as a partnership, because the agile supplier will rely on real-time data in order to maintain flexibility. The buyer and supplier will need to integrate their systems and constantly share data. Suppliers are likely to be more willing to develop agile supply and share this data if they are involved in a partnership relationship. The benefits of developing agile supply with suppliers include reduced delivery and distribution costs and increased quality control.

Behaviours

At this point the buyer will need to clarify what the expected behaviours from themselves and the supplier are as part of the partnership relationship. These behaviours will include the following.

- **Open and honest communications between both parties**. The buyer will need to establish a relationship in which the supplier feels able to be open and honest about any issues that arise during the partnership.
- **Trust.** Both parties will need to work together to establish a relationship where there is trust. This will support information and knowledge sharing.
- **Fair/non-opportunistic behaviour**. The buyer will need to be clear that it is committed to the relationship with the supplier over the long-term and will not leave the relationship to develop opportunistic relationships with other suppliers. The supplier will need to do the same.

If these behaviours are poor or missing, then the partnership is likely to fail. This is discussed in more detail in section 3.3.

Establish joint commitment to the partnership

For a partnership relationship to be successful the buyer will have to establish joint commitment from the buying organisation and the supplier. Lack of commitment is a key reason why partnership relationships fail (see section 3.3). There are a number of ways that joint commitment can be established in order to ensure that the partnership gets off to a good start.

Communication

Communication is a key part of developing a successful partnership relationship with suppliers. In order to develop commitment via communication the buyer will need to do the following.

- Establish a formal review structure. This will include a team structure, review frequency, methods of communication, escalation points and timescales.
- Provide clear information on the knowledge to be shared by the buyer and supplier (e.g., forecast demand data, market intelligence) as well as information on how this knowledge is to be managed once it has been shared.
- Both the buyer and the supplier must communicate the partnership information within their organisations to support commitment.

Setting up regular sessions attended by senior figures in the buyer and supplier organisations to communicate progress and issues will demonstrate to each party the importance and level of commitment given to the partnership.

Contractual commitment and partnership governance

In some cases, the buyer's and supplier's joint commitments, obligations and responsibilities will be outlined in a formal partnership agreement, similar to a contract, signed by both parties. If there is no partnership agreement then there should be a clear governance structure outlining roles, responsibilities and accountabilities to support the management of the partnership. By jointly agreeing to this both the buyer and the supplier are demonstrating commitment to the partnership relationship.

Driving commitment and allocation of resources from the top down

Commitment to the partnership from the buyer and the supplier will need to be driven by the senior management in each company. As already discussed, if the senior management of both the buyer and supplier are not committed to the partnership, they will not provide the resources required in terms of staff, equipment or finance.

To ensure that there is commitment from senior management the benefits of the programme should be clearly communicated to all staff from the top to the bottom of the organisation. Tevelson et al. note that:

> " *early communication from the upper levels of the buying organisation, and strong support from corporate leadership are critical in mobilising the internal team and persuading suppliers to develop a shared vision for these objectives.* "

(Source: Tevelson et al., 2013)[41]

In addition to this, resources will need to be allocated to developing the partnership at all levels in order to demonstrate its importance. These resources should be reviewed regularly to ensure that the partnership project is sufficiently resourced.

Joint objective setting

One of the first steps in developing a joint commitment will be to agree on shared objectives and goals for the partnership. What are the companies that are entering into the partnership relationship trying to achieve? As noted previously, partnership is resource and time intensive and therefore both the buyer and supplier need to see benefits for their companies in return for the effort put into developing the relationship. Developing objectives jointly will start the process of joint commitment towards shared goals and outcomes. If the buyer develops the objectives in isolation, the partner may feel that these are being imposed on it, which is not in the spirit of a buyer–supplier partnership relationship.

Objectives should be developed for the performance of the partnership. Any objectives developed should be SMART (see table 3.2), and they should be agreed by both parties.

Objective
A target that a company or partnership intends to achieve. Resources will be focused on achieving the objectives of the company

Acronym letter	Acronym meaning	Definition
S	Specific	The focus of the objective must be clearly defined and identified.
M	Measurable	The objective must allow the buyer and supplier to measure the progress made from the start to the planned end point.
A	Achievable	The objective must be achievable. Unachievable objectives are demotivating and waste valuable resources.
R	Relevant	The objective should be a target that is relevant to the company strategy. Irrelevant objectives waste valuable resources.
T	Time bound	The objective should have a defined start and end period so that progress can be measured.

Table 3.2 Developing SMART objectives

Objectives for a buyer–supplier partnership can be short-term, but others may have a longer-term focus. The following are examples of SMART objectives.

1. In the financial year 2019/20 reduce 10% of the waste in the supply chain caused by defects.

2. Improve communications by undertaking monthly reviews of all partnership KPI data throughout 2019.

3. Work together to develop and launch one new product or service by the end of 2021.

If the buyer and supplier have a type 1 or type 2 partnership (see section 3.1), the objectives are likely to be more operational, such as those outlined in points 1 and 2 above. It is important to remember that until a buyer and supplier reach a type 3 partnership, they are unlikely to have joint strategic objectives such as the objective to launch a new product or service as described above in point 3. Note, however, that type 3 partnerships can of course also include cost reduction and operational drivers as well.

Common metrics (see section 2.3) will also be needed to develop common key performance indicators to enable the buyer and supplier to assess the performance of the partnership relationship. In type 2 each firm has its own metrics that are agreed upon jointly while in type 3 the metrics are jointly developed.

Joint planning and decision-making

Developing joint plans will also serve to develop joint commitment to the partnership, as this demonstrates that both parties are entering into the relationship for the long-term. Once the partnership has been agreed plans need to be developed and implemented to ensure that the partnership benefits materialise. This will need to include regular reviews and audits. This is discussed in more detail later in the section.

The buyer and supplier will need to jointly decide and agree an implementation plan with relevant milestones and targets and assign responsibility to individuals within each company for each of the key drivers accepted as joint goals. Tevelson et al. (2013)[42] stated that relatively few buyers inform their partners of their long-term business plans. Buyers may work with their partners to reduce costs, but the suppliers are not integrated into the buying organisation. This may be appropriate in some cases for buyers who are only pursuing a type 1 or 2 partnership. However, at this stage, commitment can also be developed if both the buyer and the supplier share their long-term business plans with each other (this is a requirement for type 3 partnerships).

Partnership planning

Toyota informs its partnership suppliers of its long-term plans. This makes it easier for suppliers to improve their designs and enhance the quality of the parts and the systems they develop for Toyota. It also allows them to minimise waste. These processes operated by Toyota are characteristic of advanced collaboration initiatives. Here Toyota is maximising the benefits that it obtains from its partnership relationships with suppliers as well as developing commitment.

(Source: Tevelson et al., 2013[43])

Case study

Remember

Joint commitment needs to be established for the partnership to be successful. If both parties are not committed to the partnership relationship then they are unlikely to provide the required resources. As a result, the anticipated benefits will not be achieved.

Benefits and resource allocation

The buyer and supplier will also need to agree how the benefits of the relationship will be shared between the parties, and how the supplier will be financially incentivised to meet its objectives. Bresnen and Marshall (2000)[44] noted that in order to generate commitment to project objectives, the sharing of gains (and losses) was seen not only as desirable but necessary.

The buyer will need to demonstrate to the supplier that it is willing to share the gains of the partnership as well as the losses. Discussions here will set the standard for trust and fairness in the view of the supplier. Both trust and fairness are important aspects of gaining commitment to any successful partnership relationship.

Where suppliers are involved in these areas the partnership will need to clearly define how any costs and profits from this project will be split between the partners. A buyer needs to ensure that the benefits offered to the supplier are significant enough to motivate it to perform and commit to the objectives and goals of the partnership relationship.

As well as the allocation of benefits, there also needs to be clear agreement on what both partners are committing to the relationship in terms of capital (finance) and resources, including staff and equipment. There should be commitment from the top management of the buyer and the supplier that these resources will be allocated to the partnership, and both parties can demonstrate their commitment by making these resources available at the commencement of the partnership.

Quick wins

Joint commitment from both parties can be further consolidated by sharing information on quick wins. These quick wins demonstrate the benefits of the partnership to both the supplier and the buyer. This approach will allow confidence and trust in the partner to build. As commitment increases, partners are more likely to allocate resources in order to gain more benefits.

Joint commitment needs to be established at an early stage in the partnership to ensure that both parties are equally supporting the objectives of the relationship.

> *Check*
> Discuss methods that a buyer can use to gain commitment from a supplier to the partnership relationship.

Reviews and audits

It is important that regular reviews of the partnership are undertaken as it develops through the implementation stages towards business as usual. Reviews are required to ensure that the effort that has been put into developing the relationship by both the buyer and the supplier is resulting in tangible benefits and improvements for both partners.

These reviews will need to be undertaken regularly and supported by a suitable governance structure, such as a **project steering committee**. This project steering committee should be made up of a cross-organisational team of senior managers from both the buyer and supplier organisation. Ideally there should be equal representation from both parties, demonstrating a true partnership approach. To obtain an objective view of the progress of the relationship, the steering committee should also include members who are independent of the partnership implementation team.

Project steering committee
A group that decides on the priorities for a project and manages the general operations of the project

The partners will need to decide how regularly partnership reviews should be undertaken, as well as what aspects of the relationship should be included in the scope of the review. For example, will progress be reviewed weekly, monthly or quarterly? Performance reviews are likely to be needed more frequently in the early days of the partnership relationship. The scope of the reviews should be defined as part of the project implementation process; for example, which data sources and KPIs will be included in the review.

Reviewing the partnership relationship is important for a number of reasons.

- The saying 'what gets measured gets done' is very true. By having key performance indicators and a formal review process the partners can focus resources on the priority areas in order to achieve the required benefits.

- Reviews will ensure that the benefits and value-added objectives are achieved within the required timescales. Is the partnership hitting the agreed key milestones? If the plans are behind schedule the review can result in remedial actions to ensure that milestones and deadlines are met.

- Documenting and celebrating success is important. Demonstrating the improvements and benefits will motivate the partners and their staff to continue to progress the partnership relationship. This may also serve to reduce or eliminate any remaining resistance in the wider organisation.

- As well as success the partners need to review what is not working so well and how this can be changed to ensure success. The risk of the partnership failing will be reduced if issues are highlighted early so that plans can be put in place to bring the partnership project back on track.

- Reviews can assess current levels of support. Does the partnership relationship require any additional support or resources at its current stage? Is this likely to change over the coming weeks and months?

- Areas for further improvement and development can be identified. McKinsey (2013)[45] notes that ideas will need to be redeveloped and refreshed throughout the collaboration. McKinsey also stated that for a partnership to grow and be sustainable there needs to be a process to generate, evaluate and prioritise new ideas.

- The process of involving both organisations in the reviews via the steering committee can also serve to support the development of trust and commitment to the partnership. Once reviews have been undertaken the findings need to be communicated to the wider business to maintain support for the partnership.

- The reviews can also be used as decision points. The review process itself will provide evidence to help the project steering committee to decide to either continue with, enhance or end the partnership. This prevents the parties from continuing to waste resources on building a relationship that is not achieving the required outcomes. These resources could be better used on more successful projects.

Reviews should be undertaken separately by each partner and also jointly. The information gained regarding what has gone well and what has not gone so well can be used by the buyer when developing further partnership relationships. This could be with the supplier they are already partnering with or with other suppliers. This would form part of a **lessons learned** process.

The process of review also links to the process of **continuous improvement**. Both the buyer and the supplier must be willing to commit to the process of continuous improvement in order to continue to gain benefits from the partnership throughout its life.

As with reviews, audits of the partnership should also be undertaken. It is important to point out that this will not be the type of financial audit that many procurement professionals will be familiar with, but will instead be a **project audit**. A project audit is a more formal process than a review and would usually be undertaken by a party that is independent of the partnership project. This independent review will support the process of gaining a true insight into how well (or poorly) the partnership relationship is developing.

Project audit

The project audit will assess the extent to which the project has complied with the governance set out by the steering committee and has met its stated aims and objectives.

There will be several benefits to undertaking an audit of the partnership relationship.

- The audit will review how the partnership is progressing against the implementation plan and the key milestones.

- It provides an overview of what has gone well and what could be improved. This will support the lessons learned process (see below).

Lessons learned
Experiences gained as part of a project that should be documented and used to improve future projects

Continuous improvement
An ongoing effort to improve products, processes and services

Project audit
A more formal process than a review; this would usually be undertaken by a party that is independent of the organisation being audited

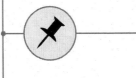

- Audits can uncover problems which can then be addressed before they derail the partnership relationship, and they can ensure that the partnership relationship is efficient and effective.

- The audit will review whether the project is complying with the governance requirements as set out by the steering committee.

- The audit will also serve to instil a sense of confidence in the management and shareholders (if applicable) that the partnership is meeting the requirements of the buying organisation.

As well as providing an overview of the above information, the audit report should also include a set of recommendations. These recommendations should be undertaken in order to ensure that the partnership project creates the maximum benefit and value-added outcomes for the partners. In order to gain the benefits of the audit process both the buyer and the supplier will need to act on the recommendations provided as part of the audit report.

As with reviews, the audit report should also outline key lessons learned. These will be useful to share with the wider organisation as they are likely to be relevant to the successful management and development of future projects. These projects could include future partnership relationships and initiatives in the business that involve change management. This will be applicable to both the buyer and the supplier.

> *Remember*
> Reviews of the partnership project should be undertaken to allow the buyer and supplier to ensure that they are receiving the expected benefits in relation to the resources allocated to the partnership relationship.

3.3 Identify the reasons why partnerships fail

Partnerships between a buyer and a supplier can fail for a variety of reasons. CIPS notes that a number of factors, both within the partner organisations or the relationship itself (intrinsic factors) and in the external environment (extrinsic factors), may hinder the progressive development of a relationship or cause problems within it. These problems could ultimately lead to the failure of the relationship.

Sima and Balan (2014)[46] stated that a partnership built or implemented incorrectly may result in additional costs and disadvantages for both the buyer and the supplier. Therefore, as discussed above, it is important to carefully manage the implementation phase to give the partnership the best chance of succeeding.

> *Check*
> Go back to section 3.1 and consider the drivers for entering a partnership.

Lambert et al[47] found two primary reasons for partnership failure; the first was that one or both partners had unrealistic expectations of what could be achieved by the partnership, and the second was that their expectations, however reasonable, were never shared with the other partner with the result that no joint plan for achieving them was ever made, with failure as the result.

Lambert et al developed the Collaboration Framework to enable organisations to share, agree, plan for, and measure the value co-created by the partnership (see figure 3.6):

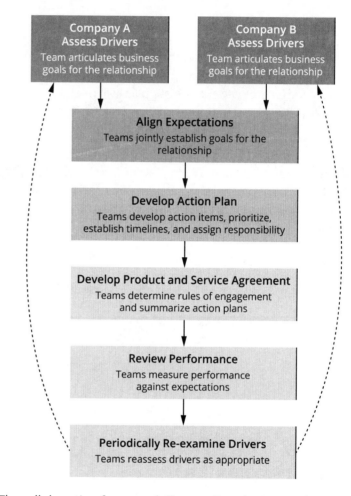

Figure 3.6 The collaboration framework (Source: Douglas M. Lambert, A. Michael Knemeyer, and John T. Gardner, Building High Performance Business Relationships, Sarasota, FL: Supply Chain Management Institute, 2010. Copyright Douglas M. Lambert. For more information about The Collaboration Framework and how it has been used to develop an 18-24 month plan for important business relationships see: www.drdouglaslambert.com)

Even after goals have been successfully recognised and agreed between the partners, there are further issues around management, communication and culture that can cause failure. Many of the issues are linked and affect each other. Poor communication can cause low levels of trust between the buyer and supplier, for example. Often there is no single reason for failure but a combination of issues, which will be discussed in this section.

Poor communication

Clear and effective communication is an important element for the success of all types of relationship, both business and personal. Oosterhuis (2009)[48] stated that communication was a basic requirement for co-operation in buyer–supplier relationships. This is particularly true in strategic relationships where the parties are highly connected.

As part of a strategic relationship, such as a partnership, the buyer and supplier must be transparent in their communications in order for the relationship to succeed. Poor communication is one of the key reasons that buyer–supplier partnerships fail. Emmett and Crocker (2006)[49] noted that both buyers and suppliers ranked poor communication as the top reason for partnership relationships failing.

Although the buyer may consider that it has communicated its message, in order for the message to be effective it must be received by the supplier. The communication cycle (figure 3.7) demonstrates that effective communication is a two-way process. Poor communication between the partners could be caused by any breakdown in the cycle.

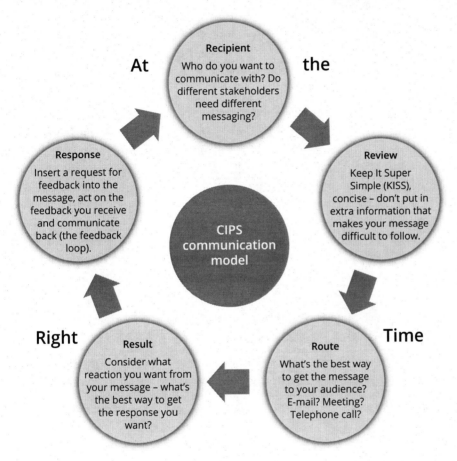

Figure 3.7 The communication cycle

> *Remember*
> Effective communication is key for the development and maintenance of any partnership relationship. Communication is required for exchanging important information, for building relationships, for persuading and for confirming requirements.

Poor communication between the buyer and supplier could be due to the presence of several common communication barriers.

- **Distortion or omission**. If information is distorted or omitted by buyer, the supplier, or both, this reduces the transparency between the companies and could also affect trust (see below).

- **Misunderstanding**. This can be the result of a lack of clarity or technical jargon.

- **Communication overload**. If too much information is provided, the important aspects of the message may be lost. Effective communication is also about limiting the content of the communication to the important points.

- **Ineffective communication**. This may mean a lack of communication skills, or use of an ineffective method of communication.

Poor communication could be an issue from the start of the partnership, or communication may deteriorate as partners become complacent. In the implementation stage, the buyer and supplier need to make sure that appropriate communication channels are in place. Forbes (2017)[50] states that for partnerships to be successful between buyer and supplier, many touchpoints need to exist between the companies. If there is only communication between the buyer and supplier with no involvement from any other staff in both businesses, then there may be a lack of information transfer between the businesses. These touchpoints will increase if the buyer and supplier relationship progresses beyond a type 1 partnership (see section 3.1).

For a successful partnership, communication is important in terms of both day-to-day informal communications and more formal, scheduled meetings and reviews. Poor formal or informal communication could cause problems within a partnership. Lambert et al. (1996)[51] note that "communication links should be across all levels of the organisations including strategic, tactical, operational, interpersonal and cultural". If one of these links is missing, then vital information may not be shared, or transparency could be affected. Although strategic communication between the leaders of the partnership initiative is important, the operational day-to-day communication is also crucial for success. It is at the operational level that the benefits of the partnership will be realised.

Communication will also involve the sharing of information that may be confidential or related to a buyer or supplier's IPR.

Poor communication can cause a multitude of issues and problems, such as those outlined below, which can feed into the reasons that partnerships may fail.

- A lack of understanding around roles and responsibilities can lead to misinterpretation of required tasks. This can result in key tasks not being undertaken, wasted time and resources, and a focus on tasks that will not bring value to the partners.

- Errors and inefficiencies can reduce the cost and profitability benefits of the partnership and could affect the company's reputation if they affect customers.

- Lack of transparency and openness can result in a lack of trust. For example, the buyer could feel that a lack of openness from a supplier was due to them trying to hide issues.

- Poor buy-in to the partnership relationship because it has not been effectively communicated to the wider business can affect commitment to the partnership project.

- Poor communication can be a source of conflict due to misunderstandings.

- If communication is poor this reduces the ability of the buyer and supplier to feed back to each other and make improvements.

Paulraj (2008)[52] stated that inter-organisational communication is a key relationship competency that can provide advantages for supply chain partners, enhancing the performance of both the buyer and supplier. If communication between partners is poor, then this will have an impact on the success of the partnership. Communication must be actively managed as part of the partnership process, for example, by putting in place a formal communications plan (see section 2.2). PwC (2013)[53] noted that in partnerships, communications plans are often not established in a structured way so that reporting lines, roles, responsibilities and communication are unclear.

> *Check*
> What partnership relationship issues can poor communication cause?

Lack of senior management support and trust

A lack of senior management support and trust can have a negative effect on a partnership relationship that can result in the failure of the partnership.

Lack of senior management support

As already discussed, buy-in and support from senior management will be crucial for the success of the partnership relationship. Sievers et al. (2015)[54] state that senior executives and management are the main influencers; it is essential that they support the vision of the partnership. If a partnership has senior management support this will filter down through the organisation. As noted previously, management techniques can be a key facilitator for the development of successful partnerships.

Senior management that have not been engaged and that resist the partnership development may seek to sabotage it. This situation may occur if stakeholder mapping and engagement has not been undertaken. PwC (2013)[55] noted that in many cases a partnership between a buyer and a supplier only involved the procurement department and the sales department, with little involvement of the wider business. This could indicate that the strategic and departmental objectives of the buying organisation are not aligned.

Lack of trust

Trust was defined in chapter 2 (see section 2.3). It can be difficult to define and measure, as it is demonstrated by the behaviour of people. Lambert et al. (1996)[56] noted that most executives intuitively knew when it existed and when it did not.

Trust is developed through clear, two-way feedback and communication between the buyer and supplier; it is developed overtime. Generally, buyers will have worked with suppliers for a number of years before developing a partnership relationship. In these cases, there is likely to be a good level of trust before entering into the partnership.

A high degree of trust between the partners is required in order for partnership relationships to be successful. Narain and Singh (2012)[57] noted that a lack of trust can affect supplier performance and ultimately the performance of the buying organisation. In a study undertaken by Brownell and Reynolds (2002)[58] trustworthiness was rated as the most important personal characteristic of a supplier for building a strong relationship.

Before entering into a partnership relationship, the buyer should engage in trust-building activities with the supplier, for example, providing assistance or involving them in early development of new products or services. Politis (2003)[59] noted that trust brought several benefits.

*   Greater creativity

*   Increased innovation

*   Increased knowledge sharing

Communication between partners, especially face-to-face communication, should support the development of trust by assisting in the development of personal relationships. The link between trust and co-operation is highlighted in figure 3.8. The graph shows that as trust increases so do levels of co-operation between a buyer and a supplier, moving from defensive win-lose situations to synergistic win-win scenarios. If partners are unable to develop trust they will continue to act defensively. This will severely reduce the benefits that buyers and suppliers are able to achieve.

If there is a lack of trust between partners this may be due to insufficient time allocated to developing business relationships at both a strategic and an operational level. Narain and Singh (2012)[60] also noted that trust could be developed by the readiness of the supplier to invest in the specific requirement of the buyer.

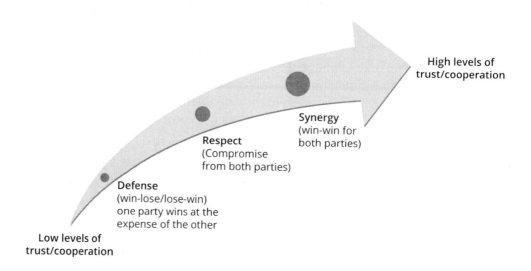

Figure 3.8 *The link between trust and co-operation*

> *Remember*
> Trust is an important aspect of any partnership relationship. Before entering into the partnership, the parties should spend time undertaking trust-building activities. There is a clear link between low levels of trust and low levels of co-operation between partners.

As the partnership develops over a period of time, so should levels of trust. However, this may not be the case. Lack of trust could occur for a number of reasons.

*   One partner may fail to share the required level of information and may behave in a way that is not transparent. This may be due to fears around increasing vulnerability.

3.3 L03

- Communication may be poor and irregular or inconsistent. Communication is an essential part of trust and relationship development (Prahinski and Benton, 2004[61]).

- There may be a lack of understanding regarding shared goals and objectives, leading to increased vulnerability (Serem et al., 2015[62]).

- One of the partners may behave opportunistically at the expense of the partnership relationship.

- One of the partners may consistently fail to meet the agreed goals and objectives of the partnership.

- A partner may disclose commercially sensitive information to a third party.

- There may be issues around payments, for example, late payments made by the buyer to the supplier.

If there is a lack of trust in the partnership relationship then the buyer and the supplier will be less willing to work together, resolve conflict and compromise to develop win-win solutions. There will also be a lack of long-term focus. Coupled with this there are likely to be increased transaction and negotiation costs, as the presence of trust in a buyer–supplier relationship can serve to reduce these costs (Madhock, 2006[63]).

Due to the shared liabilities and risks, unethical or illegal practices by one of the parties could have serious repercussions for the other party. If the partnership has been characterised by a lack of trust the parties may not have shared a significant amount of knowledge with each other. This may have resulted in a lack of benefits for both parties.

Obviously, trust is a very important element of a successful partnership relationship.

Lack of commitment by one or both partners

Entering into a type 2 and type 3 partnership is a commitment to developing longer-term and more strategic relationships. When commitment is present there are various benefits including efficiency, productivity and effectiveness (Mugarura, 2010[64]). Serem et al. (2015)[65] state that a buyer in a committed relationship will receive more relevant on-time market data and product information, as well as a more efficient service.

Partnerships cannot succeed if there is not a high enough level of **commitment** from both the buyer and the supplier. A number of studies have highlighted that there is a strong link between commitment and the continuation of a relationship (Mugarura, 2010[66]). If there is a lack of commitment by a partner they will be less motivated and will put less effort into maintaining the partnership relationship due to a belief that the relationship is not worth maintaining.

A lack of commitment suggests the partner views the relationship as transactional rather than strategic. Ross et al. (1997)[67] suggests that the commitment of a supply partner is based on its perception of the commitment of the buyer. Therefore, if a buyer demonstrates low commitment to a relationship, a supplier is likely to do the same. Conversely, if a buyer demonstrates high commitment, so will the supplier. Commitment to the partnership can be demonstrated in various ways such as providing sufficient staff resource, equipment and finance. If either the buyer or the supplier is not committing sufficient resources to the relationship, this can demonstrate a lack of commitment to the other partner.

Commitment
Willingness to dedicate financial and non-financial resources to a project

In order for the partnership to work, both the buying organisation and the supplier need to contribute. If there is a perception of an unequal level of commitment, the partnership is more likely to fail. This is because a perception of unequal commitment can lead to conflict, unrealised benefits and a lack of trust between the partners.

Lack of commitment to the partnership could be the result of a number of issues.

- The buyer and supplier do not demonstrate to each other that they are committed to the partnership, perhaps by not dedicating the agreed resources to the partnership.

- The buyer has not done enough research around supplier preferencing and has chosen the wrong supplier to partner with. As a result, the supplier is not committed to the partnership.

- Senior management lacks commitment to the partnership, on the buyer or supplier side, or both. Lack of commitment from senior management may also affect the commitment from the wider business. As a result, insufficient resources are allocated to the development of the partnership.

- There is a lack of joint decision-making. This will be an issue for the buyer and supplier trying to develop type 3 style partnerships.

- There is a lack of supplier involvement in developing objectives and key performance indicators for the partnership. Involving a supplier in this phase would generally lead to a higher level of commitment to meet these targets and goals.

- The supplier or the buyer may have been tempted away from the partnership by short-term gain and value-added benefits elsewhere. For example, another customer may suddenly become more attractive and profitable to the supplier.

Overtime the commitment to the relationship may be reduced if both parties are not actively working to manage the relationship.

The three different types of partnership were discussed in section 3.1. As a partnership moves from type 1 to type 3, the required levels of commitment from both the buyer and the supplier will increase. Therefore, buyers need to consider a supplier's current level of commitment before they move to the next stage. If there is insufficient commitment a partnership that was previously working well could fail.

> *Remember*
> Lack of commitment to a partnership relationship could be a result of several issues, including the buyer choosing the wrong supplier, a lack of commitment from senior members of staff, insufficient resources being allocated, and suppliers not being involved in objective setting or decision-making.

Poor planning

Planning is an important aspect of any successful procurement strategy, including partnership development. The buyer should develop a partnership plan document in collaboration with other departments such as operations, finance and legal. The plan should also form part of the business case for undertaking the partnership relationship, identifying key milestones and required resources. If the partnership is not fully planned then the buying organisation may miss out on valuable benefits. Once the partnership has been approved by senior management the supplier should also be involved in the planning process.

When developing a supplier partnership, a buyer can take either a strategic or a reactive approach. There are obvious benefits to undertaking a strategic approach to partnering including having the time to develop synergy in terms of vision, mission and objectives in order to be culturally compatible. This is likely to result in greater value and benefits. However, in some cases a buyer may have to take a reactive approach, due to a sudden change in the marketplace, for example. If a reactive approach is used, then there may be little time for planning as the buyer could be responding to an unforeseen event. In these cases, the plan may have to be developed quickly and modified as implementation progresses. However, if a strategic approach is used then the buyer should develop a formal, detailed plan for implementing the partnership.

Partnerships may fail due to poor planning. Planning a partnership involves a number of key steps that should be linked to a clear timeline with milestones. The following list shows what a plan for developing a partnership might include and why the partnership may fail if this plan is not in place.

1. Procurement with other key business functions should undertake product/service segmentation and supplier preferencing to ensure that the correct supplier(s) are targeted for partnership development. If this part of the planning stage is not undertaken the buyer could end up partnering with the wrong supplier, which would lead to failure. We also need to recognise the importance of engaging with our key stakeholders in this process as if undertaken purely by the procurement function it can be difficult to get buy-in after the fact.

2. Develop a cross-organisational team to manage the planning and partnership process, as discussed above. Having a cross-organisational team will ensure that the partnership meets the objectives of key internal stakeholders.

3. Outline the objectives and goals that the buying organisation has for the partnership and ensure that these are in line with the overall strategy and mission of the organisation. If the partnership does not meet the needs of the wider business, it will not be successful.

4. Develop a business case and present this to senior management in order to gain approval for the approach and support for the partnership. If the partnership is not supported by the senior management of the buying organisation it is likely to fail.

5. Undertake a stakeholder mapping exercise. Procurement will need to map the stakeholders and develop a communication plan for the different types of stakeholder. Identifying any potential resistance will support the implementation plan. If resistance is not identified and managed and there is no support from the wider business the partnership could fail.

6. Undertake the required due diligence including credit checks and an audit of supplier premises. If the buyer selects a partner that is financially unstable or involved in unethical business practices, then there could be serious repercussions for the buying organisation.

7. Develop any required contracts or non-disclosure agreements (NDAs) to protect confidential data and IPR. If these are not in place the buyer and supplier may be reluctant to share knowledge and information. If this is not shared the benefits of the partnership could be reduced.

8. Undertake joint objective and goal planning with the supplier, using the partnership model, and collaboration framework. These objectives and

goals should then be developed into performance measurements for the partnership. They will then need to be monitored and evaluated at regular intervals to check progress and assess whether it is beneficial for the buyer to continue with the partnership. If there are no clear objectives the partners may be wasting effort on unimportant tasks and initiatives.

9. Identify resources from both the buyer and supplier for the implementation of the partnership. This could include both staff and financial resources. If adequate resources are not committed by both parties the partnership could fail.

10. Develop a communications plan that sits alongside the main plan, stating the methods of communication and how often formal communication will occur. If communication is poor this could affect the development of trust between the partners, which could result in the failure of the partnership.

11. Assess whether any IT systems integration is required. This can often be more costly and time consuming than anticipated.

12. Once the partnership is in place planning will also need to be undertaken regarding operational activities to ensure that both partners are working towards the achievement of the agreed objectives.

Apply
Think about any partnership relationships that your organisation has entered into. Were these partnership relationships fully planned?

If any of these stages are not undertaken fully or are missed out, the buyer–supplier partnership may fail due to implementation and operational planning issues. If there is no implementation plan or future long-term plan, then there is likely to be a lack of focus on the key tasks that need to be undertaken.

If a clear plan for the implementation and operational management of the partnership has not been developed and agreed by both partners this could also result in unclear roles and responsibilities. If roles and responsibilities are unclear, tasks may not be undertaken and there could be delays. This could also cause conflict between the buyer and supplier. If there is conflict in a partnership that cannot be resolved this could result in the failure of the partnership. Therefore, it is clear that failing to plan, or having a poor plan, can ultimately cause the failure of a buyer–supplier partnership.

Check
List the key stages that should be included in a plan to develop a partnership relationship with a strategic supplier.

Value-added benefits
Enhancements that a supplier makes to a product or service before sale to the buyer. This could include features at no extra cost, extended warranty periods or services such as product training

Lack of value-added benefit

The ability to gain **value-added benefits** for the buying organisation is one of the main reasons that the buyer enters into a partnership relationship with a supplier. If a partnership is not bringing the expected levels of value-added benefit either party may consider the relationship a failure and decide to end the partnership.

As discussed in chapters 1 and 2, more collaborative forms of supplier relationship such as partnerships or strategic alliances, similar to type 3 partnerships, are time intensive and require more resources to develop than more traditional approaches such as adversarial or arm's-length relationships. It is necessary for partnership relationships to demonstrate that they are bringing value and benefits to the buying organisation when compared to the resources spent developing the relationship. If there is a lack of value-added benefits these resources can be better deployed on other projects and tasks.

The expected level of value-added benefits from the partnership may not materialise due to a number of reasons.

- The buyer may have selected the wrong supply partner. This could be due to a lack of due diligence undertaken in the early stages of the partnership. The supplier may be the wrong partner for a number of reasons, including cultural fit and quality of supply.

- After a period of time of working together, one or both of the partners may have become complacent. This could affect the value-added benefits that the partnership is able to achieve.

- Since the partnership was developed the market may have changed, which may have eroded the value-added benefit that the supplier is able to offer a buyer. For example, if demand for the supplier's product reduces and it is facing financial difficulties, it may be forced to start charging a buyer for services the buyer has previously not paid for. The effect of market change is discussed further in 'Changes in the market' below.

- The relationship is not being actively managed and measured. The ability to measure value-added benefits is key if both the buyer and the supplier are to understand whether the partnership relationship is bringing benefits to their companies. Therefore, issues could be caused not by a lack of benefits, but by a lack of joint performance measurement.

- Lack of value-added benefits could also be caused by the buyer expecting unrealistic levels of value-added benefits. When entering into a partnership, both parties need to be clear on their expectations and have access to good financial data for measuring.

Case study

Partnership failure

Partnership failure can have serious repercussions for a business. An example is Phones 4u and the breakdown of its relationship with both EE and Vodafone (network partners), which decided to withdraw supply. Following the supplier relationship failure, Phones 4u went into administration. Until this point the company had been making profits of over £100 million per year. It has been suggested that this was the result of Phones 4u driving a hard bargain and therefore valuing short-term gain over the benefits of a long-term partnership relationship with its network providers.

(Source: www.cips.org/supply-management/news/2014/september/phones-4u-collapse-classic-example-of-supplier-relationship-breakdown/)

Before entering into a partnership, it is key that the buyer and supplier develop a joint value-sharing model. This model will define both the financial and non-financial benefits expected from the collaboration. The model will also detail how these benefits will be split between the partners. If a partner perceives that the model does not offer a fair share of the benefits and value added, then they will be less likely to show commitment to the partnership and this could cause the partnership to fail.

Lack of value-added benefits can also cause conflict between the parties if the expected benefits are not achieved. Emmett and Crocker (2006)[68] noted that a supplier saw a lack of benefits and risk sharing as a more important reason for ending partnerships than a buyer did. This conflict around value-added benefits may ultimately end the partnership.

Huxham and Vangen (2013)[69] discuss the concept of collaborative inertia. This refers to a situation when the apparent output from collaboration is considerably less than expected. A buyer needs to look out for collaborative inertia. Although a partnership relationship may have been successful for many years, if the relationship is no longer providing benefits it may be time to draw it to a close.

> *Remember*
> Buyers and suppliers enter into partnerships in order to achieve benefits. Value-added benefits are one aspect of this. If the buyer is not gaining tangible benefits then the resources that are being used to create and maintain the partnership relationship could be deployed more effectively elsewhere.

Changes in the market

The external environment can have a big impact on a buyer and supplier, and this can be positive or negative, i.e. create opportunities and/or threats. The marketplace that a buyer and supplier operate in is a key feature of their external environment. Both a buyer and supplier should be constantly monitoring their external environment including the marketplace for threats and risks as well as opportunities. This can be done by undertaking a STEEPLE analysis regularly (see section 1.3). Once the buyer and supplier have entered into a partnership this type of analysis should be undertaken jointly and updated regularly.

Changes in the marketplace are often caused by changes in customer behaviour. In today's modern world, technology and globalisation mean that markets are changing faster than ever before. Shorter product life cycles due to changing markets and the effect of disruptive technologies were discussed in section 1.3.

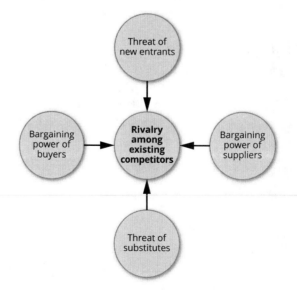

Figure 3.9 Porter's Five Forces model (Source: Porter, M.E. (1980[70]). Competitive Strategy: Techniques for Analysing Industries & Competitors. The Free Press, NY)

The structure of the external marketplace was covered in section 3.1. As noted by Emmett and Crocker (2006)[71], the external environment is made up of a number of factors.

- External elements – the STEEPLE factors: Social aspects, Technology, the Economy, the natural Environment, Politics, the Law and Ethics

- Levels of demand for the supplier – for example, reduced demand could have a negative effect on supplier profitability and survival, while increased demand could pose a problem if a supplier has no additional capacity

- Supply base of the buyer – how many suppliers are available in the market?

- The buyer and supplier – how the buyer and supplier interact in the marketplace before entering into a partnership relationship

- The partnership itself – what effect does the partnership have on the marketplace?

Table 3.3 provides some examples of each of the above bullet points (this table is not exhaustive).

Area of the market	Example of change
External	<ul><li>The economy enters a recession period.</li><li>A new technology enters the marketplace.</li><li>There is a natural disaster in the country where the supplier is based.</li><li>Import and export tariffs change.</li></ul>
Levels of demand for the supplier	<ul><li>A new buyer enters the marketplace and it is a more profitable customer for the supplier. This could increase the power of the supplier.</li><li>A key buyer exits the marketplace. This would make the partnership buyer a more important customer.</li><li>Levels of demand from buyers in the market increase or decrease.</li></ul>
Supply base of the buyer	<ul><li>New suppliers enter the marketplace and they are able to offer the buyer greater business benefits than their current partnership relationship. This could increase the power of the buyer.</li><li>A previous supplier leaves the marketplace. This would make the partnership supplier a more important supplier.</li><li>Levels of supply in the market increase or decrease.</li></ul>

Area of the market	Example of change
The buyer and supplier	• Strategic intent, e.g., exploiting competitors' weaknesses or expanding into global markets. • Strategic match, e.g., using JIT or TQM. • The buyer or the supplier gains more power in the marketplace.
The partnership relationship itself	• Performance problems. • Change of key personnel.

Table 3.3 The effect of market changes on buyer–supplier relationships (Source: adapted from Emmett and Crocker, 2006[72])

> " *Changes in any environment component can affect the expectations or perceptions of performance. They require adjustment by the buyer, the supplier or both to maintain a viable relationship.* "

(Source: Emmett and Crocker, 2006[73])

As noted by Emmett and Crocker, changes in the marketplace may result in the partnership no longer being viable. For example, a disruptive technology enters the market and changes consumer or buyer behaviour. Examples of this include Airbnb and Uber. As a result, the buyer no longer has a requirement for the supplier's product or service. The market changes could also result in one or other of the partners changing its long-term strategy for the business and therefore its requirement to maintain the partnership relationship.

Changes in the marketplace could also change the balance of power between the buyer and the supplier. This could result in conflict which could negatively affect the partnership relationship. However, changes in the marketplace could also create drivers for a buyer and supplier to enter into a partnership agreement. This could include a buyer and a supplier partnering to develop a new product faster than their competitors can.

Corporate cultural differences

Culture
The shared values, practices and beliefs within an organisation that determine how its procedures are carried out and how it is run overall

Partnership relationships are more likely to fail if the business **cultures** of the buyer and the supplier are incompatible. For a partnership to be successful, a buyer should partner with suppliers that have compatible values and cultures.

> " *The more similar the culture and objectives, the more comfortable the partners are likely to feel and the higher the chance of partnership success.* "

(Source: Lambert et al., 1996[74])

3.3 L03

The compatibility of cultures should be considered by both parties before they enter into the partnership relationship. Note, this is one of the facilitators in the partnership model.

Before discussing cultural issues and where culture can have a negative effect on business partnerships, we will discuss the types of business culture that may exist within the buyer and supplier companies (see table 3.4). This is important, as there are some business cultures that will generally not work well together. Incompatible cultures are a reason why partnerships can fail.

Handy's Cultural Type	Cultural Feature	Leadership Style
POWER	• Controlled by an individual • Agile decisions	Autocratic
ROLE	• Well-defined structure • Organisational authority	Autocratic or Paternalistic
TASK	• Matrix organisation • Cross Functional teams	Paternalistic or Democratic
PERSON	• Individual experts • Flat organisation chart	Democratic

Table 3.4 Charles Handy's four types of organisational culture

Table 3.4 provides examples of cultures that would not work well together in a partnership relationship, such as an aggressive culture and a laid-back culture, or a bureaucratic culture and a laid-back culture. Some of these cultures, like aggressive and dominating, are only going to be able to develop the type of relationships located on the left of the relationship spectrum (see section 1.1). In order to avoid partnering with a supplier that has an incompatible culture, the buyer should spend time developing relationships with the supplier before entering a partnership, for example by working closely on key projects. Cultural conflict makes it harder to achieve drivers but not impossible which is why facilitators and drivers jointly determine partnership type.

> *Remember*
> There are several types of corporate culture, including bureaucratic, paternalistic, aggressive, laid-back and dominating. Ideally, in order for a buyer–supplier partnership to work, the companies will have compatible cultures.

As already discussed, before entering a partnership the buyer and supplier should have developed a joint vision and strategy and assessed whether they have a compatible vision and culture. If this has not been done, the objectives and goals of each of the partners may not have been aligned. If the buyer and supplier are not working towards the same objectives the opportunity to deliver value for the companies will be reduced. This could have been caused by buyers and suppliers jumping into partnership relationships before they have undertaken due diligence. As discussed above there is a need to spend time working with the other party to assess whether there are synergies between the two businesses. If the buyer and supplier have significantly different business values and cultures this will affect the ability of the partnership to create a joint vision.

Partnership failure could also be caused by a change to the culture of either the buyer or the supplier. This could be linked to changes in the leadership of either of the businesses.

Lambert et al. (1996)[75] discuss the need for the presence of facilitators, which are the aspects of a company's culture that allow a partnership relationship to grow and strengthen. These facilitators cannot be developed in the short term. They either exist or they do not. Examples of these facilitators include corporate compatibility and similar management techniques which link strongly to the culture of a business.

McKinsey (2013)[76] notes that to avoid failure in buyer–supplier collaborations, the buyer should try to understand whether it has the internal capabilities and strategic alignment to make the collaboration a success. These factors are linked to culture. This includes reviewing whether the business has the type of skills required to develop a partnership relationship. The skills could include knowledge of value-sharing models and strategic supply chain practices such as Lean and just in time. They will also include the softer skills involved in relationship development such as negotiating, communication and influencing skills.

Logistics and distance barriers

Offshoring
The relocation of business, processes, for example, a customer service call centre or the manufacturing of a product, to a country where the costs of production are lower. Usually this country will be located overseas

Due to improvements in communications technology and transportation, global sourcing and **offshoring** are increasing in popularity. Buyers are entering partnership relationships with foreign suppliers in order to reduce costs. For example, lower labour costs in countries such as China and India make the costs of producing the same products there far lower than they are in the UK. This is a significant driver of partnering with suppliers in low-cost countries.

Ellram (1991)[77] noted that relationships with a supplier located geographically far away from the buyer were more complex and required additional effort and attention in order to be successful. When entering into partnerships with suppliers who are located geographically far away, partnerships may fail if the supplier has underestimated these additional challenges and complexities.

Logistics

Before entering into a partnership, the buyer needs to research the logistics process to assess whether it is viable and cost effective. Transporting goods from other countries will not only include the cost of the transportation method but also duties and taxes. The buyer will need to have strong supply chain management skills due to increased complexity and risk.

Being geographically far away also increases the possible risks in the transportation process. Products could be delivered late due to delayed transportation, so the logistics process is slower. In more serious circumstances a natural disaster in one part of the world could prevent the delivery of products in the short term. Complexity is also added; for example, the complicated nature of international shipping procedures and documentation.

In addition to increased transport costs and potential delays or non-delivery, the buyer may also have to consider making changes to packaging to ensure the products arrive in good condition. The need for this will vary depending on the nature of the products being supplied. If all of these logistical considerations have not been researched and planned for, the relationship between the buyer and supplier could fail. One reason for this could be unanticipated logistics costs eroding the financial benefit of entering into the partnership. In addition to this, if the logistics risks are not being jointly managed and shared, there could be conflict such as agreeing on who will pay any additional logistics fees due to delays.

Distance barriers

Being located physically near to a supply partner would serve to enhance the relationship as the distance barriers would be reduced. As discussed above, developing a partnership relationship takes a significant amount of resources and effort, and if partners are located in different countries the levels of effort and resources required will be increased.

Physical distance also often results in cultural distances. Lucas (2006)[78] states that cultural distance can negatively affect knowledge transfer, which is a key benefit of entering into a partnership relationship. Distance barriers make developing these relationships more difficult and more costly due to the requirement to travel.

There are a couple of distance barriers to take into consideration.

- **Time differences**. This can make it difficult to arrange meetings. For example, the time difference between the UK and Hong Kong in UK summer time is seven hours. Therefore, unless teleconferences are arranged for early in the UK working day, the buyer and supplier will be unable to speak to each other. This could result in delays in the transfer of important information and knowledge. Communication is key to partnership success, and time differences can have a negative effect on that.

- **Physical distance**. Depending on where in the world the supplier is, if the parties want to meet face to face there will be additional travel and time costs. These costs will increase the further away the supplier is from the buyer.

Where partners are located near to each other they will often meet in person to discuss objectives, actions and progress and is in fact one of the **Facilitator-points** evaluated. During these interactions personal relationships will be developed between the partners which will support the development of the partnership and the levels of trust between the buyer and supplier. Drolet and Morris (2000)[79] noted that face-to-face contact supports the development of rapport and helps negotiators to co-ordinate their responses. Without this both the buyer and supplier will have to work harder to reach any agreement.

It is more difficult to exercise control when there are distance barriers, such as undertaking unannounced audits or spot audits to ensure the correct quality processes are being followed, if the supplier is located geographically far away from the buyer. If the buyer is unaware of issues like the use of child labour it could face reputational damage.

> *Remember*
> There are a number of distance barriers including time differences and physical distances. Both of these factors can make managing a buyer–supplier partnership difficult.

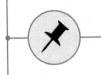

The importance of communication for a successful partnership has already been discussed. If there are physical distance barriers between a buyer and a supplier there are also likely to be language and cultural barriers. These issued can be both technical and behavioural.

- **Technical difficulties**. There are likely to be issues relating to having a clear understanding what is being offered and accepted as part of the partnership relationship. This could include issues such as technical specifications, pricing and terms and conditions. If there are misunderstandings, then a buyer could potentially overestimate the benefits of entering the relationship with the supplier. Misunderstandings can also cause conflict, which could result in the failure of the partnership.

- **Behavioural difficulties**. This relates to culture, and how people interact with each other and form productive and beneficial business relationships. For example, business behaviour in the UK involves shaking hands when you meet, but this may be different for business practices in other countries. In some countries physical contact in this way may be offensive. In Japan there is a greater link between social and business relations and the practice of avoiding a direct 'no'. If buyers are not aware of these cultural differences, there could be issues with developing trust and working relationships.

Failure due to logistics and distance barriers may also occur due to a lack of up-front preparation by the buyer. This preparation should be undertaken as part of the planning phase of the implementation of the partnership, which was discussed above.

Chapter Summary

This chapter has looked at the partnership relationships a buyer might enter into with a supplier. First, the types of situations in which a buyer may wish to develop a partnership relationship with a supplier were considered, for example, where there are a high number of drivers or products and services are high value and/or high risk. Following this, the successful implementation of partnership relationships was discussed. The final section covered the reasons why partnership relationships might fail, including poor planning, lack of trust and senior management support, and poor communication.

End of Chapter Assessment

DESCRIBE

1 Describe the three types of partnership relationship that a buyer and a supplier could choose.

EXPLAIN

2 Explain two of the benefits gained by the buyer and supplier from engaging in a partnership style relationship.

IDENTIFY

3 Identify how many stages the Kotter's model of business change has.

DESCRIBE

4 Describe two key reasons why a buyer–supplier partnership might fail.

References

1 Lambert, D. M., Emmelhainz, M. A. and Gardner, J. T. (1996), "Developing and implementing supply chain partnerships", *The International Journal of Logistics Management*, Volume 7, Issue 2, pp. 1–18

2 Ibid.

3 Ibid.

4 Ibid.

5 Ibid.

6 Ibid.

7 Ibid.

8 Ibid.

9 Serem, W., Chepkwony, J. and Bor, J. (2015), "Buyer-supplier relationship and firm's procurement performance: evidence from Kenya medium and large scale enterprises", *International Journal of Economics, Commerce and Management* Volume 3, Issue 6, pp. 416–430

10 Lambert, D. M., Emmelhainz, M. A. and Gardner, J. T. (1996), "Developing and implementing supply chain partnerships", *The International Journal of Logistics Management*, Volume 7, Issue 2, pp. 1–18

11 Ibid.

12 Kanter, R. M. (1994), "Collaborative Advantage: The Art of Alliances", *Harvard Business Review*, Vol 72, No 4 (July-August 1994), pp. 96-108

13 Brownell, J. and Reynolds, D. (2002), "Actions that Make a Difference: Strengthening the F&B Purchaser–Supplier Partnership", *Cornell Hotel and Restaurant Administration Quarterly*, Volume 43, Issue 6, pp. 49–61

14 Lambert, D. M., Emmelhainz, M. A. and Gardner, J. T. (1996), "Developing and implementing supply chain partnerships", *The International Journal of Logistics Management*, Volume 7, Issue 2, pp. 1–18

15 Ibid.

16 Noor, J. (2013) *The power of successful supplier collaboration* [online]. Retrieved from: www.mckinsey.com/practice-clients/operations/the-power-of-successful-supplier-collaboration

17 The Partnering Initiative (2018), *The benefits and risks of partnering* [online]. Retrieved from: thepartneringinitiative.org/about-us/philosophy-and-approach/the-benefits-and-risks-of-partnering/

18 Ryu, S., Park, J. E. and Min, S. (2007), "Factors of determining long-term orientation in interfirm relationships", *Journal of Business Research*, Volume 60, Issue 12, pp. 1225–1233

19 Srinivasan, M., Mukherjee, D. and Gaur, A. S. (2011), "Buyer–supplier partnership quality and supply chain performance: Moderating role of risks, and environmental uncertainty", *European Management Journal*, Volume 29, Issue 4, pp. 260–271

20 Ramsay, J. (1996), "The case against purchasing partnerships", *International Journal of Purchasing and Materials Management*, Volume 32, Issue 3, pp. 13–19

21 Skjøtt-Larsen, T., Schary, P. B., Kotzab, H. and Mikkola, J. H. (2007), *Managing the Global Supply Chain*, Copenhagen Business School Press DK

22 Van der Vaart, T. and van Donk, D. P. (2008), "A critical review of survey-based research in supply chain integration", *International Journal of Production Economics*, Volume 111, Issue 1, pp. 42–55

23 Nazli Wasti, S., Kamil Kozan, M. and Kuman, A. (2006), "Buyer-supplier relationships in the Turkish automotive industry", *International Journal of Operations & Production Management*, Volume 26, Issue 9, pp. 947–970

24 Srinivasan, M., Mukherjee, D. and Gaur, A. S. (2011), "Buyer–supplier partnership quality and supply chain performance: Moderating role of risks, and environmental uncertainty", *European Management Journal*, Volume 29, Issue 4, pp. 260–271

25 Lambert, D. M., Emmelhainz, M. A. and Gardner, J. T. (1996), "Developing and implementing supply chain partnerships", *The International Journal of Logistics Management*, Volume 7, Issue 2, pp. 1–18

26 Eben, C. (2018), *Six tips for developing successful strategic partnerships* [online]. Retrieved from: www.theglobeandmail.com/report-on-business/small-business/sb-managing/six-tips-for-creating-successful-strategic-partnerships/article17665250

27 Ibid.

28 Cousins, P., Lamming, R., Lawson, B. and Squire, B. (2008), *Strategic supply management: principles, theories and practice*. Harlow: Pearson Education

29 PwC (2013), *Supplier relationship management* [online]. Retrieved from: www.pwc.nl/nl/assets/documents/pwc-supplier-relationship-management.pdf

30 Cousins, P., Lamming, R., Lawson, B. and Squire, B. (2008), *Strategic Supply Management: Principles, Theories and Practice*. Harlow: Pearson Education

31 Ibid.

32 Tevelson, R., Alsén, A., Rosenfeld, P., Benett, S., Farrell, P. and Zygelman, J. (2013), "Buyer-supplier collaboration", *BCG Perspectives*, pp. 1–7

33 Lambert, D. M., Emmelhainz, M. A. and Gardner, J. T. (1996), "Developing and implementing supply chain partnerships", *The International Journal of Logistics Management*, Volume 7, Issue 2, pp. 1–18

34 Sima, E. and Balam, G. (2014), "The use of partnership in purchasing", *Annals of the University of Petrosani, Economics,* Volume 14, Issue 2, pp. 245–252

35 Cousins, P., Lamming, R., Lawson, B. and Squire, B. (2008), *Strategic Supply Management: Principles, Theories and Practice*. Harlow: Pearson Education

36 Webb, J. (2017), *47% of supplier collaborations fail: Build trust or expect failure* [online]. Retrieved from: www.forbes.com/sites/jwebb/2017/08/30/47-of-supplier-collaborations-fail-build-trust-or-expect-failure

37 Emmett, S. and Crocker, B. (2006), *The Relationship-Driven Supply Chain*. Aldershot: Gower

38 Lambert, D. M., Emmelhainz, M. A. and Gardner, J. T. (1996), "Developing and implementing supply chain partnerships", *The International Journal of Logistics Management*, Volume 7, Issue 2, pp. 1–18

39 Sima, E. and Balam, G. (2014), "The use of partnership in purchasing", *Annals of the University of Petrosani, Economics,* Volume 14, Issue 2, pp. 245–252

40 Carter, J. R., Smeltzer, L. and Narasimhan, R. (1998), "The role of buyer and supplier relationships in integrating TQM through the supply chain", *European Journal of Purchasing & Supply Management*, Volume 4, Issue 4, pp. 223–234

41 Tevelson, R., Alsén, A., Rosenfeld, P., Benett, S., Farrell, P. and Zygelman, J. (2013), "Buyer-supplier collaboration", *BCG Perspectives*, pp. 1–7

42 Ibid.

43 Ibid.

44 Bresnen, M. and Marshall, N. (2000), "Motivation, commitment and the use of incentives in partnerships and alliances", *Construction Management & Economics*, Volume 18, Issue 5, pp. 587–598

45 Noor, J. (2013) *The power of successful supplier collaboration* [online]. Retrieved from: www.mckinsey.com/practice-clients/operations/the-power-of-successful-supplier-collaboration

46 Sima, E. and Balam, G. (2014), "The use of partnership in purchasing", *Annals of the University of Petrosani, Economics,* Volume 14, Issue 2, pp. 245–252

47 Douglas M. Lambert, A. Michael Knemeyer, and John T. Gardner, *Building High Performance Business Relationships*, Sarasota, FL: Supply Chain Management Institute, 2010

48 Oosterhuis, M. (2009), "Communication in buyer-supplier relationships", University of Groningen

49 Emmett, S. and Crocker, B. (2006), *The Relationship-Driven Supply Chain*. Aldershot: Gower

50 Webb, J. (2017), *47% of supplier collaborations fail: Build trust or expect failure* [online]. Retrieved from: www.forbes.com/sites/jwebb/2017/08/30/47-of-supplier-collaborations-fail-build-trust-or-expect-failure

51 Lambert, D. M., Emmelhainz, M. A. and Gardner, J. T. (1996), "Developing and implementing supply chain partnerships", *The International Journal of Logistics Management*, Volume 7, Issue 2, pp. 1–18

52 Paulraj, A., Lado, A. A. and Chen, I. J. (2008), "Inter-organizational communication as a relational competency: Antecedents and performance outcomes in collaborative buyer–supplier relationships", *Journal of Operations Management*, Volume 26, Issue 1, pp. 45–64

53 PwC (2013), *Supplier relationship management* [online]. Retrieved from: www.pwc.nl/nl/assets/documents/pwc-supplier-relationship-management.pdf

54 Sievers, J., Rossiter, L., Roush, W., Beedle, C., Smidt, M., Schnabel, M., Nicolaus, K., Mitchell, T., Miller, L., Rogers, J. and Koopman, Z. (2015), "ISU On-Farm Cooperator Trials: Relationships and Partnerships–2015", *Farm Progress Reports*, Volume 2015, Issue 1

55 PwC (2013), *Supplier relationship management* [online]. Retrieved from: www.pwc.nl/nl/assets/documents/pwc-supplier-relationship-management.pdf

56 Lambert, D. M., Emmelhainz, M. A. and Gardner, J. T. (1996), "Developing and implementing supply chain partnerships", *The International Journal of Logistics Management*, Volume 7, Issue 2, pp. 1–18

57 Narain, R. and Singh, A. (2012), "Role of buyer-supplier relationship and trust in organizational performance", *Delhi Business Review*, Volume 13, Issue 2, p. 73

58 Brownell, J. and Reynolds, D. (2002), "Actions that make a difference: strengthening the F&B purchaser–supplier partnership", *Cornell Hotel and Restaurant Administration Quarterly*, Volume 43, Issue 6, pp. 49–61

59 Politis, J. D., (2003), "The connection between trust and knowledge management: what are its implications for team performance", *Journal of Knowledge Management*, Volume 7, Issue 5, pp. 55–66

60 Narain, R. and Singh, A. (2012), "Role of buyer-supplier relationship and trust in organizational performance", *Delhi Business Review*, Volume 13, Issue 2, p. 73

61 Prahinski, C. and Benton, W. C. (2004), "Supplier evaluations: communication strategies to improve supplier performance", *Journal of Operations Management*, Volume 22, Issue 1, pp. 39–62

62 Serem, W., Chepkwony, J. and Bor, J. (2015), "Buyer-supplier relationship and firm's procurement performance: evidence from Kenya medium and large scale enterprises", *International Journal of Economics, Commerce and Management* Volume 3, Issue 6, pp. 416–430

63 Madhok, A. (2006), "How much does ownership really matter? Equity and trust relations in joint venture relationships", *Journal of International Business Studies*, Volume 37, Issue 1, pp. 4–11

64 Mugarura, J. T., Ntayi, D. J. and Muhwezi, D. M. (2010), *Buyer-supplier collaboration, adaptation, trust, commitment and relationship continuity of selected private manufacturing firms in Kampala. A masters dissertation,* Makerere University Business School

65 Serem, W., Chepkwony, J. and Bor, J. (2015), "Buyer-supplier relationship and firm's procurement performance: evidence from Kenya medium and large scale enterprises", *International Journal of Economics, Commerce and Management* Volume 3, Issue 6, pp. 416–430

66 Mugarura, J. T., Ntayi, D. J. and Muhwezi, D. M. (2010), *Buyer-supplier collaboration, adaptation, trust, commitment and relationship continuity of selected private manufacturing firms in Kampala. A masters dissertation,* Makerere University Business School

67 Ross Jr, W. T., Anderson, E. and Weitz, B. (1997), "Performance in principal-agent dyads: the causes and consequences of perceived asymmetry of commitment to the relationship", *Management Science*, Volume 43, Issue 5, pp. 680–704

68 Emmett, S. and Crocker, B. (2006), *The Relationship-Driven Supply Chain*. Aldershot: Gower

69 Huxham, C. and Vangen, S. (2013), *Managing to collaborate: The Theory and Practice of Collaborative Advantage*. Abingdon: Routledge

70 Porter, M. E. (1980), *Competitive Strategy: Techniques for Analysing Industries & Competitors*. New York: The Free Press

71 Emmett, S. and Crocker, B. (2006), *The Relationship-Driven Supply Chain*. Aldershot: Gower

72 Ibid.

73 Ibid.

74 Lambert, D. M., Emmelhainz, M. A. and Gardner, J. T. (1996), "Developing and implementing supply chain partnerships", *The International Journal of Logistics management*, Volume 7, Issue 2, pp. 1–18

75 Lambert, D. M., Emmelhainz, M. A. and Gardner, J. T. (1996), "Developing and implementing supply chain partnerships", *The International Journal of Logistics management*, Volume 7, Issue 2, pp. 1–18

76 Noor, J. (2013) *The power of successful supplier collaboration* [online]. Retrieved from: www.mckinsey.com/practice-clients/operations/the-power-of-successful-supplier-collaboration

77 Ellram, L. M. (1991), "A managerial guideline for the development and implementation of purchasing partnerships", *International Journal of Purchasing and Materials Management*, Volume 27, Issue 3, pp. 2–8

78 Lucas, L. M. (2006), "The role of culture on knowledge transfer: the case of the multinational corporation", *The Learning Organization*, Volume 13, Issue 3, pp. 257–275

79 Drolet, A. L. and Morris, M. W. (2000), "Rapport in conflict resolution: accounting for how face-to-face contact fosters mutual cooperation in mixed-motive conflicts", *Journal of Experimental Social Psychology*, Volume 36, Issue 1, pp. 26–50

Recommended reading

Lambert, D. M. and Knemeyer, A. M., "We're in This Together," *Harvard Business Review*, Vol. 82, No. 12 (2004), pp. 114–122

Cousins, P., Lamming, R., Lawson, B. and Squire, B., (2008). *Strategic supply management: principles, theories and practice*. Pearson Education

Emmett, S. and Crocker, B., (2006). *The relationship-driven supply chain*. Aldershot: Gower

Glossary

Added value
Non-cash releasing benefits generated via procurement processes and supplier relationship management

Agile
An agile organisation is one that has systems and processes that enable it to react quickly to changes in its environment

Arbitration
The settling of a dispute between buyer and supplier by an impartial third party. This party may be named in the contract. The buyer and supplier agree to accept the third party's decision

Auto-renewal clauses
Clauses in a contract which state that if the buyer does not give sufficient notice, for example 90 days' written notice, then the contract will auto-renew for another period. These clauses are common in software licences

Backward integration
A situation where the buying organisation purchases one of its suppliers of raw materials. The raw materials supplier is further back in the supply chain. For example, a paper factory buying a forest plantation

Benchmarking
Comparing an element of one business, such as price, quality or service, against another

Business case
A justification for a proposed project or undertaking on the basis of its expected benefits

Business continuity planning (BCP)
A process that a company uses to develop a plan to enable it to recover from a disruption in the shortest possible time

Business cycle
The rise and fall over time of output in an economy as measured by gross domestic product (GDP)

Call-off contract
An overarching agreement in respect of price, terms and conditions that allows a buyer or user department to 'order/call off' products or services as required over a period of time. These types of contract are useful where volume over a period of time is unknown

Category management
The spend in an organisation is broken down into groups (categories) of related products and services, e.g., construction, IT, facilities management. For example, an IT category would include contracts for software, and hardware such as laptops/printers/servers, telecoms and IT consultancy

Commitment
Willingness to dedicate financial and non-financial resources to a project

Common procurement vocabulary (CPV) codes
Numerical classifications for products and services. The aim of these codes is to standardise the references used by buyers to describe the products and services that they are purchasing

Competitive advantage
Putting an organisation in a strong position against its competition

Conflict
A disagreement, or difference of opinions or principles

Connected stakeholder
This is a stakeholder that has a strong interest in a company's activities. This is due to its contractual or commercial relationship with the company. This definition includes suppliers

Consortia procurement
When a group of separate organisations come together to procure products or services. This allows them to leverage their buying power. This is common in the public sector

Continuous improvement
An ongoing effort to improve products, processes and services

Contract frustration
As a result of an unforeseen incident beyond either party's control, the obligations of the contract become impossible to perform. UK law states that when contract frustration occurs the contract can be terminated. This can be avoided by adding a force majeure clause naming the possible events. Those events are now classed as foreseen

Corporate social responsibility (CSR)
A business approach that contributes to sustainable development by delivering social, environmental

and economic benefits for all stakeholders. The CSR policy may cover fundraising for charity, ethical behaviour, social and environmental policies, etc.

Cost modelling

A process that buyers use to understand all of the costs that make up a supplier's price. The model is used to understand how the cost is broken down across the production of a product or service

Cross-organisational teams

Teams that involve individuals from different departments that work together towards a common goal. A group of people working on a defined project that come from different functions/departments of the company. It can also include members that are from outside the company, such as suppliers

Culture

The shared values, practices and beliefs within an organisation that determine how its procedures are carried out and how it is run overall

Demand risk

The risk that the forecast demand levels may not be met by actual customer demand

Disruptive technologies

New or enhanced technologies that replace or affect existing technology, making it obsolete. An example is cloud computing services, which are a disruptive technology for in-house servers

Due diligence

Undertaking a thorough appraisal or conducting an evaluation to establish all the facts prior to entering into an agreement

Dynamic purchasing system (DPS)

As its name suggests, this is dynamic. Therefore, a supplier can be on-boarded onto the system or removed at any point during its life. A supplier will be required to pass a pre-qualification questionnaire (PQQ) and, once approved, it can submit a tender for any requirements within the scope it has been short-listed for. A DPS can be for any length of time, unlike frameworks which have a maximum length of four years

Early supplier involvement (ESI)

A type of collaboration between a buyer and supplier in which the buying organisation involves the supplier in the product or service development process

Economy of scale

The trend of cost per unit being reduced as output increases due to factors such as increased bargaining power and the cost of tooling being shared between larger numbers of units

Ethical sourcing

Ensuring that products are obtained in a responsible and sustainable way that demonstrates respect for the people who produce them and for the environment

Evergreen contracts

These are contracts with no end date. Like an evergreen tree that never loses its leaves, an evergreen contract is never-ending

External supplier

A supplier that is independent of the organisation and provides products or services to it

Fit for purpose

The product or service is capable of doing what it was designed to do

Force majeure (French for 'superior force')

An exclusion clause excluding the party from liability due to 'acts of God'

Forward buying

This involves buying a quantity greater than the volume currently required in order to avoid future price increases

Globalisation

The process by which the world is becoming more interconnected, which means that events in one location are shaped by things that happen many miles away

Hedging

A hedge is deal that a buyer can undertake to try to mitigate the effect of price increases. It involves buying similar quantities of the same product in two separate markets at the same time on the basis that a price increase in one market will be offset by a price decrease in the other market

Intellectual property

Products or services created as a result of an individual's ideas

Internal supplier

A supplier that is part of the same company as its customer. It provides the products or services that co-workers within the organisation need in order to do their job

Just in time (JIT)

A system that works alongside Lean manufacturing. In order to reduce waste in the supply chain, JIT makes sure that stock is not held unnecessarily in inventory

Key performance indicators (KPIs)
These are measurable values that will enable a buyer to track how well a supplier is performing. KPIs are tracked over time and will enable the buyer to decide when remedial action may be needed to improve performance

Lessons learned
Experiences gained as part of a project that should be documented and used to improve future projects

Leverage
To use the market to one's best advantage. For example, leveraging spend involves the buyer reviewing the total spend for a product or service, e.g., across multiple business areas or sites. The spend will then be combined into one contract, which will increase the potential contract value with the supplier, increasing the buyer's power to negotiate a better deal

Liquidity ratio analysis
Referred to as 'financial ratios' – using information from a supplier's published financial statements

Make or buy
A decision about what products or services an organisation will manufacture or provide themselves in-house, and which will be purchased from outside sources

Make-or-buy decision
The action of choosing whether to manufacture a product or provide a service in-house or purchase it from an external supplier

Material breach
A material breach of contract is a failure of performance. This can be on the part of either the buyer or the supplier. This failure is considered so great that it gives the other party the right [?] to terminate the contract and/or sue for damages depending on the situation

Mediation
This involves a neutral third party which encourages the buyer and supplier not just to think about their legal rights under the contract but also their commercial interests. Mediation attempts to get both parties to reach a compromise

Monopsony
A market with only one buyer

Multi-national company (MNC)
A company that operates in more than one country, for example McDonald's

Negotiation
A negotiation between a buyer and supplier is a discussion with the aim of reaching agreement, usually on the price of a product or service

Non-disclosure agreement (NDA)
A non-disclosure agreement means that if a party to the agreement discloses confidential information there will be a penalty for doing so. The penalty is usually financial

Objective
A target that a company or partnership intends to achieve. Resources will be focused on achieving the objectives of the company

Offshoring
The relocation of business, processes, for example, a customer service call centre or the manufacturing of a product, to a country where the costs of production are lower. Usually this country will be located overseas

Open book costing
Where the supplier allows the buyer access to its finances so the buyer knows what the costs are

Pareto principle
Also called the 80/20 rule, this states that 80% of the outputs come from 20% of the inputs

Partnership relationship
A commitment between a buying organisation and a supplier entering into a long-term, collaborative relationship based on trust and mutually agreed objectives and goals for the benefit of both parties

Pre-qualification questionnaire (PQQ)
A document sent to potential suppliers asking for information necessary to support their qualification as an approved supplier

Preferred customer
A buying organisation that a supplier treats better than other customers, for example, in terms of product quality and availability, delivery or/and prices

Price elasticity
A measure of the change in demand for a product or service in relation to changes in its price. If a product is price elastic, the more the price is reduced the more demand will rise. Generally for a product to be price elastic there will need to be a number of substitute products. Price elasticity of demand (PED) is a measure of how responsive the demand for a product is in relation to its price

Private sector
Organisations that are owned by private individuals and enterprises

Product life cycle
A period of time which involves developing a product from scratch, bringing the product to the marketplace, sales in the market and the eventual decline and removal of the product from the marketplace. The model has four key stages: introduction, growth, maturity and decline

Project audit
A more formal process than a review; this would usually be undertaken by a party that is independent of the organisation being audited

Project champion
A person within an organisation that is implementing a project or business change who takes responsibility for ensuring the project or change is successful

Project steering committee
A group that decides on the priorities for a project and manages the general operations of the project

Public sector
Service organisations run by the government and usually funded by taxes

Qualitative measures
Measurements of non-numerical data that tends to be based on thoughts and feelings, for example, how satisfied the end customer is with the product manufactured by the supplier and buyer

Quantitative measures
Measurements of numerical data, for example, the percentage of deliveries from the supplier that arrive on time and in full

Relationship marketing
This looks at long-term term customer engagement including customer loyalty

Restricted marketplace
A market where there are only a small number of capable and competent suppliers

Return on relationship investment (RORI)
The financial benefits for a buyer of establishing, developing and maintaining buyer–supplier relationships

Reverse e-auction
An electronic procurement process that involves suppliers competing against each other by reducing their prices. The supplier that submits the lowest price will win the auction

Risk
A situation that involves exposure to danger

Risk management
A process involving risk identification, assessment and management

Service credits
A contract mechanism for performance management. If a supplier fails to meet the standard set in the service credits the buyer has the right to deduct set amounts of money from the payments owed to the supplier

Stakeholder
In terms of procurement, stakeholders are people who have an active interest in or a concern about what is being procured. They will be affected by the outcome of the procurement, for example, via changes to their job role or working practices. The level of stakeholder interest/concern will vary, as will their power to act on it

Supplier development
The process of working with a supplier to improve its processes and/or the products and services it delivers. The aim of supplier development is commercial benefits for the buying organisation; however, there will also be benefits for the supplier

Supplier relationship management (SRM)
Process for identifying all interactions with key suppliers and then managing them in a way that increases the value from the relationship for both parties

Supply base rationalisation
When a buyer reduces the number of suppliers it has for a product or service. This is normally done as part of an exercise to cut costs. Buying from just one supplier will allow the buyer to leverage its spend and should result in reduced prices

Supply chain management (SCM)
The ongoing development and monitoring of a supplier and the links between supply chain members to ensure that the buyers' and end customers' needs are met

Tacit knowledge
The vast amount of unwritten knowledge that is held in the minds of people. This knowledge has not been taught, but is based on previous experiences, observations, thoughts and feelings

Total quality management (TQM)
Efforts of all departments within an organisation to improve processes, products and services

Triangulation
A statistical concept based on understanding whether data is valid or not by reviewing information from multiple data sources. Data is considered to be valid if it is verified by two or more reliable sources of information

Trust
A belief that one party is acting in the best interests of another party

TUPE legislation
TUPE stands for Transfer of Undertakings (Protection of Employment). TUPE regulations protect the rights of the employees where work they were employed to undertake is transferred to a new business

Unique selling proposition/point (USP)
These are the elements of a product or service that differentiate the buying organisation's offering from that of its competitors. This could be a feature of a product or it could be related to cost or quality. USPs are a source of competitive advantage

Value for money (VFM)
The most advantageous combination of price and quality that makes a product or service fit for purpose and will achieve the buyer's required outcomes. This needs to be reviewed in terms of whole life costs

Value mapping
A process in which value is created by reducing or eliminating waste and operational inefficiencies

Value-added benefits
Enhancements that a supplier makes to a product or service before sale to the buyer. This could include features at no extra cost, extended warranty periods or services such as product training

Vertical integration
When a buyer owns companies within its supply chain. There could be forward vertical integration where a buyer owns a distributor, or backward vertical integration where a buyer owns one of its suppliers of raw materials

Whole life costing
A process that involves the buyer reviewing the costs of a product or service throughout its whole life. This will include the initial cost of the product, set-up, day-to-day running, maintenance, repair and disposal costs. This is generally applied to the purchase of equipment and machinery to assess which item will offer the best value for money over its expected life

Working capital
Capital of a business that is used in its day-to-day trading operations, calculated as the current assets minus the current liabilities

Index

A

ABC analysis   17
Accurate cost modelling   93–95
Added value   48
    outcomes   48–49
    sources of   49–59
Agile   59
Arbitration   112
Auto-renewal clauses   112
Award stage
    private sector   76–77
    public sector   77–79

B

Backward integrate   43
Behaviours   149
Benchmarking   72
Business case   142
Business continuity planning (BCP)   104–106
Business cycle   44
Buyer/supplier relationship KPI   101–104

C

Call-off contracts   21
Carter's 10 Cs   11–12
Case study
    Benefits of partnership   130
    Competitive advantage   34
    Cost leadership and differentiation strategies – travel market   32
    Cost modelling – developing procurement strategies   94
    Cross-organisational teams   90
    JIT   58
    Knowledge transfer and innovation   101
    Kraljic example   22
    Nestlé   15
    Partnership failure   165
    Partnership planning   152
    Toyota partnerships   9
    TUPE   115–116
    UK horse meat scandal and quality control   55
    Category management   19
Collaboration framework   156
Commitment   161
Common procurement vocabulary (CPV) codes   72
Communication cycle   157
Competitive advantage   30
Competitive dialogue   77
Competitive forces
    competitors rivalry   39–41
    new entrants threat   41
    Porter's Five Forces model   38–39
    power of buyers   42–43
    power of suppliers   42
    substitute products/services threat   41–42
Competitive procedure with negotiation   77
Competitive strategies
    capital   34
    case study   32
    cost leadership   30
    differentiation   31
    focus   31–32
    human resource management, staff and skills   33
    natural resources   34
    organisation culture and structure   33
    Porter's generic strategies model   31
    processes and practices   34
    products and intellectual property   34
    tacit knowledge   33
    technology   34
Competitive tender   51–52
Confidentiality   113–114
Conflict   86
    and coping processes   86–88
Connected stakeholders   64
Consortia procurement   22
Continuous improvement   154
Contract frustration   108
Contract management   53, 70–71
Corporate social responsibility (CSR)   45
Cost focus   31
Cost modelling   93
Cross-organisational teams   88–90
Culture   168

D

Demand risk   134
Differentiation focus   31
Disruptive technologies   44
Distance barriers   171–172
Due diligence   141
Dynamic purchasing system   101

E

Early supplier involvement (ESI)   97–99, 124
Economies of scale   4
Employee rights   115
ESI vs buyer-developed specifications
    information sharing and transparency   126
    joint performance measurement   126
    less contractual   126
    no adversarial negotiations   125

no defined end period   126
no tender process   125
shared costs and benefits   125
E-sourcing   52–53
Ethical sourcing   46
Evergreen contracts   112
External stakeholders   64
External supplier   2, 4–5
advantages   4–5
disadvantages   5
economies of scale   4

F

Fast-changing technology   137–138
Finances   113
Fit for purpose   37
Flexibility management   148–149
Force majeure   104
Forming   91
Forward buying   96

G

Globalisation   45

H

Hedging   96
High risk   134
High spend   132–134

I

Imperfect competition   40
Improving quality   53–54
Innovation   148
Innovative partnership procedure   77
Intellectual property (IP)   3, 98
Internal stakeholders   64
Internal suppliers   2–4
advantages   3
disadvantages   3
make-or-buy decision   2
Invitation to tender (ITT)   77
IPR   114

J

Just in time (JIT)   146, 147
Just in time (JIT)   57

K

Key performance indicators (KPIs)   9, 101
Knowledge transfer   99–101
Kotter's eight-step change model   144
Kraljic matrix   20
Kraljic model
benefits   23

case study   22
category management   19
limitations of   23–24
quadrants   21–22
risk   18–19
supplier types   20

L

Lack of commitment   161–162
Lack of support   159
Lack of trust   159–161
Lessons learned   154
Leverage   8
Liquidity ratio analysis   12
Logistics   170–171

M

Make or buy   69
Make-or-buy decision   2
Market changes   166–168
Market management matrix   27–28
Market types   39–41
Material breach   15
Mediation   112
Mendelow's theory   81, 143
Model of buyer and supplier power   43
Monopolistic competition   40
Monopoly   39
Monopsony   42
Multi-national companies (MNCs)   148

N

Negotiation   53, 77
Negotiation tactics   7
New services   136–137
Non-disclosure agreement (NDA)   113
Norming   92

O

Objective   150
Offshoring   170
Oligopoly   40
Open book costing   51
Open tender process   77
Overcoming resistance   83–85

P

Pareto analysis   17–18
Pareto principle   6
Partnering
advantages for purchaser/supplier   129–132
drivers/motivators for   127–129
fast-changing technology   137–138
high risk   133–134

high spend 132–133
new services 136–137
restricted markets 138
technically complicated supplies 135–136
types of 122–124
vs. traditional relationships 124–126
Partnership commitment
allocation of resources 150
benefits and resource allocation 152
communication 149–150
contractual commitment 150
joint objective setting 150–151
joint planning and decision-making 151–152
partnership governance 150
quick wins 153
Partnership implementation
items potentially suitable for 139–141
joint commitment 149–153
reviews and audits 153–155
selling the philosophy 141–146
standards/requirements for
relationship 146–149
Partnership life cycle model 139
Partnership model 129
Partnership relationships 122
Partnerships failures
changes in the market 166–168
corporate cultural differences 168–170
lack of commitment 161–162
lack of support/trust 159–161
lack of value-added benefit 164–166
logistics and distance barriers 170–172
poor communication 156–159
poor planning 162–164
Performance management
cost 14
delivery 13–14
environment 14
morale 14
quality 13
safety 13
Performing 92
Porter's Five Forces model 38–39, 167
Porter's generic strategies model 31
Positive relationships 80–83
Potential partners standards
ability to supply globally 148
behaviours 149
flexibility management 148–149
innovation programmes 148
just in time method 147–148
total quality management (TQM) 147
Preferred customer 25
Pre-qualification questionnaire (PQQ) 75
Price–cost iceberg 51
Price elastic 40
Price fluctuations, impact of 95–97

Private sector 71
award stage 76–77
supplier assessment 73–74
supplier identification 71–72
Procurement and supply cycle
contract management 70–71
develop strategy 70
review the market 70
understand the need 69–70
Procurement objectives 32–33
Procurement rights 37–38
Product life cycles 127
Project audit 154
Project champion 143
Project steering committee 153
Public sector 71
award stage 77–79
supplier assessment 74–75
supplier identification 72

Q
Qualitative measures 102
Quantitative measures 102

R
Relationship features 6
Relationship life cycle 10
Carter's 10 Cs 11–12
development and innovation 14–16
performance management 13–14
qualification 11–12
segmentation and risk management 12–13
Relationship marketing 26
Relationship spectrum
adversarial relationships 7
arm's-length relationships 8
closer tactical relationships 8
co-destiny relationships 9–10
Lose-lose 7
negotiation tactics 7
outsourced relationships 8–9
Pareto principle 6
partnership relationships 9
relationship features 6
single-source relationships 8
strategic alliance relationships 9
transactional relationships 8
Win-lose 7
Win-win 7
Request for information (RFI) 11
Request for proposal (RFP) 11
Restricted marketplace 138
Restricted markets 138
Restricted tender process 77
Return on relationship investment (RORI) 48
Reverse e-auctions 21

Risk 18
Risk management   12

S

Security   114
Service credits   113
SMART objectives   151
Sources of added value
    improving quality   53–55
    pricing and cost management   50–53
    procurements   58–59
    timescales   56–58
Specification development   50–51
Stakeholders   3
Starbucks value chain   36
STEEPLE analysis   46–47
    environmental   45
    ethical   46
    factors   44–45
    legislative   45
    political   45
    in practice   46–47
    social   44
    Storming   91–92
Supplier assessment
    private sector   73–74
    public sector   74–75
Supplier development   14
Supplier preferencing matrix   24
Supplier preferencing model   24–26
Supplier preferencing quadrants   25–26
Supplier relationship management (SRM)   2
Supplier relationship spectrum   5
Supplier termination process   109
    business approval to terminate   109–110
    contract management   109
    develop exit strategy   110
    manage exit   110
    new supplier   110
    new supplier on-boarding   111
    performance issues   109
    written notice of termination   110
Supply base rationalisation   105
Supply chain management (SCM)   59

T

Tacit knowledge   33
Team development
    forming   91
    norming   92
    performing   92
    storming   91–92
Technically complicated supplies   135–136
Terminating process
    legal considerations   112–115
    process of termination   108–111
    reasons for termination   107-108
    relationship impacts   111–112
    succession issues   116–117
Total quality management (TQM)   146, 147
Triangulation   95
Trust   102
Trust and co-operation link   160
Tuckman's team and group development
    model   91
TUPE legislation   9

U

Unique selling proposition/point (USP)   140

V

Value-added benefit   164–166
Value chain   35–37
Value for money (VFM)   65–66
    competition   67–68
    economy   65
    effectiveness   65
    efficiency   65
    equity   65
    negotiation   68
    procurement   66–67
    procurement cycle   68
Value mapping   69
Vertical integration   129

W

Whole life costings   12
Working capital   148

About CIPS, the Chartered Institute of Procurement & Supply

The professional body

CIPS, a not-for-profit organisation that exists for the public good, is the voice of the profession, promoting and developing high standards of skill, ability and integrity among procurement and supply chain professionals.

Quality guaranteed

Our qualifications are recognised by OFQUAL in England and regulators in various countries, demonstrating that they meet specific quality standards.

The Global Standard

CIPS Global Standard in Procurement and Supply, which is freely available, sets the benchmark for what good looks like in the profession.

A commercial organisation

CIPS helps governments, development agencies, and businesses around the world to excel in procurement and supply, supporting them to improve and deliver results and raise standards.

A global community

We are the world's largest professional body dedicated to procurement and supply with a global community of over 200,000 professionals in over 150 countries, and offices in Africa, Asia, Australia, the Middle East, Europe and USA.

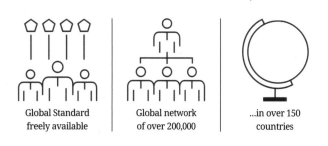

Global Standard freely available | Global network of over 200,000 | ...in over 150 countries

978-1-86124-293-8

cips.org